Mastering
Meetings

Mastering Meetings

Discovering the Hidden Potential of Effective Business Meetings

The 3M Meeting Management Team with Jeannine Drew

McGraw-Hill, Inc.

New York San Francisco Washington, D.C. Auckland Bogotá
Caracas Lisbon London Madrid Mexico City Milan
Montreal New Delhi San Juan Singapore
Sydney Tokyo Toronto

orary of Congress Cataloging-in-Publication Data

Mastering meetings : discovering the hidden potential of effective
    business meetings / the 3M Meeting Management Team with Jeannine
    Drew.
        p.   cm.
    Includes index.
    ISBN 0–07-031037-8   —ISBN 0-07-031038-6 (pbk.)
    1. Meetings. 2. Communication in management. I. Drew, Jeannine.
II. 3M Meeting Management Team.
HF5734.5.M37   1994
658.4'56—dc20   94–15757
                                                 CIP

    2 3 4 5 6 7 8 9 0   DOC/DOC   9 0 9 8 7 6 5

ISBN 0-07-031037-8 (HC)
ISBN 0-07-031038-6 (PBK)

*The sponsoring editor for this book was Betsy Brown, the editing
supervisor was Fred Dahl, and the production supervisor was Suzanne
W. Babeuf. It was set in Baskerville by Inkwell Publishing Services.*

Printed and bound by R. R. Donnelley & Sons Company.

Contents

Acknowledgments   xi

1. Meetings in Corporate America   1

Fear and Loathing in the Meeting Room   1
  The Reasons for Meeting Dread   2
Meetings *Do* Matter   3
  The Purposes of Meetings   4
  Meetings as a Control System   5
  "Out-Meeting" the Competition   5
  Career Makers—or Breakers   6
The Meeting as Ritual   7
  A Fundamental Human Need   7
  Meeting Rituals and Organizational Culture   8
Why Meetings Fail   8
The High Cost of Failure   10
  Calculating Meeting Costs   10
  The Meeting Meter   14
  Weighing Costs and Benefits   14
The Future of Meetings   17
  Challenges Ahead   18

2. Before and After the Meeting   21

To Meet or Not to Meet   21
  Legitimate Reasons to Meet   21
  Should I Call This Meeting?   24
When to Meet   24
  The Best (and Worst) Times to Hold a Meeting   24
  How Long to Meet   25

Preparing the Agenda   26
  General Guidelines   26
  What to Include   27
  When to Distribute   28
Who (and How Many) Should Be Invited?   29
Where to Meet: Room Selection and Setup   31
  How to Size Up a Meeting Room   32
  Optimizing Seating Arrangements   37
  Insist on Your Setup   40
Summing Up: Meeting Minutes   42
  Guidelines for Taking Minutes   44
  The Post-Meeting Action Plan   45
Evaluating the Meeting   47
  Simple Evaluations   47
  Formal Evaluation   49
  Guidelines for Designing and Conducting Evaluations   50
Room for Improvement   51

3. Choosing and Using Meeting Procedures   53

"Recipes" for Managing Meetings   54
Powerful Tools   55
The Benefits of Using Procedures   55
  Imparting a Sense of Control   56
  Overcoming Mindless Behavior   56
  Balancing Independence and Group Work   56
  Maximizing Participation   57
  Maximizing Defensiveness   57
  Minimizing Defensiveness   57
  Managing Conflict   57
  Preventing "Groupthink"   58
  Fostering Self-Evaluation   58
  Providing a Feeling of Closure   58
A Sample of Meeting Procedures   59
  Roberts' Rules of Order   59
  Brainstorming   59
  Nominal Group Technique (NGT)   60
  Multiattribute Decision Analysis (MDA)   61
  Hall's Consensus Rules   63
  Devil's Advocate   64
  Synectics   64
  Delphi Technique   65
How Procedures Vary   66
How to Choose the Right Procedure   67
  Match the Procedure to the Task   67
  Choose a Procedure That Fits the Group   68
  Fit the Procedure to the Desired Outcome   69
  Match the Procedure to the Organizational Culture   69
Why Groups Resist Procedures   70
Eight Ways to Promote Use of Procedures   72

Contents $\quad$

4. Meeting Roles: How to Lead, Facilitate, or Participate 77

Leading the Meeting 77
  The Servant of the Group 78
  Getting the Meeting Off to a Good Start 79
  Encouraging Participation 80

Drawing Silent Types into the Discussion 82
  Joining the Discussion 83
  Managing Emotions 84
  Dealing with Latecomers 85
  Managing Conflict 86
  Injecting Humor 87
  Ending the Meeting 89

The Role of the Facilitator 90
  Neutral Third Party 91
  Other Benefits of Facilitation 91
  The 16 Functions of an Effective Facilitator 92
  Graphic Facilitation 95
  Developing Facilitation Skills 96

Active Participation 97
  Empathic Listening 97
  Communicating Accountably 100
  Risk Taking 101

5. The Rise of Electronic Meetings 103

The Growth of Meeting Technology 104
  If We Build It, They Will Come ... 105

Audioconferencing 105
  The Power of Verbal Cues 106
  The Price Is Right 106
  Potential Drawbacks 107
  How to Plan an Audioconference 107
  Advice for Participants 108

Videoconferencing 109
  Videoconference Applications 109
  One-Way Video 110
  Two-Way Video 111
  Producing a Videoconference 111
  Tips for Success 112
  The Future of Videoconferencing 113

Computer Conferencing 114
  The "Interpersonal" Computer 114
  A Flexible Tool 115

Groupware 115

A Sampling of Groupware Products 116
  OptionFinder 116
  Lotus Notes 121
  GroupSystems V 123

But Does It Work? 123
  Key Advantages 123

Potential Drawbacks   126
Getting the Most Out of Groupware   127
The Future of Groupware   128
The Limits of Technology   129

6. How to Develop and Deliver Powerful Presentations   133

The Effective Presentation   134
Developing an Effective Presentation   135
  Analyzing Your Audience   135
  Developing a Structure   135
  Creating a Logic Tree   137
  Crafting a Beginning and Ending   138
Creating Visuals   139
  When to Use Visuals   140
  Visual Design Principles   140
Adding Color   143
  The Impact of Color   143
  Uses of Color   145
Common Types of Visual Aids   147
  Pie Charts   147
  Bar Charts   147
  Line Charts   150
  Title and Text Charts   151
  Tables   152
  Diagrams   153
  Maps   153
  Standard Drawings   153
  Photographs   154
Choosing the Right Graphic Medium   154
  Overhead Transparencies   154
  35 Millimeter Slides   156
  Computer Graphics   157
  How to Choose a Presentation Software Program   157
  Graphic Mistakes   158
  Video and Laser Disk   159
  LCD Projection Panels and Projectors   159
  Multimedia   160
Delivering Your Presentation   161
  Controlling Your Nerves   161
  Monitoring and Involving the Audience   162
  Evaluating and Improving Your Performance   163

7. Emerging Issues in Meeting Management   167

Diversity in the Meeting Room   168
  An Equal Right to Be Different   168
  The Gender Gap   169
  "A Marriage Without Courtship"   171
International Meetings   173
  Bridging the Language Gap   173

Watch Your Pronunciation   173
Make Yourself Understandable   175
Avoid Idioms, Acronyms, Jargon, and Slang   175
Hear the One About the German and the Scot?
Keep It to Yourself   175

Other Ways to Bridge the Language Gap   176
Visual Aids   176
Technology   176
Software Translation   177
Interpreters   177
Language Training   178
Body Language   178

Customs   179
The Ghost of the Ugly American   179
International Meeting Styles   180
Planning an International Meeting   181
Where to Go for Help   182

Team Meetings   182
The Team Performance Model   183
Different Stages, Different Meeting Needs   186
Cross-Company Team Meetings   186
Training and Rewards   187

Two-Person Meetings   191
Differences Between Dyads and Large Groups   191
Work Tools for Dyads   192
The Need for More Research   193

8. Improving Meeting Systems   195

The Meeting Audit   195
The Meeting Systems Profile   196
The Improvement Plan   196

Typical Audit Findings   197
Recommendations   198
Raising Awareness   198

Guidelines for Conducting a Meeting Audit   204
Choosing Observers   205
A Tool for Continuous Improvement   206

Training: The Missing Link   206
Address Problems, Not Symptoms   207

Smart Meetings   207
Winning Companies   209
A High Priority   209

Notes   211
Index   227

Acknowledgments

Developing a book is a team effort. We wish to acknowledge the many people whose contributions are reflected in these pages. Special thanks to Paul Carlson, John Dreiling, Bob Richards, and Mike Wadino for offering their "real world" insights into meeting management. We are grateful to Susan Putnam and Fran Upton for fielding an endless stream of requests for information, and to Jerry Tapley for his technical support throughout the project. We wish to acknowledge Barbara Langham for her invaluable editorial advice and contributions; Jeannine Drew, for helping us to put our thoughts into words; and Betsy Brown of McGraw-Hill for guiding the project. Last but by no means least, we would like to thank the many researchers and meeting management experts who allowed us to include their material in the book.

The 3M Meeting Management Team

Mastering
Meetings

1

Meetings in Corporate America

The meeting was so boring that the person in front of me pulled out literature she had received from a funeral home and began to plan her funeral.

LAWRENCE A. WIGET
Anchorage School District

Fear and Loathing in the Meeting Room

The modern corporate meeting, according to humorist Dave Barry, can be compared to a funeral, "in the sense that you have a gathering of people who are wearing uncomfortable clothing and would rather be somewhere else." The major differences, he notes, are that most funerals "have a definite purpose (to say nice things about a dead person) and reach a definite conclusion (this person is put in the ground), whereas meetings generally drone on until the legs of the highest-ranking person present fall asleep."

Barry claims:

> Also, nothing is ever really buried in a meeting, An idea may *look* dead, but it will always reappear at another meeting later on. If you have ever seen the movie *Night of the Living Dead* you have a rough idea of how modern meetings operate, with projects and proposals that everybody thought were killed rising constantly from their graves to stagger back into meetings and eat the brains of the living.[1]

arry's critique may be tongue-in-cheek, but his cynical view of meetings widely shared. When we asked readers of our newsletter, *Meeting Management News*, to tell us about their most boring meeting experience, they were eager to recount their tales of woe.

The quote that begins this chapter was our favorite reader response. We also were fond of two other contributions. A subscriber in Minneapolis told us she'd gone to a meeting so boring that "even the speaker lost interest. At point 13 of 17 he said, 'You've heard enough of this stuff,' and quit!" Another correspondent, from Chicago, wrote that "it took me 20 minutes before I came out of my coma and realized that I was at the wrong meeting ...." Perhaps Dave Barry is not so far off the mark.

Why the universal disdain for meetings? The short answer is that too many people, like our hapless correspondents, have sat through too many meetings that proved to be an utter waste of time.

Milo Frank, in his insightful book, *How to Run a Successful Meeting in Half the Time*, tells the story of his grandfather, an American businessman who owned a legging factory that outfitted. American soldiers in World War I. He was approached by the Russian General Staff about the possibility of making bulletproof vests for the Russian army.

After much investigating, Frank's grandfather determined that he could convert the factory and turn out the vests at just three dollars each—a real bargain at the time. What followed was a series of meetings with the Russians—"days, weeks, and months of meetings" on everything from design and material to guarantees and delivery dates.

Ultimately the proposal was turned down. Frank's puzzled grandfather asked why, pointing out that the vests would save lives. "Because," he was told, "no Russian soldier's life is worth three dollars." Milo Frank cites the story as his first lesson in what a waste of time meetings can be.[2]

The Reasons for Meeting Dread

Not all meetings are wasteful, and not everyone dreads them. How people feel about meetings depends in part on where they work. In organizations that foster open communication, people may view meetings in a positive light, as a productive forum for sharing ideas and solving problems. In organizations where communications are poor and political in-fighting is the norm, people will likely have an aversion to participating in meetings for fear that what they say in the conference room today may be used against them tomorrow.

Lynn Oppenheim, vice president of the Wharton Center for Applied Research in Philadelphia, writes about this concern in *Making Meetings Matter*, a study sponsored by the 3M Meeting Management Institute and conducted by the Wharton Center: "Meetings can ... create tension when a manager experiences himself as having two directives which are in conflict. He may believe that honest feedback is necessary to his boss to prevent the organization from making a serious mistake, but he may be afraid to say something which may be 'unspeakable.'" Managers at one of the study sites referred to this as the fear of making "a career limiting utterance."[3]

While such fears are justifiable, other reasons for meeting dread are less worthy. Oppenheim, who headed the Wharton study, concluded that some people dislike meetings because they serve the legitimate purpose of monitoring and controlling behavior:

> To the extent that meetings function as [a] control mechanism, it is quite understandable that managers dislike them. Few people write odes of praise about their company's MBO system or about individual appraisals. They may recognize their own need for feedback, and their organization's legitimate need for integration and control, but there is an element of tension as well. Perhaps some disdain for meetings is an attempt to discount their legitimacy and thereby undermine their power.[4]

The Wharton study, which gathered information from a broad mix of middle and senior managers in nine locations, offers another explanation for the widespread fear and loathing of meetings: the possibility that they will generate more work. One middle manager who participated in the study admitted "[t]here is a problem in attending some meetings because you might be called upon to do more work as a result of the follow-up." Others noted: "You get so you don't say anything ... because of the risk of creating more work and responsibility for yourself." One manager went even further, explaining that meetings don't always lead to decisions because "[p]eople do not want more work, and they don't want to commit."[5]

Meetings *Do* Matter

Despite all the fear and loathing, the fact is that meetings *do* matter to an organization. Peter Drucker, in *The Effective Executive*, tells why: "We meet because people holding different jobs have to cooperate to get a specific task done. We meet because the knowledge and experience needed in a specific situation are not available in one head, but have to be pieced together out of the knowledge and experience of several people."[6]

These basic purposes of meetings remain unchanged, despite the massive organizational, technological, and social changes that have occurred since Drucker wrote that passage in 1967. If anything, today there is an even greater need for organizations to cooperate and share knowledge in meetings, as a result of burgeoning information, increased pressure to innovate, and a pace of change so rapid that products may be obsolete by the time they're introduced.

The Purposes of Meetings

What purposes do meetings serve in the 1990s? To find the answer to this question and others, we commissioned the Annenberg School of Communications at the University of Southern California to conduct research into the nature, importance, and frequency of meetings in corporate America.[7] Participants included 903 employees, selected randomly from 36 small, medium, and large public and private organizations in California and Minnesota. Each participant was asked to complete a detailed survey describing the last meeting he or she attended. (For purposes of the study, a meeting was defined as "a gathering of three or more people.")* From these surveys, the research team constructed a profile of meetings in U.S. organizations.

The study found that nearly two-thirds (66%) of meetings in corporate America are held to reconcile a conflict (29%); reach a group judgment or decision (26%); or solve a problem (11%)—purposes that coincide with Peter Drucker's assessment of meetings as a forum for cooperating in order to get work done.

Meeting Purposes	
▪ Reconcile a conflict	29%
▪ Reach a group judgment or decision	26
▪ Solve a problem	11
▪ Ensure that everyone understands	11
▪ Facilitate staff communication	5
▪ Gain support for a program	4
▪ Explore new ideas and concepts	4
▪ Accept reports	2
▪ Demonstrate a project or system	2

Figure 1.1. Meeting purposes cited by Annenberg study participants. (*Source:* A Profile of Meetings in Corporate America.)

* In this book we will focus primarily on meetings involving three or more people. (Chapter 7 includes a discussion of two-person meetings.)

Meetings as a Control System

Managers tend to think of meetings as discrete events, but in most cases they are interconnected. Lynn Oppenheim writes: "Meetings are rarely isolated events. At the very least, they are embedded in a cycle of preparation and follow up. More often, individual meeting cycles are connected over a period of time in 'meeting systems' revolving around specific issues or problems."[8]

When meeting systems are "taken together across many issues," they serve as a managerial control system, allocating "scarce management resources to some issues rather than others" and "creating successive deadlines to ensure that managers stay on task."[9] Meetings exert control in part by determining whether and when work is performed:

> Given that most managers face competition for their time from several sources, the timing of work that is outside the meeting boundary will often be governed by when a meeting is held. That is, managers may do very little work on a certain issue the day after a meeting on that topic, and increase their work on that topic shortly before the next scheduled meeting. Hence, the "scallop" pattern of work on an issue, a pattern in which the flow of work is punctuated by the meeting.[10]

In other words, meetings control the work flow (see Fig. 1.2).

"Out-Meeting" the Competition

If meetings direct the flow of work in an organization there should be a positive correlation between how well they are run and the level of success

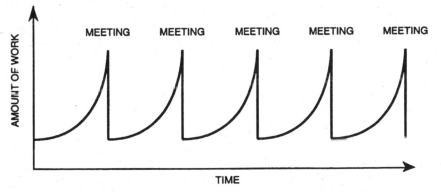

Figure 1.2. Meetings and the timing of work. (*Source*: Making Meetings Matter, *p. 15*.)

the organization achieves. That's the view of Dick Byrd and John Johnson, Minneapolis-based management consultants who contend that effective meeting management is a powerful competitive strategy. They write:

> When companies choose the core capabilities that give them competitive advantage, they typically focus on their unique capacities in such areas as distribution methodology, inventory management, customer service, production technology, purchasing power, and flexible resource management. But an equally important capability is meeting systems management—an organization's ability to consciously manage its intelligence and decision making across functions with speed and surefootedness ... [B]y making a strategic choice to "out-meet" the competition, an organization gains distinct advantage.[11]

Career Makers—or Breakers

Meetings are vehicles for individual advancement as well as organizational achievement. Many a career has sizzled or fizzled on the basis of a single performance in a critical meeting.

The skills practiced in the meeting room are the same as those required in the executive suite: the ability to communicate and persuade, to lead and inspire, to handle objectives, manage conflict, and bring a group to consensus. Former ITT Chairman Harold Geneen has said, "It was in our meetings that we ran ITT." The implication, writes George Kieffer, who solicited the comment from Geneen: "If you can't handle a meeting, you can't handle the company."[12]

Meetings are an organization's showcase for managerial talent, the forum in which employees get to audition before peers and senior management. The person who aspires to advance in the organization had best come to the audition well prepared.

Harold Williams, former CEO of Norton Simon Industries and ex-dean of the UCLA School of Management, notes: "Any time you're in a meeting, you're sending a message about who you are, what your abilities are, and what league you belong in." He adds: "Whether I'm dealing with employees or international business associates, I am always evaluating the people at the table with a view to future responsibilities and relationships."[13]

Many executives actively scout for rising young stars at meetings. In a survey of business leaders conducted jointly by Harrison Conference Services and Hofstra University, 87 percent of respondents said they gauge people's management abilities according to how well they lead meetings. Almost the same percentage (81%) said they assess managerial ability on the basis of how well people participate at meetings.[14] Clearly, meetings are the training ground for managers.

The Meeting as Ritual

A Fundamental Human Need

Beyond serving the business purposes of individuals and organizations, meetings fulfill a more fundamental human need for socializing and communicating. Antony Jay, writing in *Harvard Business Review*, reflects that human beings are a social species: "In every organization and every human culture of which we have record, people come together in small groups at regular and frequent intervals, and in larger 'tribal' gatherings from time to time. If there are no meetings in the places where they work," says Jay, "people's attachment to the organizations they work for will be small, and they will meet in regular formal or informal gatherings in associations, societies, teams, clubs, or pubs when work is over."[15]

Tribal or religious rituals have several functions: They create a sense of belonging to the group; convey the values of the tribe or religion; show what is acceptable and what is taboo; and mark rites of passage. Likewise, meetings—the organizational version of rituals—help employees to bond with one another; communicate the values of the organization; let employees know what behavior is allowed and what is considered unacceptable. And, like religious rituals, they acknowledge rites of passage. An orientation meeting can be likened to a baptism. A promotion is analogous to a confirmation or bar mitzvah, in which the group acknowledges the new status of one of its members. A meeting to celebrate a merger might be compared to a wedding; a retirement party, to a funeral.

Meetings are similar to religious rituals in other ways. They are often held in a temple or on hallowed ground (the conference room). They follow a ceremonial order (the agenda). Ritual foods (coffee and snacks or sandwiches) may be served and ritual objects (handouts or overhead transparencies) may be used. A shaman or priest (the meeting leader) presides over the ceremony. There might be a homily (presentation). Participants may dress in religious clothing (business suits) and recite chants such as "I'll take care of it right away."[16] If it is a ceremonial meeting, such as a new product kickoff or an awards banquet, they may sing hymns (company songs).

Ceremonial meetings serve two important purposes. First, they provide "a way to recognize belonging," says Lynn Oppenheim. "In organizational life, a gathering like this says, 'we belong to this group and others do not.'"[17]

Ceremonial meetings also communicate overt or subtle messages about what it takes to get ahead in the organization. By observing who is invited to and acknowledged at ceremonial meetings, employees infer who is considered important, and learn what behavior and attributes are required to become a star.[18] Says Oppenheim: "The message is that you, too, can be acknowledged if you do the things the honorees have done."[19]

Meeting Rituals and
Organizational Culture

Just as rituals vary from tribe to tribe, so do meetings differ from one organization to the next, depending on the organizational culture. "Meetings reflect the organization's culture more than any other set of events," according to Michael Leimbach, director of program research and measurement of Wilson Learning Corporation. "They are the windows into the soul of a company. As pre-agrarian hunter-gatherer societies expressed their culture through ritual dances and song, today's organizations conduct meetings with much the same outcome."[20]

Leimbach defines organizational culture as "the collective values that consciously and unconsciously guide behavior, influence how people act, and affect how people interact within a group setting." He believes that meetings reflect the culture of the organization "more than any other set of events."[21]

Leimbach says he can quickly determine "what values are held most dear to an organization" by observing what goes on in the meeting room. For example, in companies that value informality and creativity, "meetings come to order gradually (if at all), chairs and tables are used for purposes other than their design, and the agenda (if one exists) is probably not followed," writes Leimbach. "In contrast, meetings in other organizations make the chain of command obvious from the very first moment. Agenda points are checked off the list one by one, and when the last item is checked off, everyone files out in near silence."[22] (We agree with Leimbach's point about organizational values, but we believe neither approach is optimal. We'll discuss the proper use of agendas in Chap. 2.)

If organizational culture is transmitted through meetings, modifying the style and focus of meetings may be an effective means of changing the culture, if needed or desired. For example, if a company wishes to develop a stronger customer service ethic, it might begin by emphasizing service in the content and style of its meetings. If it wants to become more team-oriented, it can start by practicing the skills of teamwork in the meeting room.[23] Viewed in this light, meetings become a potentially powerful tool for transforming the organization—if they are effectively managed.

Why Meetings Fail

While meetings ideally serve as control mechanisms for the organization, they do not always succeed in this role: "Not all meetings in organizations appear to be well thought out, careful exercises of control. Many, in fact, seem quite out of control, and some almost in opposition to the best interests of the organization."[24] In other words, meetings fail.

Meetings fail for some of the same reasons they are disliked. For example, they may lack a purpose, or participants may be reluctant to speak candidly.

To this list can be added a host of sources of failure. It could be that the meeting was held at the wrong time or place. Perhaps the wrong people were there and the right ones were not. Maybe there was no agenda, or the agenda wasn't followed. There may have been inadequate preparation, ineffective leadership, or insufficient follow-up. Or, the meeting may have succumbed to what George Kieffer calls the "phenomenon of collective incompetence," whereby the collective intelligence of the group turns out to be less than the sum of its members' IQs.[25]

The Annenberg study suggests some of the most common reasons for meeting failures:

- *Lack of notification.* On average, participants in the study received just two hours' notice that a meeting was to be held, leaving little time for preparation.

- *No agenda.* Nearly one-third of participants (32%) reported that their meetings had no stated agenda; nearly two-thirds (63%) said no written agenda was distributed in advance.

- *Wrong people in attendance.* One-third of participants (34%) stated that only a few (4%) or some (30%) of the relevant people attended the meeting.

- *Lack of control.* One-third of participants (32%) felt they have minimal (20%) or no (12%) influence on the decision-making process in meetings.

- *Political pressure.* More than a third (37%) said they felt pressure to express views with which they disagreed; 24 percent stated they experienced "mild" pressure, 10 percent experienced "strong pressure," and 3 percent experienced "very great" pressure.

- *Hidden agendas.* Two-thirds of the respondents (63%) indicated that underlying issues were present at the meeting. Nearly a third (30%) said these were present to a small extent; 21 percent stated that they were present to some extent; and 12 percent reported that underlying issues were present to a great extent.

The last finding may be the most troubling. In some cases, meetings fail because they are intended to fail. For example, they may be used as a tactic to delay action instead of a vehicle to achieve results.

One group of senior managers described situations where there are

certain tough policy decisions which require infinite study. The company can't afford not to think about these topics. Even though they are currently on the back burner, they will eventually make it to the front. Since no one individual is able, or willing, to decide on an acceptable corporate policy, meetings are held. A series of meetings are held to set deadlines, to delay the decision-making, to show that the topic is under review, to gather support for a decision and to give a facade for progress.[26]

Some organizations are more prone to meeting failures than others. The healthier the organization in general, the more productive its meetings, according to Lynn Oppenheim, who writes: "In organizations where there are other control issues—frequent contests for control, absence of clear direction, uncertainty about authority or responsibility—meetings are likely to be less productive than in organizations where there is greater consensus."[27]
She also notes:

> When there is a stable, dominant coalition, when organizational priorities are clear, and when norms for behavior are shared and well accepted, meetings will function more smoothly as a control mechanism and are more likely to be productive.
> In contrast, when there are struggles over power and authority, different coalitions will call, or attempt to call, meetings that seem to be at odds with each other. The struggles for organizational control will be evidenced in meetings that seem out of control.[28]

While improving meeting productivity is a worthy goal, some inefficiency is unavoidable, according to Oppenheim:

> Some of these unproductive meetings, this waste of time and resources, is inevitable. People in organizations make mistakes, they take risks and lose, they try to get something going and can't make it happen. We accept as inevitable the pages thrown out from poorly drafted reports or memos. It is, of course, harder for us to accept as inevitable the waste of our own time.[29]

The High Cost of Failure

In our experience, most managers underestimate the cost of holding meetings and thus discount the price of meeting failures. As the following discussion will make clear, unproductive meetings can cost an organization dearly, not just in terms of wasted dollars but also in lost time, decreased morale, and ultimately, reduced productivity.

Calculating Meeting Costs

In determining the economic cost of a meeting, the following factors must be entered into the equation:

- The hourly wages or salaries (including benefits) of those attending the meeting.
- The wages and salaries of those who prepared for the meeting (attendees, secretaries, people who set up the meeting room, etc.).
- The cost of materials used in the meeting, from handouts to visuals.
- The overhead costs of the meeting room or facility, for the length of the meeting.
- The cost of the speaker or facilitator, if any.
- The cost of travel, hotel rooms, meals, and the like, if the meeting is held away from the office.
- Any other miscellaneous expenses in connection with holding the meeting.

Calculating these individual costs can be cumbersome and time-consuming. For this reason, we've established a simple formula for estimating the per hour cost of an in-house meeting: take the average base pay of participants and double it. This will roughly account for overhead, benefits, preparation time, and meeting materials. (For an off-site meeting, the cost of travel, hotels, meals, keynote speakers, etc. must be added.)

Figure 1.3 shows the application of this formula to groups of various sizes and salary ranges. Costs are calculated on the basis of a 50-week, 2000-hour work year. Thus a manager who makes $60,000 per year would earn $30 per hour ($60,000/2000 hours).

The figures in the chart become more meaningful when you consider how much of a manager's time is spent in meetings. The typical manager attends five meetings per week and averages two hours and 14 minutes each day in the meeting room.[30] Managers probably spend even more time than that in meetings, according to Peter Monge, the USC professor of communica-

Average annual salary	Hourly cost of meeting					
$75,000	150	300	450	600	750	1500
$62,500	125	250	375	500	625	1250
$50,000	100	200	300	400	500	1000
$37,500	75	150	225	300	375	750
$25,000	50	100	150	200	250	500
$12,500	25	50	75	100	125	250
	2	4	6	8	10	20
			Number of attendees			

Figure 1.3. Meeting costs.

tion who headed the Annenberg study, because the findings don't reflect the large number of two-person meetings that are held every day in the typical organization. (We'll discuss two-person meetings in Chap. 7.)

To understand the cost implications of having management spend over two hours a day in the meeting room, let's do some calculations. Suppose the average salary of a manager is $45,000. If each manager spends two hours per day, five days a week in meetings, the cost per manager per week is $450; per year, $22,500.

Applying the same formula, a small company with just 10 managers at the $45,000 level would spend $225,000 per year on meetings. A mid-sized organization with 100 managers would spend $2.25 million per year. And a major corporation that employs thousands of managers would spend tens of millions of dollars annually on meetings.

Of its 84,000 employees worldwide, some 3500 people held middle-management positions within 3M in 1993. If their profile is similar to employees in the Annenberg study (and we believe it is), these managers are spending more than 4.4 million hours in meetings each year. Using the average managerial salary figure of $45,000, these meetings are costing the company a staggering $78.8 million annually.

These figures are not exaggerated; if anything, they are conservative estimates of meeting costs. For one thing, we slightly underestimated the number of hours managers spend in the meeting room, as reported in the Annenberg study, for ease of calculation. For another, the estimates do not include preparation time, which could add several hours and hundreds or thousands of dollars to the cost of a single meeting. Also, as noted earlier, the figures don't take into consideration the added cost of off-site meetings, which are inherently more expensive than in-house gatherings. Nor do they account for the fact that the average managerial salary in large corporations is higher than the figure of $45,000 used in the example. Finally, the estimates do not include the hidden costs of ineffective meetings. According to John Johnson, meeting costs can be grouped into five successively deeper levels:

1. *Actual cost outlay per time unit:* The most obvious meeting costs include the individual's time spent in preparation, participation, and follow-up work, plus the cost of food, travel, and housing.

2. *Ineffectiveness:* At a slightly deeper level are the additional hidden expenses of too many people meeting too much for a needlessly extended time period because of inefficient and ineffective meeting processes.

3. *Delayed decisions:* Deeper, and better hidden, are the incurred costs and missed opportunities that result from taking eight months instead of two to make a major decision.

4. *Poor decisions:* At a deeper level still, poor meeting processes lead to poor business decisions, no matter how long they take to make. The costs and/or lost revenues that result from poor decisions are often huge— sometimes catastrophic to the business.

5. *Perpetuation of ineffectiveness:* Finally, at the most complex and systemic level, chronically ineffective meetings and meeting cultures cause dysfunction at the personal, interpersonal, and intergroup dimensions of the organization. Individuals do not produce well, do not use their resources well, and often leave. Ineffective meeting processes precipitate ineffective groups, which in turn lead to ineffective organizations as a whole. The costs of poor meetings and meeting system management eventually prove disastrous to the business if they are allowed to go on unchecked. (See Fig. 1.4.)

From this discussion, it should be clear that meetings are a source of considerable expense for an organization. But that means they also are a source of potential savings.

Continuing with our earlier example, if the number or length of meetings could be cut by half, even a small company with only 10 managers could cut its costs by more than $100,000. For large corporations, the potential savings are enormous. Of course, these savings would not transfer directly to the bottom line, but they would affect the bottom line by raising productivity.

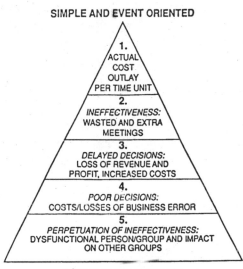

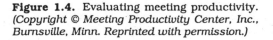

Figure 1.4. Evaluating meeting productivity.
(Copyright © Meeting Productivity Center, Inc., Burnsville, Minn. Reprinted with permission.)

The Meeting Meter

To help organizations become aware of how much meetings are costing them, management consultant Bernie DeKoven created the Meeting Meter®. DeKoven modeled the product after the "old-fashioned taxi meter" as a graphic reminder that "meetings are not free."[31]

The Meeting Meter is a software program designed to run on an IBM or Macintosh computer. The program displays how much a meeting is costing every second as the meeting goes on. Participants enter their hourly salaries before the meeting (on a computerized, confidential sign-up sheet) and activate the meter when the meeting starts.

For example, six managers earning $50,000 a year will see a "fare" of nearly $600 on the screen after two hours. (Besides hourly salaries, the meter takes into account payroll taxes, fringe benefits, and overhead costs.)

"It's a little like a joke, and most people who call to order it are chuckling," says DeKoven, director of the Institute for Better Meetings in Palo Alto, California. "It tickles their fancy." As an example, he cites secretaries who have ordered the meter for bosses as a spoof to their constant complaints about how much time they spend in meetings.

Indeed, the software's packaging refers to it as "almost a laughing matter"—*almost* because the meter has a serious purpose. "It's intended to make people aware of the value of their collective time," says DeKoven, and ultimately to change their unproductive meeting habits.

"One culturally accepted—but subtly destructive—practice in some organizations," he says, "is coming late to meetings—arriving at 9:35 or 9:45 for a 9:30 meeting. Those who come early feel abused because their time is being wasted; they sense a lack of respect on the part of the latecomers."

By turning on the Meeting Meter at the scheduled start time and letting it tick off the dollars while everyone waits, participants have a graphic way of showing late arrivals how much their tardiness has cost.

The meter is especially useful in meetings of 20 or more people and in all meetings of highly paid executives because the money accumulates so dramatically. One enterprising commercial photographer used the meter during a day's shooting that involved several actors, horses, and scenery. Every time someone said, "Wait, we need to fix that makeup," or "Hold it, his hat is on wrong," the photographer ran the meter. At day's end, he was able to show his clients the huge cost of those interruptions.

Weighing Costs and Benefits

It's important to note that an organization saves money only by cutting down on the number of *unproductive* meetings it holds. In some cases, it may be better to hold more meetings rather than fewer. For example, younger companies tend to have more meetings because there are more issues to decide and authority patterns are not as established as in older firms. And when a company is going through a major transition such as a reorganization or a widespread layoff of workers, it's wise to hold extra meetings in order to keep communication channels open and ensure a smooth transition.[32]

In determining whether or not to hold a given meeting, managers must measure the potential benefits, not just the projected costs. An expensive meeting may be well worth its hefty price tag, if it leads to cost-saving suggestions, innovative product ideas, or the development of an effective new strategy—three potential benefits of a well-planned, skillfully executed meeting.

In a downturn, budget-conscious companies may be tempted to cut back on expensive meetings, particularly off-site conferences, viewing them as a luxury they cannot afford. But this view may be shortsighted, even "deadly," according to Gerald Celente, director of the Socio-Economic Research Institute, a trend research and forecasting group in Rhinebeck, New York.[33]

Educational conferences and professional meetings serve as a marketplace for exchanging information, generating ideas, and learning what others are doing, according to Celente. These meetings are necessary in order for people to keep current in an era of whirlwind change. "To survive change, you don't just look for new markets for existing products," Celente says. "You look for new markets for *new* products, and meetings are where you do that."[34]

Coleman Finkel agrees that off-site conferences are important vehicles for keeping employees informed and up-to-date. Finkel is president of the Conference Center Development Corporation, a New York firm that plans and designs meeting facilities. He worries that organizations "can be so set on cutting cost that you cut the heart out of your company." But he acknowledges that not all conferences are equal. Far too many, he says, are "put together by amateurs" and fail to realize their educational potential.[35]

Both consultants would agree that meetings should be assessed on the basis of their benefit versus their cost to the organization. Unfortunately, it's easier to calculate the cost of a meeting than to quantify its benefits. What is the monetary value of an off-site retreat that boosts morale and spurs productivity? What is the benefit, in dollars and cents, of a brainstorming session that may or may not result in a breakthrough product idea, or the solution to a tough problem? How many sales will be generated by a dazzling new product introduction held in a posh hotel ballroom? How much goodwill? The answers to such questions are difficult to reduce to numbers.

How to Beat the High Cost of Off-Site Meetings

✓ Go with the trend to shorter and more intense meetings.

✓ Avoid meeting at peak times (September, October, and April through June).

✓ Meet in small cities and small hotels. They offer less glitz but also lower prices.

✓ Universities, churches, and community centers are usually the least expensive sites for meetings.

✓ Try a conference room at an airport. American Airlines' conference rooms at La Guardia Airport in New York and O'Hare International Airport in Chicago have audiovisual equipment, controlled lighting, and flipcharts. They rent by the hour.

✓ Read the fine print in any contract for the hidden costs. Check the cancellation clause carefully. Note the minimum that will be charged for food and beverage service.

✓ Shop around for the best prices on coffee breaks. The mark-up is usually 100 percent.

✓ Have lunch in the room you are meeting in and ask the hotel staff to waive the room rental. If they're making enough on the lunch, they might agree.

✓ Double-check to be sure that presenters really intend to use the equipment they've ordered. Once it's in the room, you pay for it whether it's used or not.

✓ Request flipcharts at no extra charge.

✓ Negotiate, negotiate, negotiate. Don't be persuaded by seemingly attractive offers of extra services, if they are not documented in a contract. Don't make a decision or sign a contract without careful thought and comparison. And keep checking to see if anything in your plans can be altered to obtain better rates or advantages.

Figure 1.5. (*Adapted and reprinted from* Training & Development, *"How to Make the Most of Your Meetings." Copyright © October 1992, the American Society for Training and Development. Reprinted with permission. All rights reserved.*)

The fact that meeting benefits are not easily quantified is no reason to discount or ignore them. Nor is it necessary to capture the value of meetings in tidy equations. Experience and sound judgment can be used to predict whether the benefits of a given meeting will outweigh the costs. In organizations that focus on making every meeting a productive one, overall productivity will inevitably improve, whether or not the contributions of meetings are isolated. (In Chap. 8 we'll introduce the concept of the meeting audit, a tool to enhance meeting productivity throughout the organization.)

The Future of Meetings

"Some people think they can eliminate meeting problems by eliminating meetings," says Dick Byrd. "But doing that makes as much sense as saying we're going to eliminate criminals by getting rid of laws."[36]

Costly or cheap, productive or problematic, meetings will continue to be a central feature of corporate life in the twenty-first century. In fact, meetings are likely to increase in number and importance in the future, and to change in nature, as a result of several factors:

Rapid Change.   Organizations of the future will require more meetings simply to keep up with the rapid pace of change. Managers will have to meet more frequently to develop, analyze, and adjust their strategies. The planning cycle will be continuous rather than semiannual (i.e., spring and fall). Planning meetings will be held whenever internal or external factors require it, rather than on a fixed schedule.[37]

Information Overload.   The greater the amount of information available to an organization, the greater the need to hold meetings to sort, analyze, and disseminate it. As the quantity of information continues to multiply at an accelerating rate, we can expect more, and more frequent, information-related meetings.

Flattening of the Hierarchy.   The flattening of the organizational hierarchy, which began in the 1980s and continues in the 1990s, guarantees more lateral meetings in the future, across functions, departments and divisions, in order to coordinate activities previously directed by middle managers.

Emergence of Teams.   There will continue to be a heavy emphasis on cross-functional teams, as organizations look for ways to compress the product development cycle and improve product quality. The meeting will be the forum in which teams make key product decisions, resolve design, manufacturing, and marketing problems, identify quality defects, undertake quality improvements, and develop and refine new product ideas.

Cross-Company Alliances.   Increasingly, companies will forge partnerships with one another, including teams for the joint development of products and services, in order to compete more effectively. These cross-company teams, even more than their intracompany counterparts, will conduct business in the context of meetings.

Demographic Shifts.   According to Census Department estimates, by the year 2005 Asians, Hispanics, African-Americans, and other nonwhite groups will account for up to 47 percent of the total U.S. population.[38] The Labor Department projects that 85 percent of new entrants into the U.S. workforce by the year 2000 will be minorities, immigrants, and women. These shifting demographics will be reflected in the workplace, which will become increasingly diverse in the twenty-first century.

Meetings in the future will have to accommodate a diversity of communication styles and cultural and ethnic differences. We can also expect to see more training meetings to help diverse groups of employees work together more effectively.

Globalization. As organizations expand their activities around the world, they will call meetings to discuss mergers, develop marketing strategies, learn the fine points of international law, resolve intercultural or cross-national disputes, work out mutually beneficial sales arrangements, and address a host of complex issues pertaining to international business transactions.

Technology Advances. Advances in communications technology, such as videoconferencing, will make it easier, faster, and (as technology costs decline) cheaper to conduct meetings across national and international boundaries. Inflated air travel costs in the coming decades will make remote "electronic" meetings all the more inviting.

Organizations of the future will have access to a broad range of technology to assist them in the meeting room. Group decision support systems ("groupware") and other interactive meeting tools will become increasingly popular as a new, computer-literate generation of employees makes its way into the ranks of management.

Challenges Ahead

The outlined trends ensure that meetings will play an integral role in the twenty-first century organization. Each of the trends presents new opportunities for meeting managers, and each poses special challenges.

For example, quick and easy access to an abundance of data, and the technology to process it, may make meetings more productive—or it could make them more chaotic, as participants struggle under the burden of information overload. The growth of teams to carry out the fundamental work of the organization promises to make meetings more functional than in the past—unless the team can't manage meetings, in which case they may be *less* functional than before. Computer technology has the potential to bring people closer together. But it could also drive them further apart, by encouraging them to work in isolation and avoid human contact. We'll examine all of these prospects and problems in subsequent chapters.

Of course, preventing boredom will continue to be a central challenge for meeting managers in the twenty-first century. In a 1989 study of 200 corporate vice presidents by Motivational Systems, 40 percent of participants admitted to falling asleep or dozing off during a meeting presentation. We can't guarantee this won't happen in the future, but we can offer a suggestion from Dave Barry about how to handle the problem if it does arise:

> Have everybody leave the room, then collect a group of total strangers, from right off the street, and have them sit around the sleeping person and stare at him until he wakes up. Then have one of them say to him, in a very somber voice, "Bob, your plan is very, very risky, but you've given us no choice but to try it. I only hope, for your sake, that you know what you're getting yourself into." Then they should file quietly from the room.[39]

2
Before and After
the Meeting

When more than 1000 executives were asked in a survey to rank nine aspects of meetings in order of importance, they rated "adequate preparation" first and "agreement on follow-up" second.[1] When meetings are viewed as a system rather than a series of discrete events, what goes on before and after the meeting is as important as the work done behind the conference room door. Without adequate preparation and follow-up, the meeting system cannot effectively control the organizational work flow, and meeting productivity suffers.[2]

To Meet or Not to Meet

The most important aspect of preparing for a meeting is determining whether or not to hold it.[3] Despite widespread disdain for meetings, the knee-jerk reaction of many managers to every problem that arises is to call a meeting to address it. As a result, many meetings are held for the wrong reasons—because they are regularly scheduled, for example, or because holding a meeting gives the appearance of action.

Legitimate Reasons to Meet

In Chap. 1, we noted that meetings in corporate America serve a variety of purposes. Let's expand on some of the legitimate reasons to hold a meeting:

- *To reconcile conflicting views.* Meetings are an appropriate forum for airing grievances and reconciling conflicts. Bringing all parties together in the same room increases the likelihood of resolving their differences, if the meeting is skillfully managed. (If the conflict is serious, a facilitator may be required. We'll discuss the role of the facilitator in Chap. 4.)

- *To reach a group decision.* This is high on the list of legitimate reasons to call a meeting. As organizations form teams to carry out much of their work, group decision-making meetings will grow in number and importance.

  One caution: Don't call a meeting to "decide" on an issue if a decision has already been made, or participants will rightfully be resentful. It's fine to meet in order to review a decision, or to seek approval for one, but make this purpose clear in advance.

- *To solve a problem.* Many problems, especially complex problems, are more readily solved by groups than by individuals. A group of people is also more likely than an individual to identify problems that are vague or that cross departments or functions.

- *To communicate important or sensitive information.* There's no need to call a meeting every time you have information to communicate. But some information must be delivered face-to-face, including bad news (of a layoff, for example), explanations of important policy or benefit changes, and other information of a sensitive nature that will have a serious impact on the lives of employees.*

  It's also legitimate to call a meeting to deflect rumors. In general, any information that's subject to misinterpretation should be relayed in a meeting, so that whoever delivers the information can provide clarification and prevent misunderstanding.

- *To gain support for an idea or project.* A meeting is a proper forum for seeking approval of a proposed project or bolstering support of one that's underway. By selling your idea to everyone at once, in the meeting room, you minimize your chances of being undermined later.

  The meeting is also a useful vehicle for "testing the waters," for eliciting a group reaction to a proposed idea, policy, program, or project before much time or money has been expended on it.

- *To explore new ideas and concepts.* When it comes to developing and refining ideas for new products, programs, promotions, and the like, bringing people together in a brainstorming session is far more effective than soliciting ideas from individual contributors. (We'll discuss brainstorm-

---

*Management consultant John Johnson cautions that bad news should only be communicated in small group meetings, since "whatever is announced in a large gathering is multiplied"—including bad feelings.

ing in Chap. 3.) The synergy that is created when individuals freely exchange ideas results in a greater number and quality of ideas.

- *To report on progress.* Progress reports help to ensure smooth implementation of projects. Meetings to report on progress can also be used to modify or refine objectives, and to identify and correct problems before they escalate out of control.

- *To demonstrate a product or system.* A meeting is an efficient forum for demonstrating products to customers and employees, and for introducing new products to dealers, distributors, the press, and the public. Although product introduction meetings are expensive, they can generate publicity on a scale that would be difficult to achieve by any other means.

Meetings can serve many other legitimate purposes. For example, they can be used to build morale, confer awards, or offer recognition, plan projects and strategies, or provide training to employees, suppliers, and customers. The common denominator is the group. If there is a clear need for a group of people to assemble, a meeting is called for. If there isn't, a meeting should not be called. (See Fig. 2.1.)

Meetings (versus *presentations*) should be used for work that requires people to interact. As management consultant John Johnson writes:

> The meeting setting is best used in dialogue and vigorous exchange and interaction among interested and contributing people. Most of the meeting time should be spent in that fashion. Monologues are valuable only as tools for the interaction. Getting together to hear indi-

DO hold a meeting if you need to...	DON'T hold a meeting...
• Reconcile conflicting views	• Unless you have a clear objective
• Reach a group decision	• If no group decision is needed
• Identify or solve a problem	• If there's a better alternative
• Communicate important or sensitive information	• Just because it's regularly scheduled
• Gain support for an idea or project	• If key participants are unable to attend
• Explore new ideas and concepts	• If the costs outweigh the potential benefits
• Report on progress	
• Demonstrate a product or system	• If failure to hold it will produce no negative effects

Figure 2.1. When to hold a meeting.

vidual reports and speeches with an occasional question regarding the information presented is not a good use of meeting time. It's like driving a sports car at 30 mph. Poor investment. Several individuals are available in one place and/or one time for interaction. Use the time for interaction. That way the whole of the group, its product, is greater than the sum of its parts. Things are created at meetings that could never be created by individuals outside the meetings if the power of the interaction is tapped.

Should I Call This Meeting?

Before you call a meeting, ask yourself the following questions:

What is my objective? Your objective is simply what you want participants to know, do, or believe as a result of your meeting. If you cannot write a one-sentence objective, don't hold the meeting.

Is there a better way to achieve my objective? Even if you have a clear objective, it might be accomplished more efficiently through another route. Letters, telephone calls, one-on-one conversations, faxes, memos, E-mail—all are suitable substitutes for certain meetings. Especially if a group decision is not required, think hard before you call a meeting.

Is the timing right? Are the time and circumstances right for a meeting? Are participants ready to discuss the issues? Do they have all the information they need to make a decision? Are key people available to attend? If the answer to any of these questions is "no," it's not yet time for a meeting.

How much will the meeting cost? Even if the timing is right, the cost may be wrong. Using the chart in Fig. 1.2, estimate the cost of the proposed meeting. Does the estimated cost outweigh the potential benefits? Could participants be spending their time more productively doing something else? If the answer to either question is "yes," don't hold the meeting.

What will happen if I don't call the meeting? A final question to ask yourself: What are the potential negative consequences of *not* holding a meeting? If they are significant (e.g., a major decision will be delayed), it's appropriate to call a meeting. If they are insignificant, there's no good reason to meet.

When to Meet

The Best (and Worst) Times to Hold a Meeting

If you decide to call a meeting, you must determine the best time to hold it. If a meeting is triggered by a crisis or immediate opportunity, you won't have much leeway in terms of scheduling. But whenever possible, carefully consider the timing of your meeting because it can have a significant impact on the meeting outcome. Here are some scheduling guidelines:

- *Meet when participants are at their best.* Do not call a meeting on Monday morning or Friday afternoon, when participants are likely to have little motivation. Don't schedule a meeting for the hour immediately after lunch, when most people feel lethargic.

- *Start at an unusual time, and end at a natural break point.* There is no law that says a meeting must start on the hour or half hour. Select an unusual starting time, and participants are more likely to show up on time—especially if the meeting is scheduled to end at a natural break point, such as lunch or the close of the workday. So, for example, if you want to hold an efficient 20-minute meeting, schedule it for 11:40.

- *Allow ample time for preparation.* Make sure you allow participants sufficient time to prepare. Preparation time will vary according to the nature of the meeting. The longer or more involved the meeting, the more time required to develop handouts, prepare scripts, create visuals, rehearse, and so on.

- *Avoid surprise meetings.* Nobody appreciates a surprise meeting. On-the-spot meetings interrupt the flow of the workday, leave people insufficient time to prepare, and ensure that most participants will enter the meeting room with a negative attitude.

How Long to Meet

The appropriate length for a meeting depends on the type of meeting and on the number, complexity, and sensitivity of agenda items. The more complex or controversial the items, the fewer you can address in a given time period. If you have more topics than you can effectively cover in a single meeting, schedule a second meeting rather than try to cram too much information into the first.

The greater the number of participants, the shorter the meeting should be. In a small meeting, a high level of interaction is possible, and this makes the time pass quickly. In a large meeting, interaction is restricted, and it's more difficult to maintain interest. Five people working on a problem may be absorbed for hours. Five hundred people listening to a lecture can become distracted within minutes.

When scheduling your meeting, allow sufficient time for breaks. Psychologists have found that productivity levels off after an hour and a half and falls off dramatically after two hours. For this reason, make sure to schedule a break at least every two hours.

In scheduling breaks, consider the makeup of the group. "It's an error to apply a patent medicine approach to breaks," says Fred Pryor, board chairman of Fred Pryor Seminars in Shawnee Mission, Kansas. "Some people need a two-minute break after 50 minutes of work, and some need a 20-minute break after five minutes of work."[4]

The length of the break also depends on the nature of the activity. Five minutes is long enough to stand and stretch, but 20 or 25 minutes may be necessary to do a creative exercise.

It's important to let participants know when the session will resume. Instead of saying "let's take a 15-minute break," tell the group "we'll pick up where we left off at 2:15."

For all-day meetings, allow at least an hour for lunch, but preferably an hour and a half or two hours. This gives participants time to recover from post-lunch fatigue and ensures more productive afternoon sessions. Keep afternoon sessions short (an hour is a good length) to prevent boredom and fatigue.

Preparing the Agenda

A written agenda, distributed in advance, is the single best predictor of a successful meeting. The agenda keeps the meeting on course and helps to ensure that stated objectives are accomplished. It also serves as a planning tool for participants and a control tool for the leader.

General Guidelines

The first step in developing an agenda is to refine your meeting objectives. If participants know your objectives in advance and view them as important, they will come to the meeting better prepared and will be more productive participants, according to Bob Bostrom.

Bostrom, who is a professor of business management at the University of Georgia, believes it's important for participants to know exactly "what they're going to walk out the door with"—a rough draft of a report, for example, or a list of ranked ideas. "The more tangible, the better," he says.[5]

With meeting objectives clearly defined, you can begin to develop an agenda, keeping the following guidelines in mind:

- *Limit the number of agenda items.* Focus on a few crucial items—three to six is a good rule of thumb. Separate the "need to know" from the "nice to know," and include only the former items. The remaining topics can be summarized and included with the agenda as supplementary material, or held for a future meeting agenda.

- *Don't dwell on the past.* A meeting should not be a forum for rehashing past problems, rethinking yesterday's decisions, or otherwise dwelling on dead issues. If a meeting is to be productive, it must focus on actions and decisions that will affect the future. The meeting agenda should reflect this future orientation.

- *Present opportunities, not problems.* If an agenda item is framed in negative terms, participants may come to the meeting room in a negative frame of mind, and this can affect their ability to address the issue productively. To avoid this, keep the agenda upbeat. Instead of focusing on problems, recast them as opportunities. Every problem represents an opportunity of some kind—to improve a process or prevent a future problem, for example. If it is presented in this light, there's a better chance that it will be resolved.

- *Allocate ample time.* An agenda should be well organized, but not so rigid that it inhibits creativity or discourages full participation. If you expect an agenda item to take up 20 minutes of meeting time, schedule 30 minutes to allow for questions, creative discussion, and the like. If you don't need the extra time, you can end the meeting early and be a hero.

- *Include sufficient detail.* Include enough detail in the agenda so that participants understand exactly what you want to accomplish. Listing "advertising budget" as an agenda item doesn't give participants the specific information they need to prepare for the meeting. "Allocate the advertising budget among direct mail, print, radio, and television" is a more appropriate item. With this level of information, participants can gather the appropriate data for the meeting and prepare their arguments for or against each advertising medium.

Once you've refined your objective and developed a list of agenda topics, circulate the list to participants and invite them to refine it or suggest additions. This will ensure that no important items are left out. And if participants have a role in shaping the agenda, they will feel a greater sense of ownership in the meeting room.

Be sure to ask for the input of those who may be problem participants. Including them early in the process will help to prevent conflict later.

What to Include

Your agenda should include the items listed in Fig. 2.2. Note the reference to a "meeting recorder." This is the person (usually assigned by the leader) who takes the minutes of the meeting or prepares the Post-Meeting Action Plan, which we'll discuss later in the chapter.

To ensure that the group remains focused on the agenda, consider including a list of "Nonagenda Items" as a reminder that certain issues are not to be discussed in the meeting. For example, if it's already been determined that a new facility will be built and you are meeting to decide on its location, you might include "Need for a New Facility" as a nonagenda item. If a product has failed, you might list "Determine Why Product Failed" as an agenda item, and "Placing Blame" as a nonagenda item.

If possible, the first agenda item should be a topic that will unite rather than divide the group. Schedule the most important, difficult, and/or urgent items early in the meeting when participants are alert and energetic. This is especially important if the meeting is scheduled near the end of the day. If there are guest speakers, schedule them near the beginning or end of the meeting to minimize disruptions.

Make sure the order of agenda items is logical. Don't decide on the number of new hires before discussing the departmental budget. Finally, schedule items that are not top priority, and those which may cause unduly long discussions, near the end of the agenda.

When to Distribute

If possible, deliver the agenda one week before the meeting. The more preparation required for the meeting, the further in advance you should distribute the agenda. If the meeting is a large event lasting half a day or more, send the agenda, through the mail or E-mail, two to three weeks in advance to allow participants to adjust their schedules accordingly. For major events, send the agenda four to six months in advance.

Include with the agenda any supplementary material that will help participants prepare for the meeting—but don't overdo it.

✓ Meeting objective(s)
✓ Location
✓ Starting and ending time
✓ Timing of breaks, if any
✓ Name of leader
✓ Name of facilitator, if applicable
✓ Names of participants
✓ Summary of topics, with presenter names
✓ Time to be allocated to each topic
✓ Category of topic (Decision, Information, or Discussion)
✓ Name of meeting recorder
✓ Instructions on how to prepare for the meeting and/or materials to bring.

Figure 2.2. Agenda items.

If you send a stack of materials two inches thick, don't expect participants to wade through it. It's better to condense the information, which will give it greater impact and help ensure that it's read.

Do not give out advance copies of visuals you plan to use in the meeting; otherwise, participants may focus on the handouts instead of your presentation.* If you wish to distribute copies of visuals, do so after the meeting. (We'll discuss the preparation of visuals in Chap. 6.)

The form shown in Fig. 2.3 can be used to notify participants of the meeting and to supply them with all of the information needed to prepare for it.

Who (and How Many) Should Be Invited?

One of the primary causes of unproductive meetings is not having the right people in attendance.[6] This is a frequent problem, according to the Annenberg study. More than a third of participants in that study (34%) said that only a few (4%) or some (30%) of the relevant people attended the meeting on which they were reporting.

One reason the wrong people show up in the meeting room is that invitations are often based on politics rather than purpose. Lynn Oppenheim writes in *Making Meetings Matter*:

> Despite the importance of having the right people (and only the right people) at a meeting, the public nature of meetings allows their use for "display." Much as peacocks display their feathers to assert their standing, so managers use meetings for displays of organizational standing.[7]

As a result, people get invited (or don't get invited) to meetings for other than legitimate reasons.

Who are the "right" people to invite to a meeting? They include:

- Those who have enough knowledge of the subject to make a meaningful contribution to the meeting.
- Those with the power to make decisions or approve projects.
- Those responsible for implementing decisions made in the meeting.
- Those who will be affected by the decisions made, or their representative.
- Those who need information that will be presented in the meeting in order to perform their jobs more effectively.

*International meetings are an exception to this rule. Handing out visuals in advance can enhance the communication process.

Meeting Notification

To: _____ [List participants] _____

From: _____ [Leader] _____

Date: _____ [of Notice] _____

Date: _____ [of Meeting] _____

Time: Start:_____   End: _____

Location: _____

Agenda

Topic: For: Presenter: Time:

_____

_____

_____

_____

_____

_____

Meeting Objective:

_____

_____

_____

_____

_____

_____

Premeeting Preparation:

_____

_____

_____

_____

_____

_____

_____

_____

Recorder: _____

Figure 2.3.

In addition to inviting the right people, it's important to invite the right number. The optimum number of participants varies according to the type of meeting.

For decision-making and problem-solving meetings, we recommend five persons or fewer; for problem identification meetings, a maximum of 10 people. More than that may result in too many conflicting opinions and may bog down the meeting process.

Training seminars should be limited to 15 people, especially if they involve hands-on exercises. Restricting the size of the group will enable the instructor to give participants more individual attention.

For informational meetings, reviews, and presentations, limit the audience to 30, in order to promote interaction. There is no limit to the number of people you can invite to a motivational meeting; the more, the better. (See Fig. 2.4.)

Where to Meet:
Room Selection and Setup

According to Lynn Oppenheim, you can determine how an organization views meetings by observing its primary meeting space: the conference room. Says Oppenheim:

> If the conference room has technical equipment for presenting information and the room can be reconfigured to make groups of different sizes comfortable, meetings are important to that organization. But if it looks like the meeting room doubles as a library, that tells you,

Optimal Meeting Size	
Meeting type	Maximum # of participants
Problem solving	5
Decision making	10
Problem identification	10
Training seminar	15
Informational	30
Review or Presentation	30
Motivational	No limit

Figure 2.4.

"Meetings are not what we're about. We have to have meetings, but they're not critical to our organization."[8]

Where people meet is as crucial as why and when. The choice of a meeting room has a significant impact on the overall quality of the meeting. Among other things, a meeting room can enhance or inhibit productivity, encourage or discourage communication, promote or stifle creativity, and make participants feel relaxed or tense. Because the room plays such an important role in meeting productivity, it's important take great care in its selection and setup.

How to Size Up a Meeting Room

There are several guidelines to follow in selecting a meeting room. The first and most important is to make sure the room is appropriate for the size of the group.

The room should be neither too small nor too large for effective communication between participants. If it is too small people will feel uncomfortable or claustrophobic, and it will be hard for them to concentrate. If it is too large they will spread out, and the group will lose its sense of cohesion. (If you're stuck with a large space, use room dividers or other devices to create a space of appropriate size.)

A good rule of thumb is to allow 25 ft^2 per person for meetings that require discussion or group interaction. For a lecture or presentation, 8 ft^2 per person is adequate.

Other factors to consider when choosing and setting up a meeting room:

Lighting.   Lighting should be controllable. In some cases, you may require the front and the back of the room to have separate lighting controls.

Be sure to cut the glare from wall fixtures behind participants and presenters so that their faces can be seen without squinting. Avoid fluorescent lighting, if possible; it is hard on the eyes and ears, and results in a loss of energy and concentration after an hour and a half or so.

Windows.   According to conventional wisdom, a meeting should be held in a windowless space to minimize glare if visuals are used, and to prevent distractions. But a windowless space feels confining and can become downright depressing if the meeting is a long one. And there is little evidence to suggest that a beautiful view inhibits discussion. As Paul Radde, a management consultant and expert on meeting room design, points out:

> The belief that adult participants would be distracted by a view to the outside world is a holdover from elementary school teacher anxiety over maintaining attention from school children. Adults can feast their eyes on the Colorado Rockies, city skylines, the Gulf of Mexico, the hill

country of Texas, the autumn foliage of New England, and still participate fully in the meeting. No one can stay totally focused on the meeting
without relief anyway.

If glare is a problem, simply drape the windows when visuals are presented.
And if you must hold a meeting in a windowless space, make it brief.

Ventilation.   The room should have adequate ventilation so that participants don't become drowsy. Make sure that the air and temperature can be
controlled. Smoking in the meeting room should be prohibited.

Access.   Make sure there's good access to the room, and restrooms
nearby. The entrance should be at the back of the room so that latecomers
don't disturb those already seated.

Paul Radde suggests leaving wider aisles near the doors to accommodate
heavier traffic, and varying the angle of the aisle in the direction of the exits
to facilitate traffic flow.

Acoustics.   Participants should be able to hear everything that's said
without straining. Carpeting and drapes will help to absorb sounds and
prevent echoes. And many buildings today are engineered with "white
noise," a faint, rushing sound that fades into the background but drowns
out any sound coming from the rooms next door.

There may be different acoustic qualities in different parts of the room.
Check it out in advance, and position your group accordingly.

Sound System.   Check the sound system for buzz, hum, feedback, and
static. Know where the controls are located so you can troubleshoot any
problems that occur in the meeting. The controls may be separate from those
that bring in background music or public address announcements. Find out
ahead of time.

Test out the sound system exactly as you will be using it during the
meeting. Turn the wireless system on long enough to determine if it brings
in the radios of local taxis, or passing CB radios. If there is a public address
system, silence it during the meeting.

If microphones are required, make sure all ceiling speakers are in
working order. Test out the microphones in advance, and know the spots
in the room where feedback, hum, or shriek begins. If there are other
meetings going on that will utilize wireless microphones, check out their
broadcast frequencies so that your meeting will not be invaded by their
sound systems.

Adjust sound levels upward to accommodate the dampening effect that
an audience will have on the echo of an empty room. Visit the room when
a meeting is in progress to get an idea of how the sound system resonates
with people present.

Distractions.   Make sure that noise won't carry over from other rooms.
Check room dividers for soundproofing. Find out who is scheduled to meet

next door while your meeting is in progress. If it's a rock and roll convention, you may want to reconsider renting the space.

The room next door might have speakers aimed in the direction of your room. With advance planning, both rooms can be set up so that the presenters in each have their backs to the same wall or an adjoining wall.

Disconnect the phones or block incoming calls from the meeting room. Give meeting participants a phone number in advance where they can receive messages during the meeting, and where they can pick up messages during breaks.

Presentation Equipment.   If you are not bringing your own equipment, does the room have the equipment you need? Is it large enough to accommodate the equipment?

Projection Screens.   Projection screens are traditionally set up in the front and center of the room. It's better to put them in the corner and place them at an angle. In this way, neither speaker nor projector will block the audience's view.

Tilt the screen forward at the top (or back at the bottom) so that your projector doesn't produce a "keystone" image (an image that is noticeably wider at the top than the bottom). Not only does this look unprofessional, but it makes it difficult to focus; when the top of the image is focused, the bottom blurs, and vice versa. Or, use a screen with a built-in tilting device called a keystone eliminator.

The bottom of the screen should be a minimum of three feet above the floor. If there is any ceiling light above the screen, it should be dimmed or removed.

In general, the distance between the audience and the screen should be no more than six times the width of the projected image. For example, if an image is 4 feet wide, the audience should be within 24 feet of the screen.*

Dual overhead projectors can be used in most room arrangements, as shown in Fig. 2.5. This enables the meeting leader to present a concept (e.g., a car model) on one screen while using the other screen to show the details of the concept (e.g., a graphic cross-section of the transmission).

Electrical Outlets.   Make sure the room has enough electrical outlets— at least two per wall. The typical meeting room has several outlets at the front of the room to accommodate audiovisual equipment. If you are using large coffee urns, you will need some heavy-duty outlets.

Storage Space.   Be sure the meeting room has enough storage space for coffee supplies; audiovisual equipment; note pads and other meeting supplies; and any other items that will be used in the meeting.

---

*Many manufacturers of screens and projection devices supply information about room size and equipment placement with the purchase of their products.

Figure 2-5. Dual overhead projector arrangement.

Chairs. Uncomfortable chairs distract participants and reduce their ability to concentrate. In choosing chairs, remember that support is better than sag, and that cushioning beats hard board, especially for a long meeting. For a small meeting, chairs that swivel and roll on casters make it easy for participants to interact. If storage is a concern, foldable, stackable chairs are a good idea.

Other Amenities. If the meeting is held off-site, find out whether the facility offers other amenities for your guests' convenience, such as telephones, photocopiers, and fax machines.

Special Needs. Make sure the room accommodates wheelchairs and participants who have other special needs, such as translation.

Once you decide on a room, whether it's within the company or outside the office, reserve it early. If the room you want is not available, locate a similar site or consider postponing the meeting.

Common Seating Arrangements. The type of meeting affects not only the choice of a meeting room but how the room is arranged. Following are some common layouts for different sizes and types of meeting rooms. Note that in each case, the overhead projector is set up at an angle, as previously described, so that the speaker can display visuals while remaining the centerpiece of the room.

Office. In a small office that has no conference table, you can set up a reflective overhead projector at one end of a desk. The speaker may then sit behind the desk and images can be projected onto a screen behind him or her (as shown in Fig. 2.6). This works well for informal gatherings of no more than six people.

Figure 2.6. Office setup.

Figure 2.7. Conference room setups.

Conference Room. For a conference room, a center table or U-shaped table is a common setup. The center table (Fig. 2.7a) is appropriate for small meetings involving 6 to 12 people. A circular table will enable all participants to see one another and encourage interaction among participants. This is an ideal arrangement for problem-solving and decision-making meetings, or other discussion meetings involving no more than seven people.

For larger groups of 10 to 30 people, we recommend a U-shape of small tables (Fig. 2.7b). Groups of this size, whose purpose is generally to share information, need a clearly identified leader. The U-shape gives the leader eye contact with everyone and helps to create a feeling of equality among participants.

Classroom. The classroom setup, shown in Fig. 2.8, is best for large groups and long meetings. It is also effective for training sessions and other meetings that require work space.

Auditorium or Theater. This setup is appropriate for large meetings in which little discussion is expected. The main concern is that the screen be clearly visible to everyone in the room, as seen in Fig. 2.9.

Amphitheater. An amphitheater arrangement is best used for presentations of short to moderate length. It is not recommended for long

Figure 2.8. Classroom setup.

Figure 2.9. Auditorium or theater setup.

meetings and is unsuitable for meetings that require work space for participants (see Fig. 2.10).

Optimizing Seating Arrangements

"First we shape the seating, and then the seating shapes the dynamics of the meeting," says Paul Radde. "Seating formations impact visibility, contact, interaction, networking and bonding between participants, as well as safety, access, and special effects."

According to Radde, seating layouts help to determine how well participants can see and hear a presentation; how well and how much they learn; their relative degree of physical comfort; and the quality and frequency of contact with other participants. He believes that many conventional arrangements detract from the quality of the meeting experience.

The worst offender, he says, is the tradition of seating participants in straight rows. "As long as there are straight rows in the seating arrangement, you can write off communication or contact with everyone more than one person away," says Radde. He adds:

> The next time you sit in a straight row, look at and talk with the second person to your right or left. Someone has to lean forward, or lean back just to make eye contact. And you are only one person away. Lengthen the row and you increase the difficulty of seeing everyone in it.

Figure 2.10. Amphitheater setup.

This problem occurs with every straight row setup, including some, such as the hollow square, the U-shaped table, and the rectangular boardroom table, which are commonly thought to promote interaction.

Radde offers the following principles for arranging or troubleshooting a room setup to improve access, heighten interaction, and increase visual contact:

Principle #1: Semicircle or Curve the Seating to Promote Interaction and Visual Contact.   A semicircular or concave seating arrangement puts people in visual contact and exponentially increases the connection between presenter and participants, and among participants. This may require only a slight variation on a traditional seating arrangement. The hollow square becomes a circle. The U-shaped design, shown in Fig. 2.7, is slightly more bowed to mimic a horseshoe design, providing direct eye contact among all participants (Fig. 2.11). (The audiovisual setup for this would remain the same as for the U-shape.)

Principle #2: Close Up the Middle or Center Aisle to Contain the Energy of the Presentation.   In her book, *How to Organize and Manage a Seminar: What to Do and When to Do It* (Prentice-Hall, 1983), Sheila Bethel maintains that the "energy flow of the speaker goes down the aisle rather

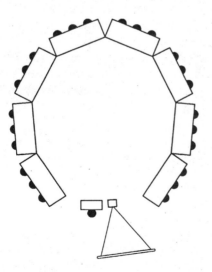

Figure 2.11. Horseshoe setup. (*Figures 2.11 to 2.14 were produced using Adobe Illustrator 5.0. Reprinted courtesy of Adobe Systems, Incorporated, copyright © 1987-1993, Adobe Systems Incorporated. All rights reserved.*)

From standard ...

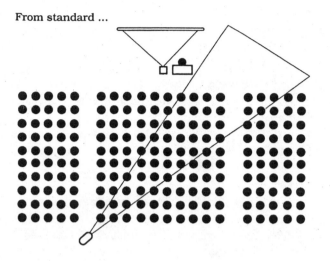

... to state of the art

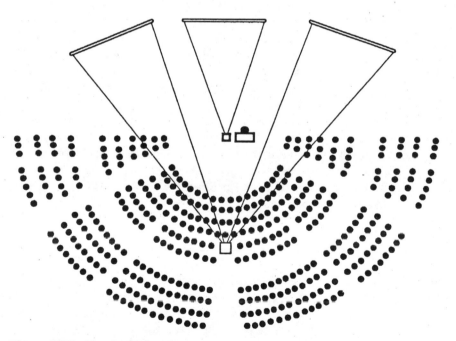

Figure 2.12. Theater style setup.

than into the audience." To contain the energy, close up the center and flank the aisles slightly outside the middle, or semicircle the seating and leave several aisles, as shown in Fig. 2.12.

Principle #3: Set the Room to the Long Side.   To increase personal contact with the presenter, set the room to the long side rather than toward the narrow end. This eliminates the impersonality of long distances, and alleviates difficulties with visibility and hearing. Use rounds or tables, as shown in Fig. 2.13. (*Note:* You may have to set up dual overhead projectors to ensure that everyone in the room can see the presentation.)

Principle #4: Face Each Chair Directly Toward the Presentation. Place chairs so that each participant will face the presentation head on. While most seating diagrams are judged on their seeming symmetry, the actual setup needs to be more functional. Rather than slavishly following a series of concentric semicircles because it looks good on a diagram, try sitting in some of the chairs to determine if they are directly facing the presentation. (That eliminates straight rows, says Radde, which require some participants to watch the presentation with their necks or spines bent or twisted.)

Principle #5: Cut in Single-Chair Aisles for Access.   Even in a small gathering, latecomers often have to struggle across several seated participants to reach an empty chair. No participant should have to go across more than six chairs to find a seat, says Radde, and no latecomer should have to cross more than two people.

To ensure this, limit each row to 11 chairs, if possible, and cut single-chair aisles across the center or sides of each seating section, as shown in Fig. 2.14. Latecomers can use the aisles in the back of the room, and participants near the front will be able to come and go easily at breaks, or in the event of an emergency. The aisles can always be filled back in if there should be a premium on space in the room.

Insist on Your Setup

Paul Radde warns that meeting planners should anticipate resistance to nontraditional seating arrangements. Most meeting rooms are set up with straight rows in mind. Hotels and conference centers often buy carpeting that has squared-off designs, to make it easier for setup crews to place chairs.

Meeting space is calculated solely on the basis of straight-row arrangements. In most cases, no one has determined the number of people who can be accommodated under a semicircular seating arrangement. Meeting space sales managers will protest that alternative seating arrangements

Better

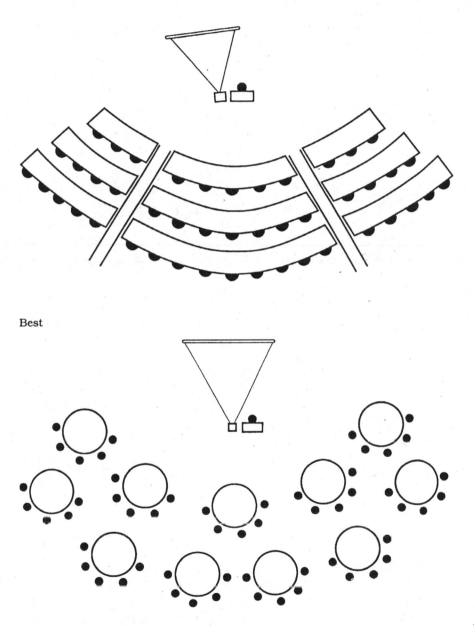

Best

Figure 2.13. Room set to the long side.

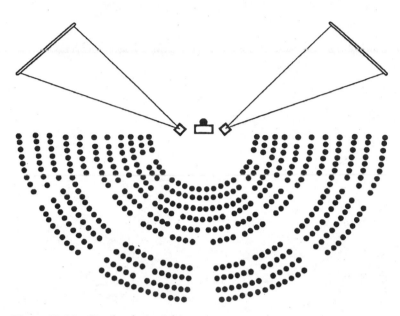

Figure 2.14. Single-chair aisles.

simply "can't be done." "Does that mean it's impossible, or that it's a service you will not provide?" Radde asks. He adds: "You may have to insist on your setup, or persist by arranging the seating yourself."

Figure 2.15 is a sample checklist you can use to ensure that all of your meeting room, equipment, and visuals requirements are met.

Summing Up:
Meeting Minutes[9]

"I thought we took care of that at the last meeting." "Wasn't Kevin supposed to check on that?" "That's not the decision I thought we made." If these comments sound familiar, you have likely participated in a meeting in which no one bothered to take minutes.

Minutes are usually taken as a matter of course in large, formal meetings but are often ignored in small, informal ones. This is a mistake. As we noted in the beginning of this chapter, without appropriate follow-up, the meeting system breaks down. Meeting minutes are the primary tool for ensuring follow-up.

Meeting Room, Equipment, and Visuals Checklist

Room Requirements

1. Room reserved for (facility, address, date/time): _____
   _____
   _____

2. Date/time for premeeting inspection: _____

3. Number of people attending: _____

4. Product(s) to be displayed, and square footage required:
   _____
   _____

5. Demonstration(s) needed and square footage required: _____
   _____
   _____
   _____

6. Food service required:
   ☐ None
   ☐ Full lunch/dinner
   ☐ Coffee/beverages only
   ☐ Continental breakfast
   ☐ Snack _____

7. Room setup required:
   ☐ U-shape
   ☐ Classroom
   ☐ Center table
   ☐ Auditorium
   ☐ Other _____

Room Layout

(Designate smoking sections, if applicable.)

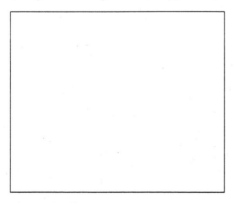

Equipment Requirements

1. Equipment needed:
   ☐ Projector(s) and spare lamps
   ☐ LCD panel
   ☐ Computer with presentation software
   ☐ Video tape player (VHS, Beta, PAL, SECAM, or U-Matic)
   ☐ Video disk player
   ☐ Film projector (8mm, Super 8mm, or 16mm)
   ☐ Video monitors
   ☐ Projection screen(s) size: _____
   ☐ Easel pad
   ☐ Chalkboard with chalk and eraser
   ☐ Lectern
   ☐ Microphone
   ☐ Extension cords
   ☐ Marking pens
   ☐ Pointer

2. Other meeting materials:
   ☐ Note pads
   ☐ Pencils/pens
   ☐ Name/place cards
   ☐ Name badges
   ☐ Other: _____

3. Equipment technician required:
   Contact person _____
   Phone number _____

4. Equipment setup time: _____
   (Allow time to practice using equipment.)

Visual Requirements

1. Visual aids needed:
   ☐ Overhead transparencies
   ☐ Slides
   ☐ Video cassette/laser disk
   ☐ Motion picture film reel
   ☐ Presentation binder
   ☐ Flip-Frame™ Transparency Protector
   ☐ Handouts

2. Transparencies needed:
   ☐ Photos
   ☐ Artwork
   ☐ Title and text charts
   ☐ Table charts
   ☐ Bar charts
   ☐ Line charts
   ☐ Pie charts

3. Deadline for production of visuals: _____
   (Allow for premeeting rehearsal time.)

Figure 2.15.

Minutes prevent people from forgetting or being confused about what went on in the meeting. They "help keep groups from having the same meeting repeatedly," says Nancy Sylvester, speech professor and team trainer at Rock Valley College, Rockford, Illinois, and author of *Handbook for Effective Meetings*.

Minutes are useful during the meeting as well. They serve as a group memory that helps to keep the meeting on course. John Johnson writes:

> All meetings should have this group memory capacity available. It is not just for the sake of keeping a record for a post-meeting report. It is primarily for the purpose of mapping progress during the meeting itself so that the group knows where it has traveled and can build on and change previous ideas and decisions, moving toward convergence on complex subjects. The group can then back track and address previous subjects with more mature and informed insights, just like an individual's thought process ... except that during a meeting it is thinking as a group. Without the group memory a meeting is much less productive.

"Many people don't keep minutes because they think of them as a scary, official document that contains everything everybody says," Sylvester notes. "Since they can't write everything, they don't write anything."

Minutes do not need to be elaborate—they may be as simple as a list maintained on a transparency during the meeting, with copies provided to attendees. Or, the meeting recorder can note decisions made or actions taken beside each agenda item, then compile the minutes from these notes. In computer-supported meetings, it's possible to generate instant minutes (we'll discuss this more in Chap. 5). As long as the minutes *summarize the decisions made and actions taken* in a meeting, *fix accountability* for post-meeting tasks, and *document deadlines* for accomplishing the tasks, the form they take doesn't matter.

Personal computers have made meeting documentation simpler. Using a variety of software packages, it's now easy to produce instant minutes that can be distributed to participants at the end of the meeting.

Guidelines for Taking Minutes

Nancy Sylvester offers the following guidelines for the person assigned to take minutes:

- Include brief summaries of any reports from participants. These summaries can be useful in preparing for and beginning the next meeting. They help the leader and participants quickly catch up on the group's progress on an issue, providing a snapshot of "where we are."

- Word decisions exactly as the group makes them. If any uncertainty exists, check with the group, preferably before the meeting adjourns. "People forget that one or two words can make a big difference," says Sylvester. She cites as an example a committee delegated to "purchase a new computer" versus one delegated to "investigate the purchase of a new computer." Record the name of any participant assigned to perform a follow-up task, along with a reporting date, so "the issue doesn't die." The assigned person knows that the group will expect either a full or status report by the date named.

   "It may be okay for the person to say, 'I haven't finished it yet,' but the group will tolerate that response only so long," says Sylvester.

- Don't include your opinions, interpretations, or judgmental statements such as "valuable comment" or "heated debate." Objectivity helps the group focus on the issues and not the persons involved.

- Consider whether key visual aids, executive summaries, and handouts need to be copied and distributed with the minutes.

- Record the date, time, and place of the next meeting if the group makes that decision.

The Post-Meeting Action Plan

We've designed a simple Post-Meeting Action Plan (Fig. 2.16), that can take the place of meeting minutes. This form is designed to capture the essential decisions and discussions of the meeting and to itemize the tasks to be completed by each participant before the next meeting.

The meeting recorder is responsible for completing the form, noting decisions reached and assignments made during the meeting. This assignment can be made in advance, or the third or fourth person who walks into the meeting can be the designated recorder (this encourages early arrivals). At the end of the meeting, the recorder turns over the Post-Meeting Action Plan to the meeting leader, who keeps the original to use for follow-up, and sends copies to all participants as minutes.

The minutes or Post-Meeting Action Plan should be sent to all participants within a day or two, while the meeting is still fresh in everyone's minds. Prompt follow-up allows participants to spot errors or ask for clarification, if necessary.

Date of meeting: _____

Time started/ended: _____

Meeting objective: _____

_____

Action to be taken	Person responsible	Deadline	Completed

Key issues of discussion: _____

_____

_____

_____

_____

_____

_____

_____

_____

_____

_____

_____

_____

_____

_____

_____

Next meeting scheduled for: _____

List of attendees attached

Figure 2.16. Post-Meeting Action Plan.

Evaluating the Meeting

Simple Evaluations

In addition to assigning follow-up tasks, it's important to evaluate the quality of the meeting so that future meetings will be more productive (and your career more successful). An evaluation doesn't have to be elaborate to be effective. The meeting leader might simply keep notes about how well participants were prepared, which discussions were most productive, what topics weren't covered, and so on. Participants might take turns at the end of the meeting telling what worked and what they feel needs improvement.

The advisory board of the 3M Meeting Management Institute uses the form shown in Fig. 2.17 when evaluating its meetings. This evaluation is simple, but it gets to the heart of meeting productivity by focusing on whether or not participants' time was well spent. A more in-depth meeting assessment form is shown in Fig. 2.18.

Another way to evaluate a meeting is to have the leader and participants compare the completed Post-Meeting Action Plan with the agenda, focusing on the following questions:

- Did the meeting achieve the objective(s) stated in the agenda? Did the right people attend? If not, who was missing and why?
- Did the meeting start and end on time? If not, why not? Were all agenda items covered? If not, which items were not covered, and why?
- Were the discussions held and decisions made productive? Were participants prepared for the meeting? If not, why not?
- What can be done differently to improve the quality of the next meeting?

Meeting Evaluation
Circle one:
0   1   2   3   4   5   6   7
I shouldn't have come   Excellent use of my time
Recommendations for the future: _____   _____   _____   _____

Figure 2.17. MMI advisory board meeting evaluation.

Meeting Assessment Form

Please use this form to answer questions about the
meeting just concluded. Your answers are confidential.   *Circle one of the following:*

Date: _____   Not at all   1

Meeting: _____   Not really   2

_____   Somewhat   3

Pretty much   4

Very much   5

Not applicable NA

1. Was the meeting necessary?	1 2 3 4 5 NA
2. Was the purpose clear?	1 2 3 4 5 NA
3. Was the meeting manager prepared?	1 2 3 4 5 NA
4. Were participants prepared?	1 2 3 4 5 NA
5. Were all needed people present?	1 2 3 4 5 NA
6. Were participants motivated?	1 2 3 4 5 NA
7. Was control of the meeting adequate?	1 2 3 4 5 NA
8. Were people involved in discussion?	1 2 3 4 5 NA
9. Was needed information available?	1 2 3 4 5 NA
10. Was there a clear work process?	1 2 3 4 5 NA
11. Were your resources and ideas used?	1 2 3 4 5 NA
12. Were differences of opinion elicited?	1 2 3 4 5 NA
13. Were problems solved?	1 2 3 4 5 NA
14. Were decisions reached on agenda issues?	1 2 3 4 5 NA
15. Was commitment to decisions obtained?	1 2 3 4 5 NA
16. Was the time used efficiently?	1 2 3 4 5 NA
17. Was closure reached on issues?	1 2 3 4 5 NA
18. Were follow-up work assignments clear?	1 2 3 4 5 NA
19. Were the room and facilities adequate?	1 2 3 4 5 NA
20. Was the purpose of the meeting attained?	1 2 3 4 5 NA

Use the back of this form for comments and suggestions.

Figure 2.18. Meeting assessment form. (*Copyright, 1990, The Meeting Productivity Center.*)

By answering these questions, the group can measure the success of the meeting and highlight areas that need improvement.

Formal Evaluation[10]

A more formal evaluation may be worthwhile for large and expensive meetings and conferences. Often, organizations spend huge sums of money planning a conference, but don't bother to find out what participants liked or disliked about it, what was effective or ineffective.

"Typically, evaluation is an afterthought," says Dana Gaines Robinson, president of Partners in Change, a human resource consulting firm in Pittsburgh. Instead of carefully considering what information they need, meeting planners may throw together two or three questions on a sheet of paper and then get information they "don't know what to do with," says Robinson.

"Evaluation builds in rigor," she adds. "It's an integral part of the whole quality effort. If you don't measure, how do you know whether what you've done is worthwhile?" Evaluation helps organizations "do a better job next time," says Anver Suleiman, president of the Marketing Federation, a conference planning and marketing firm in St. Petersburg Beach, Florida. Evaluation also enables groups to spot new educational opportunities and fill the needs of their markets.

The first step in the process, Robinson says, is to identify the purpose of the evaluation. Often, the purpose is to measure how well the conference met its objective—to update tax lawyers on new IRS regulations, for example, or to train bank tellers how to introduce additional services to customers.

The next step is to identify the sources of information for the evaluation. In many cases, the source will be participants. In the case of training meetings, the sources might include instructors or supervisors. If fund raising is the goal of the conference, the source would be financial records.

In evaluating a meeting, it's especially important to focus on *results*, according to Anver Suleiman: "We need to find out whether participants got the information they expected and whether they will use it."

One way to confirm whether or not the information or skills learned in a meeting are being applied on the job is to evaluate results over time. For example, if a skills training session for salespeople was intended to boost revenues, an easy way to evaluate its success is to track revenues after the meeting.

Suleiman also stresses the need to pay close attention to negative input from participants. In tabulating responses, evaluators commonly score "excellent" as 4, "good" 3, "fair" 2, and "poor" 1. But Suleiman would assign those responses scores of 4, 2, -2, and -4. Giving extra weight to negative input emphasizes what conference planners need to avoid in the future.

"If someone has an overall negative experience, they will tell others about it," says Suleiman. To prevent that from happening, he suggests giving dissatisfied participants a refund or free registration for a future conference.

Suleiman also recommends a follow-up mail questionnaire or telephone interview to find out how participants are using what they learned. This not only produces useful information but it motivates participants to "do things differently."

Aside from focusing on results, planners should think about how they will tabulate the data. For a conference of 1000 people, "it's a mistake to ask three open-ended questions unless you do a content analysis," Robinson says. (*Content analysis* is a tedious method of categorizing and tallying responses.)

Instead, she advises evaluators to ask closed questions that require respondents to check or circle an item, then tabulate responses by computer.

Guidelines for Designing and Conducting Evaluations

Other suggestions from Robinson and Suleiman for designing and conducting evaluations:

- *Make questions specific.* Instead of trying to measure participants' general level of satisfaction, list specific objectives (e.g., "increasing knowledge of Regulation X" or "better understanding of audit procedure") and ask how well the conference met each objective.

- *Make it easy for participants to complete the evaluation.* Consider placing computers around the room so that participants can input their responses after each session. The computers can then tabulate the responses and provide instant feedback.

- *Allow participants ample time for evaluation.* When people are hurrying to catch planes or feeling exhausted because a session has run longer than the stated time, their answers may not reflect their true feelings. Be sure to set aside a reasonable amount of time for evaluations.

- *Avoid "one-size-fits-all" questionnaires.* At least a portion of the evaluation questionnaire should be specific to the session content and presenter.

- *Ask participants if they're ready to apply what they learned.* If confidence in the new knowledge or skill is low, participants probably won't use what they've learned.

- *Determine the barriers in participants' work environment that may affect their use of new knowledge and skills.* Barriers might include lack of management support, low priority among job duties, and lack of proper tools or equipment.

- *Encourage participants to sign their evaluations.* Offer the option of remaining anonymous, but encourage participants to sign their evaluations. Signing will motivate them to think carefully about their responses, and will enable planners to follow up for further discussion.

Room for Improvement

When it comes to preparation and follow-up, there appears to be a large gap between what managers think *should* be done and what *is* done.[11] One-third of the typical meetings in corporate America have no stated agenda. Fewer than a third have written agendas that are distributed in advance.[12] And one-third of managers spend no time at all preparing for the average meeting.[13]

Nor is follow-up an apparent priority to many managers. Despite the importance of minutes as a tool for follow-up, many managers assign them a low priority. Of fourteen rules for effective meetings posed by the Wharton study, middle managers rated taking minutes thirteenth.[14]

Lack of time is surely a factor in poor preparation and follow-up. As noted in Chap. 1, the typical meeting in corporate America is called just two hours before it's held (unless it's a regularly scheduled meeting). This leaves little time for preparation.

A more fundamental reason for inadequate preparation is the sheer number of meetings that take place in the average organization. One middle manager told us it's common for him to attend three meetings a day and "not unusual" to have five or six. Given the large volume of meetings, he says, it's unrealistic to think that preparation won't suffer. Several middle managers in the Wharton study also reported "conflicting or overlapping meetings, with too little time to prepare adequately for any of them."[15]

Reducing the number of meetings won't necessarily solve the problem. Most of the reasons for inadequate preparation and follow-up are symptoms of a deeper problem: viewing meetings as isolated events. Once organizations embrace the concept of meetings as an interconnected system for controlling the work flow, they will coordinate meetings more carefully—and take preparation and follow-up more seriously.

3

Choosing and Using Meeting Procedures

JEFF: As you know, I've called this meeting to decide how we're going to spend next year's advertising budget. The first item on the agenda is to discuss your thoughts on how we allocated last year's budget. Does anybody have any ideas they want to put on the table?

KEVIN: Those radio ads were a waste of money, if you ask me.

BILL: Wait a minute. Weren't you the one who criticized us for spending so much on television commercials? That's the reason we switched to radio.

DEBBIE: I didn't think those commercials were so bad.

JANICE: Are you kidding me? Where did they come up with that actor? The whole thing looked so contrived ...

KEVIN: Has anybody tracked our response rates from TV and radio?

BILL: Maybe we should just stick to print ads this year.

DEBBIE: Get rid of the one that showed the two brothers at the family reunion. So corny ...

BILL: Jeff, how much money do we have to spend this year?

JEFF: The budget hasn't been finalized yet. I know Marketing is getting a 10-percent increase, and I assume we will too.

KEVIN: Don't count on it. Marketing is getting all of the perks these days, since John Avery came onboard. He doesn't even know this industry.

BILL: I don't think that's fair. He's done a good job, from what I can tell ...

Have you ever sat in a meeting that deteriorated into a random conversation such as that? If so, you will probably appreciate the need for groups to follow at least a minimum of procedures to keep their meetings on track.

An agenda alone is no guarantee that a meeting will flow smoothly and be productive. As management consultant John Johnson writes:

> Each item on the agenda needs to have a process. How will ideas be generated? How will the differences of opinion be brought out and managed? How will the generation of ideas be separated from the evaluation of ideas? How will an apparently far out idea with potential be worked with until the negative aspects of it are removed? How will the stage be set for the anticipated conflict that needs to be aired? How will participants be helped to speak honestly and directly on tough subjects? How will issues be brought to closure? Will the decision be made by consensus or majority vote or how? What involvement of participants might be needed prior to the meeting so that they are able to function optimally at the meeting?

Procedures address all of these vital questions.

"Recipes" for Managing Meetings

Meeting procedures are "sets of rules or guidelines which specify how a group should organize its process to achieve a particular goal," writes Scott Poole, professor of speech-communication at the University of Minnesota and an expert on meeting management.[1] Putting it more simply, Poole describes procedures as "recipes for how to run a meeting."[2]

Edward McDonald compares meeting procedures to a computer's operating system. McDonald is assistant general manager of Texaco Inc.'s Information Technology Department and a well regarded practitioner of meeting management. He writes:

> The problems faced by any group in effectively communicating are analogous to those faced by the designers of a multiprocessing computer system. Without the appropriate system control software (operating system), little or no useable results will be achieved. In group interaction, procedures can be compared to the computer's operating system software.[3]

McDonald observes that much time is wasted in meetings because the group doesn't understand the importance of using appropriate procedures. And he stresses that the larger the group, the greater the need for procedures:

As with computing systems, the simplest techniques are adequate in relatively well-ordered environments. The personal computer upon which this paper was prepared has a relatively simple structure, and only a small amount of memory is consumed by the basic operating system (in this case, MS-DOS) which interfaces with the keyboard and the screen used by the word processing program.

Likewise, if only two people are involved in a meeting, then frequently a simple dialogue will suffice. As the number of "processors" increases beyond two, it becomes imperative that a more highly structured interaction be utilized.[4]

Powerful Tools

Scott Poole calls procedures the "most powerful tools we have to improve the conduct of meetings."[5] Even a simple procedure, such as creating an agenda, enhances meeting productivity. "Planning may take a half hour longer," says Poole, "but the meeting usually ends sooner."[6]

Research supports the idea that using procedures improves the quality of meetings. Charles Pavitt, assistant professor of communication of the University of Delaware, performed an extensive review of the literature on meeting procedures. His conclusion: Groups that use formal procedures "probably do make better decisions than groups that do not." These groups also "tend to be more satisfied" with the decisions they make, and are likely to be more committed to implementing them.[7]

Procedures help groups to develop a single focus and avoid the "tendency to go off in all directions simultaneously," according to Michael Doyle and David Straus, who wrote the classic *How to Make Meetings Work.*[8] To achieve a common focus, say the authors, group members must agree not only on *what* they are going to discuss but on *how* they are going to discuss it.[9] In other words, they must agree on meeting procedures.

The Benefits of Using Procedures[10]

Most groups use procedures, however informal, whether they know it or not. "In almost every activity groups follow some procedure, even if only a fragmentary one stemming from members' intuitions that 'this group needs an agenda' or that 'a vote must be taken now.'" Pole continues to say, "In such cases the group is relying on procedures that have become part of the folklore of business and civic life."

The advantages of meeting procedures range from giving groups greater control over their fate to helping them manage conflict to providing a feeling of closure. Let's take a closer look at the many benefits of using procedures.

Imparting a Sense of Control

Without procedures, meeting groups may feel disorganized and disoriented. Procedures give groups a specific blueprint to follow, which helps them to "get a handle" on their problems. This creates an increased sense of control—and when people feel they have control over their situations, their productivity rises.

Overcoming Mindless Behavior

"One of the great barriers to creativity is mindless, habitual behavior," according to Scott Poole. "Most groups fall into habits rather quickly, especially when they have a designated leader and a set power structure." He adds: "One of the greatest challenges to leaders and meeting consultants alike is to produce a reflective attitude, in which groups are conscious of their meeting process and sensitive to the need for managing it."

Procedures make group members aware of the process they use to arrive at decisions and perform other meeting tasks. And they spell out alternative ways of running meetings, some of which may differ greatly from the everyday experience of participants. This raises the group's level of awareness of the options available to them and the need to choose carefully from among them.

Balancing Independence and Group Work

In effective meetings, members think along their own lines and contribute their ideas to a common, developing line of reasoning. Too much independence may shatter group cohesion. But too much structured work can regiment group thinking and stifle novel ideas. To be effective, a group must maintain a balance between independent thinking and structured, coordinated work. Procedures can help.

A good procedure provides explicit instructions for when individuals are to work alone and when the group should work together as a team. For example, the steps of the Nominal Group Technique (discussed later in the chapter, along with several other procedures) lay out in detail what group members should be working on individually, and when the group should evaluate and make decisions *as a group*. Roberts' Rules of Order limits the topics of discussion and determines when they are to be presented. Procedures thus help to provide for independent thinking while encouraging coordination of efforts.

Maximizing Participation

Research shows that a few members of a group tend to be high participators while the rest of the group contributes to a lesser extent or not at all. This effect becomes more pronounced as the group gets larger. One study found that in groups of six or more, the most talkative three members make two-thirds of all the comments.

Unless all participants get a chance to contribute to the meeting, a wealth of ideas and viewpoints may be lost. Participation also increases the commitment of group members. If only a few participants contribute to the meeting, there will likely be a low level of commitment from the group as a whole.

Many meeting procedures help to ensure a balance of participation among group members. For example, the nominal group technique incorporates a round robin rule to ensure that the ideas of all group members are addressed. Roberts' Rules of Order prescribes the order in which members of the group are allowed to speak. And the Delphi Technique guarantees the participation of all members and encourages candor by providing for anonymity.

Minimizing Defensiveness

Because procedures provide objective ground rules for meetings, they help to minimize the defensiveness participants might feel if they were criticized by the meeting leader or their peers. Such defensiveness can divert attention from the work of the meeting, as those reprimanded become preoccupied with getting even or saving face instead of achieving the group's goals.

Good procedures minimize defensive behavior. An agreed-upon procedure offers an objective set of rules that serve as a basis for correcting and redirecting inappropriate behavior. Participants who deviate from the rules are restrained not by the group, but by the rules. Such impersonal criticism is easier for people to accept.

Managing Conflict

Groups, like individuals, tend to have a difficult time in addressing conflict productively. Procedures help to surface and resolve conflicts which might otherwise create bad feelings and polarize the group.

Many procedures directly surface disagreements. If a straw poll is taken, for instance, it becomes clear immediately whether or not members agree with one another. And the devil's advocate procedure deliberately fosters disagreements by encouraging the development of counterarguments. Once conflict has been brought into the open, the group has no choice but to deal with it.

Some procedures incorporate specific guidelines for managing conflicts once they've surfaced. Hall's Consensus Rules incorporates a number of guidelines for dealing with disagreements. Straw votes can be used to build consensus. Repetitive voting, which is a feature of the Nominal Group Technique and the Delphi Technique, can also help to resolve disagreements and build consensus.

Preventing "Groupthink"

It's important for meeting participants to work together as a group. But too much dependence on the group can lead to the phenomenon of *groupthink*, whereby the group stifles dissent and coerces members to agree. Groupthink springs in part from the natural human desire for belonging. But this need for belonging, carried too far, can lead group members to agree in order not to be rejected by the group.

Groupthink prevents the group from fully exploring problems and can result in premature agreement on issues in the name of avoiding conflict and maintaining group cohesion. Both effects can lead to inferior decision making and problem solving.

According to Irving Janis, the Yale professor who developed the concept, one of the traits of groups that are most subject to groupthink is that they follow no formal decision-making procedures. Procedures help to minimize the reliance of individual participants on the group or its leader. When procedures are used, group members focus their efforts on following the procedures rather than caving in to pressure from the group.

Fostering Self-Evaluation

Procedures help to foster self-evaluation by providing a benchmark against which group performance can be measured. When groups become aware of the superior results they can achieve by using procedures properly, they have a basis for judging their performance when they don't use procedures, and for suggesting improvements.

Providing a Feeling of Closure

In many cases meeting groups must tackle uncertain, poorly defined tasks for which it is hard to identify distinct subtasks or to determine when the task has been completed. Individuals and groups will become frustrated if they are kept from completing a task or cannot see the end of a distinct piece of work.

In these situations, it's helpful for the group to identify discrete "chunks" of work that can be completed, so the group can experience a sense of accomplishment. Several procedures help to subdivide tasks into discrete, manageable subtasks, such as problem identification and the evaluation of alternative decisions.

A Sampling of Meeting Procedures

Meeting leaders, scientists, and those who study group dynamics have developed a wide array of simple and complex procedures to make meetings more productive. One excellent compendium, by Ohio State University professor Paul Nutt, details at least 47 distinct procedures for managing various decision-making functions.[11] The following eight examples of meeting procedures show the range of options available:

Roberts' Rules of Order

Roberts' Rules of Order, also known as "parliamentary procedure," is designed to help structure deliberations during every step of the decision-making process. This procedure specifies how proposals must be phrased; the order in which they may be considered; the order of speaking; how decisions are made; and how rules should be enforced, clarified, questioned, or suspended. In short, Roberts' Rules addresses the issue of *how* the meeting is conducted rather than its content.

While Roberts' Rules of Order is intended to promote democracy in large and small groups, the procedure has been criticized for being too complex and for being subject to manipulation. Nevertheless, it remains among the most popular of meeting procedures.

Brainstorming

Alex Osborn is credited with developing the concept of brainstorming, which he outlined in his classic book, *Applied Imagination*.[12] It is a useful procedure for generating and refining ideas.

Brainstorming is governed by two key principles: 1) deferring judgment improves the quality of participant input, and 2) quantity of ideas breeds quality. In a brainstorming session, participants must refrain from evaluating ideas and/or those who proposed them before the ideas have been fully developed and have had a fair hearing. The intent is to reduce fear of criticism and rejection by brainstormers from those eager to give reasons why a new idea "will cost too much" or "will never work."

The idea that quantity breeds quality is based on the notion that the first ideas we come up with are usually the most obvious, and that truly creative ideas will come only after we have gotten the obvious suggestions out. Research substantiates this claim.

The leader of a brainstorming session enforces four basic rules:

1. No evaluation of one's own or others' ideas is permitted. Critical evaluation is reserved until after the brainstorming session.
2. Participants are to contribute as many ideas as possible. After members have "run dry," they are encouraged to continue pressing for more ideas.
3. Wild ideas are encouraged, no matter how far-fetched they may seem.
4. Building on previously listed ideas ("hitchhiking") or combining ideas is encouraged because it promotes integration and refinement of ideas.

Brainstorming is usually facilitated by a group leader, who writes all ideas on a flip chart, storyboard (a foam board to which index cards can be pinned and easily rearranged), or other display in order to stimulate additional ideas and interaction among group members. Groups as large as 15 persons may be used. The more diverse the membership, the better. Ideally, the group should be composed of people who don't interact with one another on a daily basis.

Studies of brainstorming suggest that it produces a wide range of ideas and heightens group enthusiasm, although it is not clear from the research that groups using brainstorming out perform the same number of individuals working alone.

Nominal Group Technique (NGT)

Nominal Group Technique (NGT) is based on research findings that *idea creation* is optimized when individuals are stimulated by the presence of others but do not have to interact with them, while *idea evaluation* is best carried out in an interacting group. The procedure is designed to separate idea creation and evaluation into distinct steps, each governed by its own unique process. It is most effective when used in groups of seven to ten people.

Nominal Group Technique proceeds as follows: First, group members record their ideas in writing, without talking to one another. Then, each member of the group, in turn, reviews his or her list of ideas. The merits of the ideas are discussed, and the group votes on a priority listing of the ideas.

The first two steps of the NGT procedure (see Fig. 3.1) are devoted to idea generation and the rest to clarification and evaluation. The evaluation process may go through several cycles in order to narrow the list to the single best idea.

Multiattribute Decision Analysis (MDA)

Multiattribute Decision Analysis (MDA) is a formal procedure for choosing among alternative decisions. The group generates a list of alternative decisions, a list of outcomes associated with each decision, the probabilities that these outcomes will actually occur, and the value of each outcome.

From this information, the expected value of each alternative can be calculated and used to compare the alternatives. Expected value is simply the value assigned to the outcome multiplied by the probability that the outcome will occur. This information can be displayed as a decision tree, as shown in Fig. 3.2.

Here's a simple example to show how the procedure works: Suppose you are buying a house, and three criteria (outcomes) are important to you: aesthetics, resale value, and quality of schools in the area. The first step in the MDA process is to assign a relative weight to each criterion, depending on how important it is to you, with the total weights adding up to "1" (see Fig. 3.3). The next step is to evaluate each house (alternative decision) you are considering in terms of how well it satisfies each criterion, on a scale of 1 to 10 ("Satisfaction Probability" in Fig. 3.3). For example, if resale value is likely to be high, you might assign this criterion a score of 8. If the house is not aesthetically pleasing, you might give this factor a score of 2. If the schools in the area are average quality, this criterion would rate a score of 5.

The final step is to multiply the weight assigned to each criterion by its satisfaction probability score, then add the subtotals to arrive at the expected value of the house, as shown in Fig. 3.3.

Steps of Nominal Group Technique

Step 1: Silent generation of ideas in writing.
Step 2: Round-robin recording of ideas on a flip chart.
Step 3: Serial discussion/clarification of ideas.
Step 4: Preliminary vote on the importance of each idea.
Step 5: Discussion of preliminary vote.
Step 6: Repeat Steps 4 and 5.
Step 7: Final vote.

Figure 3.1.

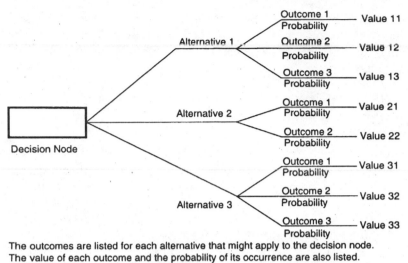

The outcomes are listed for each alternative that might apply to the decision node.
The value of each outcome and the probability of its occurrence are also listed.
Based on this information, an expected value can be calculated for each alternative.

Figure 3.2. A simple decision tree.

You would follow the same procedure for each house you consider. The house with the highest expected value would be your optimal choice, based on the criteria you set and the weights you assigned them. You might also conduct a *sensitivity analysis* to determine how the expected values of various houses would change under more pessimistic or optimistic assumptions about the probability of each criterion being satisfied.

Multiattribute Decision Analysis is usually conducted by one person, but groups can decide what the entries should be. The preceding example is a simple one, but the procedure can become quite involved. There are several

Criterion	Weight	Satisfaction probability (scale of 1 to 10)	Weight × probability
Aesthetics	.25	2	.50
Resale value	.35	8	2.80
School quality	.4	5	+ 2.00
	1.00		Expected value = 5.30

Figure 3.3. Determining expected value.

computer software packages available for groups who wish to conduct more sophisticated analyses.

Hall's Consensus Rules

Hall's Consensus Rules (Fig. 3.4) is a set of guidelines for groups to apply in the decision-making process. Unlike the previous procedures, which set out definite steps groups must follow, Hall's Rules is a general philosophy that groups can apply in the decision-making process in order to achieve consensus. Several research studies have shown that the use of Hall's Rules enhances the quality of group decisions.

Hall's Consensus Rules

Guidelines for reaching consensus:

1. Avoid arguing for your individual judgments. Approach the decision on the basis of logic.

2. Avoid changing your mind only in order to reach agreement and to avoid conflict. Support only solutions with which you are able to agree to some extent.

3. Avoid "conflict-reducing" techniques such as majority vote, averaging, or trading in reaching decisions.

4. View differences of opinion as helpful rather than as a hindrance in decision making. Differences of opinion are natural and expected. Seek them out and try to involve everyone in the decision process.

5. Disagreements can help the group's decision because a wide range of information and opinions increases the chance that the group will find more effective solutions.

Figure 3.4.

Devil's Advocate

The devil's advocate procedure assigns one member of the group as the designated critic. This person consciously opposes or criticizes the accepted stances of the group. He or she suggests disadvantages to alternatives, offers different analyses of problems, questions the value of evidence, and generally helps to "keep the group honest." This procedure differs from the others discussed so far, in that only one member of the group is responsible for implementing it.

Studies have shown that use of a devil's advocate improves the quality of group decisions, compared to the decisions of groups who use no procedures. It is an especially effective tool to use in planning and policy making.

Synectics

Synectics is a procedure that attempts to jar group members out of their mental "ruts" and to permit the free flow of ideas and associations that might occur if they were not so inhibited. The procedure is designed to encourage creativity in problem formulation through the use of analogies and metaphors. It does this through a structured seven-step procedure:

1. The leader describes the problem briefly.
2. The group reviews information about the problem and discusses it in concrete terms.
3. Members list all of the solutions that occur to them immediately and discuss their limitations. This gets the obvious answers on the table and clears the way for more creative solutions.
4. Each member is asked to describe the problem as he or she sees it, and to offer a "wishful" solution.
5. Members are asked to dismiss the problem from their minds and to begin a "mental excursion" in which they free associate and come up with analogies to the problem. Members are encouraged to roam far afield and suggest unusual analogies. This makes the familiar strange and causes members to see different sides of the problem, to view it in a new light. The group and leader select a few good analogies for further examination.
6. The group force fits the problem to the analogy and discusses the insights this produces.
7. The group develops a viewpoint on the problem, which involves the creation of practical strategies for solving the problem.

There are many historical examples of products produced and problems solved as the result of metaphors and analogies. For example, the inventor of Velcro, George de Mestral, came up with the idea by observing how cockleburs adhere to clothing.

A typical synectics group is composed of five to seven people, and a session may last up to four hours. The group should be chosen with care. The key criterion for membership is expertise; everyone in the group should have a good understanding of the problem under consideration. It also helps to recruit only high-energy, flexible people. Those who are uncomfortable with ambiguity should not be included in the group.[13]

The leader of the group should also be chosen with care. The leader's role is very important in synectics; his or her insight and experience with the process is critical to its success.

Delphi Technique

The Delphi Technique is a survey procedure that is used to solicit and pool information and opinions from the members of a group, without any discussion among group members. The process is carried out through the use of questionnaires, with written feedback given to each member. The "group" using this technique need never meet, since the entire process is done by mail.

First, members are given the Delphi question, the initial inquiry that starts the process (e.g., "List the problems in meeting the demand for prenatal care" or "What are the strengths and weaknesses of various videodisc technologies?"). The question is accompanied by a survey form that members complete and return by a specified date. The facilitator then tabulates the responses and includes them on a second questionnaire that asks members to vote for or rate the importance of the various items. In some cases members are also asked to write arguments or position papers justifying their responses. The facilitator then tabulates the ratings, summarizes the arguments, and requests that members reevaluate their choices. This process continues until no new information is forthcoming, a consensus is reached, or the group runs out of time.

The value of the Delphi Technique has been demonstrated in numerous case studies and in some experiments. It is a good procedure to follow for groups that want to gather a broad range of information. Another advantage is that, as with NGT, group members get the chance to benefit from others' insights without having to interact with them. One disadvantage is that there are no clear guidelines for interpreting the survey responses. The quality of the analysis depends heavily on the skill of the person who performs it.

How Procedures Vary

This representative sample of meeting procedures highlights five dimensions in which procedures vary. Procedures can be divided into different groups, based on these dimensions:

1. *Scope (general versus specific purpose)*. First, procedures differ in scope, the extent to which they are general purpose rather than designed for a specific meeting task. One good measure of scope is the number of functions to which a procedure can be applied. For example, Roberts' Rules of Order is a high-scope procedure because it can be applied to almost any decision-making function, from developing proposals to dealing with disputes and taking votes. Brainstorming is a low-scope procedure; it focuses only a specific subtask of a meeting—generating ideas.

2. *Degree of restrictiveness*. Procedures vary in their degree of restrictiveness, the extent to which they limit the group's activity. Roberts' Rules of Order and the Nominal Group Technique are highly restrictive. At the other extreme is the devil's advocate procedure; it controls only the advocate's behavior and does not tightly specify that behavior.

3. *Level of comprehensiveness*. Procedures vary in terms of *comprehensiveness*. Roberts' Rules of Order, the Nominal Group Technique, and Multiattribute Decision Analysis are all highly comprehensive; they specify precise rules and steps for carrying out meeting functions. Devil's advocate and Hall's Consensus Rules are low in comprehensiveness; they give general guidelines but no specific directions for interaction. Brainstorming is somewhere in between. Its rules are specific, but they govern only a limited range of behavior during the brainstorming session, such as prohibiting evaluation of ideas and encouraging wild ideas.

4. *Level of group control*. Procedures differ in terms of *group control*, the degree to which the group can apply the procedure without the help of a facilitator or expert to run the process. Multiattribute Decision Analysis is low in this dimension; it usually requires the assistance of a facilitator or consultant. Roberts' Rules is moderate in terms of group control. The chairperson and parliamentarian are required to facilitate the use of the rules, but they are chosen from the group, and members can consult and use the rules themselves. Hall's Consensus Rules is high in group control; group members enact and enforce the rules themselves. The Nominal Group Technique varies in terms of the level of group control, depending on how it is applied. Although it can be managed by a neutral facilitator, the steps are clear enough that a group can apply the procedure itself.

5. *Degree of participant involvement*. Finally, procedures vary according to the degree of *member involvement*, that is, the number of members who must

PROCEDURES DIMENSION	Roberts' Rules of Order	Brain-storming	NGT	MDA	Hall's Consensus Rules	Devil's advocate	Synectics	Delphi Technique
SCOPE	H	L	M	L	H	L	M	H
RESTRICTIVENESS	H	H	H	H	L	L	H	H
COMPREHENSIVENESS	H	H	H	H	L	L	L	H
GROUP CONTROL	M	H	M	L	H	H	M	L
MEMBER INVOLVEMENT	H	H	H	H	H	L	H	H
H = High, M = Moderate, L = Low								

Figure 3.5. Procedures rated on dimensions.

cooperate in order to apply the procedure. Procedures like the Nominal Group Technique, the Delphi Technique, and Hall's Consensus Rules are high involvement, requiring the cooperation of all members. Devil's advocate is at the other extreme; it requires only a single member's cooperation.

Figure 3.5 shows the eight procedures rated on the five dimensions. These dimensions provide a useful means of comparing procedures and designing new ones. For example, to help ensure balanced participation, the meeting leader can choose procedures that are high in restrictiveness, comprehensiveness, and group involvement, and low in group control. To prevent negative behavior, procedures that are highly restrictive and comprehensive, but low in group control, can be used (having a leader or facilitator guide the procedure ensures that negative behavior is suppressed).

How to Choose the Right Procedure

Effective use of procedures starts with selection of the correct technique. In addition to considering the attributes of procedures, it's important to match procedures to the task being performed, the group performing the task, and the outcome desired.

Match the Procedure to the Task

What tasks does the meeting involve and what procedures are suited for these tasks? Procedures are developed with certain tasks in mind. Some procedures, such as Roberts' Rules, are designed for managing entire meetings. Other procedures are intended only for specific tasks. Nominal Group Technique is effective for developing and evaluating ideas, but it's ineffective for planning implementation. Devil's advocate is most effective when the group's thinking is beginning to gel. The Delphi Technique is the optimal procedure for coordinating extensive debates when many viewpoints exist.

Too often, people try to use a procedure on a task for which it is not suited. Roberts' Rules of Order is often abused in this way. It is a wonderful system for running meetings where proposals are clearly differentiated and sides are clearly defined. However, it is not as useful if a conflict must be managed. It is also a poor procedure to use if a detailed plan must be worked out (Roberts' Rules explicitly recommends referring such a task to a subcommittee not governed by the Rules). Nevertheless, because this procedure works so well in many meetings, meeting leaders often try to apply it in all situations, with results ranging from mediocre to disastrous.

Some meeting leaders tend to adopt the procedures that are most familiar to them, whether or not they are the most appropriate for the situation. To justify the use of the familiar procedure, they may simply redefine the task so that the procedure appears to be the most appropriate choice.

Suppose a leader wants to develop a new product idea and is uncertain what such an undertaking involves. If the leader is comfortable with synectics, he or she may define generating product ideas as a "creativity task" to justify using the procedure. If the leader wants to use Nominal Group Technique, the task will be defined in terms of idea generation and evaluation. The two approaches will yield distinctly different results.

Meeting leaders must be aware that all procedures are designed for a limited range of conditions, and choose accordingly. It's a good idea for the leader to become familiar with a variety of procedures in order to avoid the temptation to fall back on those that are the most comfortable but not necessarily the most appropriate.

Choose a Procedure That Fits the Group

Charles Pavitt, of the University of Delaware, cautions: "Just as a procedure may be good in some circumstances and bad in others, a procedure may be good for some people and bad for others."[14] Not all procedures are appropriate for all types of groups. Some procedures work best with small groups and some with large groups. Some are more effective with creative people who loathe structure. Others are best used in groups that thrive in a highly structured environment.

Some procedures require that the group have special training, while others can be used with little advance preparation. It's vital to match the procedure to the group that will be applying it. In selecting meeting procedures, it's also important to consider the social climate in which the group is operating—such as, how open communications really are, how motivated the group is, and the attitudes of members toward one another.

Choosing a procedure without understanding these dynamics can do the group more harm than good. For example, a group in which members hold deep-seated resentments toward each other should not use Devil's advocate because members will likely use it as an opportunity to take potshots at one another.

Fit the Procedure to the Desired Outcome

What outcomes does the group hope to achieve? The answer to that question should inform the choice of meeting procedures. If a high-quality decision is of primary importance, Multiattribute Decision Analysis may be a good choice, but this procedure does not maximize group participation. If member commitment is more important than decision quality, a procedure that encourages individual participation may be just as useful as MDA. Paul Nutt provides some excellent choice trees for selecting procedures on the basis of desired outcomes for various decision subtasks.[15]

Match the Procedure to the Organizational Culture[16]

Procedures should be matched to the culture of the organization, according to Michael Leimbach of Wilson Learning. Leimbach speculates that more effective meetings occur when there is a strong match between the organization's values and the values implicit in meeting procedures.

Leimbach notes that many studies of meeting effectiveness fail to consider organizational culture as a variable. He suggests that matching meeting procedures to the organization's culture may be more important than the procedure chosen. "Thus," writes Leimbach, "all meeting procedures might be effective or ineffective, depending on the relationship between the procedure and the group's culture (and the strength of the cultural element)."

Meeting procedures, by their very nature, endorse or emphasize certain values. Brainstorming techniques require (or assume the values of) open communication and equal status of group members. In contrast, Roberts' Rules of Order assumes a strict hierarchy of group membership and values eloquence in expression. Hall's Rules puts a premium on consensus building.

If the values implicit in a procedure clash with the predominant values of the organization, the procedure may be ineffective. Suppose seniority is a primary cultural value in an organization. Brainstorming may not be effective in such an organization because the technique considers all participants equal. If brainstorming or similar techniques are used, they must be positioned carefully, taking into account the perceived inequality of comments from high- and low-status participants.

The values of the organization may change over time, and meeting procedures should change along with them. For example, young organizations typically value creativity, informality, and learning by trial and error. Meeting procedures such as brainstorming and synectics, which emphasize these values, are more likely to result in effective meetings if the organization is in its early stages.

As an organization grows and becomes more established, it tends to adopt values such as quantifiability, formality, and learning through practice. Such an organization may get more benefit from using formal, systematic approaches such as Multiattribute Decision Analysis and the Delphi Technique than less structured procedures.

Leimbach believes that organizations can change their culture by deliberately using procedures that emphasize the new values they wish to adopt. For example, if the organization wishes to stress the value of participation, procedures such as Nominal Group Technique, which requires the participation of everyone in the group, can be used. If the organization wants its employees to be more creative, procedures such as brainstorming can be used to stimulate creativity. By incorporating meeting procedures that emphasize the desired values, the meeting process supports the organization's overall strategy to change its culture.

A cultural shift cannot be accomplished solely in meetings. But without the support of meeting procedures, changing the organization's culture is much more difficult, perhaps even impossible. As Leimbach writes: "Can an organization effectively change its culture without changing the procedures that guide activity in meetings? Given the prominence of meetings in organizational life, the answer is probably no."

Why Groups Resist Procedures

Despite the many proven benefits of using meeting procedures, groups tend to ignore or reject them. Scott Poole explains why: "People tend to act so as to conserve time and energy. And, because most group activities are time and energy intensive, the additional energy required to select, learn, run, and enforce procedures may seem excessive." Poole continues, "This is unfortunate because well chosen procedures can save a great deal of time and energy over the long run. However, groups seldom think in the long-term. Instead, groups find various reasons for rejecting procedures."

In some cases, groups reject procedures outright. In others, resistance to procedures takes a subtle form, such as adopting a procedure, then violating some of its key provisions, rendering it ineffective. (For example, it's fairly common for members of brainstorming groups to evaluate ideas regardless of the leader's directions against doing so.)

Poole cites a number of excuses that people typically offer for their failure to adopt meeting procedures:

- *"This is unnatural; it doesn't feel right."* Group members often complain that procedures inhibit them. And in many cases, they're right. Procedures designed to balance participation will seem unnatural to talkative members. A rule mandating anonymous votes will cramp the style of powerful members who are used to pressuring those who don't agree with them. Whenever procedures jar the group out of its ruts, they may seem unnatural, and members will be tempted to abandon them.

- *"This is too hard; we don't need anything this complex."* Managing procedures requires effort. Members who would normally operate independently must coordinate with each other. Managing procedures also diverts energy the group would normally devote to the task or to other goals, such as socializing. Even worse, the payoff from this diversion comes only in the future, in higher quality, creativity, or commitment. Given these distant and intangible rewards, it's not surprising that groups often choose to focus on their work and disregard procedures.

- *"We are under severe time pressure. Using this procedure will only slow us down."* Again, procedures must plead guilty on all counts. Procedures are intended to slow groups down somewhat. Many of the worst habits of groups thrive in the midst of time pressure. The group feels it must hurry, and so divergent ideas must be discouraged, unity enhanced, and a solution developed quickly, no matter what the cost.

  There's nothing wrong with the group having a sense of urgency, but panic produces poor decisions and inferior solutions. When time pressures are great, the best thing a procedure can do is to slow the group down, make it more conscious of its process and aware of the need for considering diverse ideas.

  Research shows that when in a crisis mode, groups perceive that they have less time available to them than they actually do have. Even in a crisis, there is usually time for the group to use some procedures, and a well-chosen procedure may result in more efficient use of the time available. Nevertheless, in the heat of the moment, groups can hardly be blamed for dispensing with procedures.

- *"Using this procedure will cause a conflict."* Procedures that might make underlying disagreements surface seem threatening. Groups instinctively try to reduce conflicts as quickly as possible. But often a conflict must surface and cause some discomfort before members will feel sufficient tension to do something about it. The discomfort that a procedure causes in the short run sometimes leads to a stronger group over the long-term, provided the conflict can be managed effectively.

    Of course, in some cases surfacing conflicts is counterproductive. For instance, in a task force that must get out a report before it disbands in three days, surfacing a conflict would likely serve no productive end.

- *"Leadership is what makes the real difference in groups; procedures won't make much of an impact."* It is a Western myth that the leader—the great man or woman—is responsible for what groups or nations accomplish. People tend to attribute outcomes, both good and bad, to meeting leaders when, in fact, the group produces most outcomes through a complicated process of interaction. Procedures to guide this interaction may well make far more difference than any leader would. However, it is difficult for many people to see this because of our national focus on individual achievement.

Eight Ways to Promote Use of Procedures

Meeting procedures present a paradox. The reasons that groups commonly cite for rejecting procedures ("too hard," "too time-consuming," "unnatural," etc.) are precisely the reasons that procedures work, according to Scott Poole. Given this paradox, what can the organization do to encourage the use of meeting procedures? Poole offers the following eight guidelines for promoting the "faithful and appropriate use of procedures":

1. *Create a successful experience.* Nothing succeeds like success. If a group has trouble coming up with ideas and brainstorming helps members generate dozens of new thoughts, they are likely to use the procedure in the future. If a group has experienced problems with a task, it is more likely to embrace a procedure that promises to reduce problems or speed up work on the task. Letting a group experience a task without procedures is sometimes a useful prerequisite to introducing the procedure.

2. *Find (or create) a procedural champion.* Research on organizational change has shown that innovations have a much greater chance of being imple-

mented if they have a champion. A champion is simply a person who advocates the innovation and puts extra energy into getting it adopted.

Although finding a procedural champion is usually a matter of luck, champions can sometimes be made. Training one or two members in a procedure makes them experts, and they may decide to exercise this expertise. Because attitudes often follow behavior, they may talk themselves into becoming champions once they see that the procedure helps the group (and, perhaps, elevates their status within the group).

3. *Share control over the procedure.* The greater the number of group members who understand and control procedures, the more likely the group is to use them. As noted earlier in the chapter, the potential for member control varies for different procedures. Some procedures, including those that require a facilitator, do not allow for a high level of control by the group. However, even in these cases, member control can be maximized if the facilitator is responsive to the group.

4. *Tailor the procedure to the group's needs.* "Procedures are not all-or-nothing items that have to be used fully or not used at all," says Poole. Groups usually adapt procedures as they use them, selecting and combining features of a variety of procedures. For example, they may use the round robin feature of the Nominal Group Technique for listing ideas, then have a devil's advocate critique the ideas. This "salad bar approach" is effective, says Poole, "as long as you preserve the spirit of each procedure."[17]

Poole cautions groups to be aware that changes in procedures can undermine their intent:

> I have documented several cases in which one person has become "master facilitator" of all procedures used by a group—brainstorming, Nominal Group Technique, force field analysis. This role was a source of power to the "master"; he or she could manipulate the group through subtle management of procedures. Ironically, in most cases, the master facilitator did not intend for this to occur; they intended to use the procedures to help the group and often were not aware that they were using procedures manipulatively. Such is the power of small, gradual adaptations.

Groups must be aware of the potential for such misuse and make tailoring procedures a conscious process.

5. *Get the group interested in its own processes.* Group members tend to be so focused on the content of the task, the ideas discussed, and the actions considered that they ignore the group processes that generate these ideas and actions. It's a major challenge to sell meeting participants on the importance of attending to group process. But once they become aware of process, they will be much more open to procedures.

Procedures themselves can help groups become sensitive to process issues. Because they spell out rules and behavioral guidelines, procedures can make members aware of the need to control process.

6. *Use the procedure as a tool for self-evaluation.* Poole refers to procedures as "'idealized' molds into which we pour our meetings." Because procedures represent ideals, they contain implicit norms for evaluating other group work. For example, implicit in brainstorming is the norm that premature criticism kills ideas and discourages people from speaking out.

If this norm is used as a standard for self-evaluation, it will improve the general group operation, and the value of brainstorming will be reinforced in the eyes of the group. A good way to encourage this is to schedule a formal evaluation period at the end of meetings.

7. *Have a neutral facilitator apply procedures in sensitive situations.* There are occasions when procedures are called for, yet members fear they will not be applied fairly. In some conflict situations, there is little basis for trust, and group members will not have much faith in procedures that could be manipulated by others. It helps to have a facilitator, a neutral third party who can ensure the procedure is run properly. (We'll discuss the role of the facilitator in Chap. 4.) Studies of conflict indicate that a mediator or other neutral person increases the likelihood that all parties will agree to go through a conflict management process.

8. *Set reasonable expectations.* Unless group members have an accurate picture of the time and effort required to use a procedure, they may withdraw from the process in midstream if it becomes too difficult. They should also have a realistic understanding of the expected outcome of using the procedure.

It is a mistake to oversell a procedure, although there is a temptation to do so in the face of a reluctant group. Promising that a procedure will solve their problems may convince group members to use it, but it may also create a performance gap between expectations and reality. In the long run, this may result in rejection of the procedure.

While these guidelines are useful, procedures will continue to seem "foreign and disruptive" to many groups. "Adoption of one procedure does not necessarily mean a group will be open to others in the future. It may mean simply that the group has added one more wrinkle to its habitual behavior with no real change in other dysfunctional habits. Implementing procedures in groups is an ongoing process, and each procedure presents a new challenge."[18]

Computer software technology may make groups more receptive to using procedures in the future. (We'll discuss this emerging technology in Chap. 5.) But no matter how sophisticated the technology used to apply it, a procedure is not likely to be effective unless the group is motivated to perform its work. As Charles Pavitt points out, "the adoption of a formal procedure will not help a group make high-quality decisions if the group merely goes through the motions of performing it. A group is more likely to apply itself when its decision matters to its members."

Research supports Pavitt's contention. When asked in an open-ended survey question about what made a meeting productive, 43 percent of senior managers and 34 percent of middle managers cited *relevance, importance,* and *interest.*[19]

The moral? To make procedures work, hold meetings that matter.

4

Meeting Roles: How to Lead, Facilitate, or Participate

All the world's a stage, And all the men and
women merely players ...
　　　　　　　—WILLIAM SHAKESPEARE
　　　　　　　　　　As You Like It

The quality of a meeting is largely determined by how well the players act out their roles. In this chapter we'll explore the three primary meeting roles—leader, facilitator, and participant—and show how each contributes to success (or failure) in the meeting room.

Leading the Meeting

The quality of the leader has an enormous impact on the outcome of the meeting. Effective leadership is a major predictor of meeting success, and lack of leadership a significant contributor to meeting failures.

If the meeting leader is unskilled, the group may feel directionless and the meeting will likely be unproductive. If there is no leader, or more than one leader vying for control of the meeting, priorities will be unclear and goals left unmet.[1] Without effective leadership, the group will have a difficult time achieving its objectives.

The Servant of the Group

An effective leader is one who serves the group, according to Antony Jay, who writes in *Harvard Business Review*:

> If the chairman is to make sure that the meeting achieves valuable objectives, he will be more effective seeing himself as the servant of the group rather than as its master. His role then becomes that of assisting the group toward the best conclusion or decision in the most efficient manner possible: to interpret and clarify; to move the discussion forward; and to bring it to a resolution that everyone understands and accepts as being the will of the meeting, even if the individuals do not necessarily agree with it.[2]

Self-serving leaders who force their personal priorities on the group fail to win the respect of its members. By contrast, leaders who make it clear they are committed to the group's goals, not their own, gain the respect of members and have an easier time controlling the group. Control is then simply a matter of "imposing the group's will on any individual who is in danger of diverting or delaying the progress of the discussion and so from realizing the objective."[3] It does not require a charismatic leader, only a committed one.

In helping the group to achieve its goals, meeting leaders must wear a variety of hats. They must be visionaries, capable of helping the group see the big picture—what the meeting is meant to accomplish. They must be amateur psychologists, sensitive to the feelings of individual members and capable of reading the mood of the group. They must be moderators, negotiators, and conflict managers, monitoring disputes and helping warring factions work together. These are just a few of their diverse responsibilities.

Leading a meeting is a delicate balancing act. Meeting leaders must influence the group's thinking—not dictate it. They must encourage participation but discourage domination of the discussion by any single member. They must welcome ideas but also question them, challenge them, and insist on evidence to back them up. They must control the meeting but take care not to overcontrol it.

This last responsibility is a particular challenge. While the leader must maintain control over the meeting, there is such a thing as too much control. As Ann Depta, owner of Meridian Consulting Group in Charlotte, North Carolina writes: "Procedures and an agenda are important, but if leaders are so bound to these that they cannot allow for flexibility and spontaneity, the team will soon find its meetings to be drudgery and will lose interest in attending." Depta concludes: "The meeting leader must be willing to respond to what is happening in the here and now."[4]

In some cases, a leader may use agendas as a way of "controlling the discussion so that nothing unexpected or unpleasant" has a chance to arise.[5] But sometimes it's crucial for unexpected or unpleasant topics to be discussed if the meeting is to be productive. The leader who is too controlling may thus inhibit productivity rather than enhance it.

In the name of efficiency, leaders may move the meeting along too rapidly, forgetting or ignoring the social dimension which is so vital to a meeting's success. Management guru Tom Peters reflects: "'Efficient meetings' falls in the same category as an efficient relationship with a spouse or significant other." He adds: "Meetings in my opinion aren't for getting things done; they are for checking things out, checking people out. So a lot of what we call wasted time and boring meetings is really people doing the social stuff that's needed to gain consensus."

Time spent building consensus is not wasted, says Peters, and he cites the Japanese to prove his point: "The conventional theory is that the Japanese take forever to make a decision. In fact, they are checking stuff out and passing it up and down the line and getting emotionally used to the decision and removing objections." Once they finally reach consensus, though, "they implement overnight." Americans, on the other hand, "make a fast decision but nothing ever happens." Both are caricatures, Peters admits, "but there's more than one grain of truth there too."

Getting the Meeting Off to a Good Start

The leader must establish control of the meeting from the start, by setting the tone and stating the ground rules and objectives. "The chair can create the right environment and ground rules for the meeting with a 3- to 5-minute opening statement," says Roger Mosvick, professor of speech communications at Macalester College in St. Paul, Minnesota and a meeting management consultant.

"A brief 'orientation' speech by the chair can get rid of half of the needless talk that occurs" at the start of meetings, Mosvick claims. "The chair must set up the meeting, state the problems, general objectives and procedures, provide the relevant information base of the discussion and note the boundaries and constraints of discussion."[6]

If the meeting is large, or if participants don't know each other, the leader might introduce an icebreaker exercise to stimulate interaction and ease the awkwardness. One effective exercise, called "Coincidences," has people pair off and begin talking to one another, looking for things they have in common.

Even in a small group, it's easy to find coincidences. ("I was surprised to find another female pilot here,"; "Bill Thomas and I were born in Providence Hospital in Portland, Maine—within a week of each other ....") By the time the first agenda item is addressed or the first speaker introduced, nervousness has been replaced by a sense of togetherness.[7]

Icebreakers work because they focus people's attention on doing a job rather than on meeting people, which comes naturally in the course of the exercise. And meeting participants invariably enjoy such exercises. (At one course where "Coincidences" was used, participants were so eager to meet everybody in the room that they insisted on continuing, and the facilitator had to reschedule the next session.)[8]

Encouraging Participation

In the view of one middle manager who is a veteran of meetings: "An effective meeting leader is an orchestrator, someone who makes sure everyone is contributing, if indeed everyone needs to contribute." Encouraging participation is one of the leader's main obligations (see Fig. 4.1). Unfortu-

---

Ten Tips for Encouraging Participation

1. Don't monopolize the discussion.

2. Don't show verbal or nonverbal disapproval of ideas, even if you disagree with it.

3. Ask open-ended questions to stimulate discussion.

4. Frame problems in positive terms. Don't ask if it's possible to achieve a goal. Ask "How can we achieve our goal?"

5. Identify the introverts in the group. Make a point of asking for their input.

6. Don't let extroverts monopolize the discussion.

7. Don't allow senior members of the group to dominate the discussion.

8. Use meeting procedures that require the participation of all group members.

9. Probe to find out what's bothering those who exhibit "hostile silence."

10. Rotate leadership.

Figure 4.1.

nately, not all meeting leaders know how to go about it. According to Ann Depta: "A frequent lament among managers is their inability to get people to participate in meetings."[9]

In some cases, meeting leaders unwittingly discourage participation by their own actions. For example, they may spend "95 percent of a meeting telling or selling," according to Depta. "Then in the last few minutes, the leader asks, 'Are there any questions?'"[10] By dominating the meeting, such leaders leave little room for the participation of others.

There are more subtle ways in which leaders discourage participation. For example, if the leader shows even a hint of disapproval when someone asks a question or presents an idea, the entire group may shut down. Even if the leader doesn't agree with what is being said, Ann Depta argues, he or she must listen and "project acceptance, verbally and nonverbally."

Depta offers a number of other suggestions for encouraging participation:[11]

- *Ask open-ended questions.* Instead of asking the group questions that require simple "yes" or "no" answers, the leader should ask open-ended questions, such as "What do you think of this idea?" or "What do you see as the drawbacks of this approach?" to stimulate discussion.

- *Pose problems as opportunities.* As noted in Chap. 2, it's important to frame agenda items in positive terms that will stimulate creative responses. Meeting leaders must consider how language can stifle the ability to solve problems creatively. For example, groups create limits to their capability to accomplish things when they ask, "Is it possible to reach our target number?" Instead, the question can be worded, "How would it be possible to reach our target number?" This way of asking the question assumes it is possible to accomplish the goal; it's just a matter of finding a way to make it happen. By asking questions in this manner, people stretch their thinking beyond the limits they tend to impose on themselves.

- *Recognize differences in participation styles.* Meeting leaders must be aware that "participation means different things to different people," says Depta. For example, extroverts and introverts participate in "starkly different" ways: "Because extroverts 'talk to think,' they are usually going to be much more willing to speak without having to think through exactly what they want to say." Thus, the meeting leader must manage the process so that extroverts don't dominate the meeting.

  "Meanwhile, introverts with important things to contribute can't get their thoughts on the table because by the time an introvert 'thinks to talk,' some extrovert has jumped in." Once meeting leaders recognize the differences between extroverts and introverts, they can use procedures, such as Nominal Group Technique, that require everyone's participation.

Leaders must also remember to *ask* introverts in the group what they are thinking. "If leaders do not know what extroverts are thinking, they are not listening because extroverts will tell them. If leaders do not know what introverts are thinking, they didn't ask." Depta continues: "Introverts frequently have profound things to say because they have been busy thinking things through before speaking."

- *Rotate leadership.* Another way to encourage participation is to rotate leadership from one meeting to the next. "Where is it written that the manager must always run the meeting?" Depta asks. Managers who are secure enough to allow their people to grow and develop through the process of learning to conduct team meetings will reap the benefits of increased involvement and ownership of the meeting's outcome.

- *Change the seating arrangement.* "The sameness of seating patterns promotes a sameness of thinking that stays with the group meeting after meeting," Depta claims. Participants can become rigid in their patterns of reacting and participating. Creativity and flexibility are stifled as people enter each meeting with preconceived opinions from the last gathering. Changing seats causes people to approach things from a different perspective. "Meeting leaders should understand that their meetings are really metaphors for change. People resist change for many good reasons, but today's workers are going to have to become more comfortable with change, to accept it," says Depta, "and even to embrace it. If members of a group are encouraged to be more flexible by the simple act of sitting in a different place every week, the message about change will become a part of their thinking."

Drawing Silent Types into the Discussion

How does the leader handle the silent types who are reluctant to participate? That depends on the reason for their silence.

Antony Jay divides silence into three categories. The first is the silence that indicates "general agreement, or no important contribution to make, or the need to wait and hear more before saying anything, or too good a lunch …"[12] This form of silence should not worry the leader, says Jay. But there are two other forms that should: the "silence of diffidence" and the "silence of hostility."

The silence of diffidence indicates that the person "may have a valuable contribution to make but be sufficiently nervous about its possible reception to keep it to himself."[13] In this case, the leader should gently draw the person into the discussion and make it clear that the person's input is valued.

The silence of hostility signals that a person is "detached from the whole proceedings" and usually indicates that the person is experiencing "some feeling of affront." The meeting leader should try to get to the root of the problem, Jay argues: "If you probe it, you will usually find that there is something bursting to come out, and that it is better out than in."[14]

Joining the Discussion

Is it appropriate for the meeting leader to join the discussion? The answer is a qualified "yes": The leader can join the discussion but must be careful not to advocate his or her ideas at the expense of the group.

In most cases, it's better for the leader to stay out of the discussion and remain in the neutral, facilitative role. Antony Jay asserts that one of the best chairs he's ever served under "makes it a rule to restrict her interventions to a single sentence, or at most two. She forbids herself ever to contribute a paragraph to a meeting she is chairing. It is a harsh rule," says Jay, "but you would be hard put to find a regular attender of her meetings (or anyone else's) who thought it was a bad one."[15]

If the leader wants to advocate a point, it's best for him or her to do so later in the discussion, when others have introduced the point, so as not to unduly influence the group's thinking. One exception: If the leader has relevant knowledge or experience, the group may feel the leader is obliged to share it with them. "If so," write V. A. Howard and J. H. Barton, authors of *Thinking Together*, "you cannot remain aloof from the proceedings as an *impartial* moderator; but you can show yourself to be a *fair-minded, even-handed* participant who advocates for the common good."[16]

Even if the leader doesn't actively participate in the discussion, he or she can still play a central role, according to Howard and Barton:

Refraining from joining the discussion and from advocating, elaborating, and defending your own views does not prevent you from helping people to *draw conclusions* and *make decisions*. For example, in judicial fashion you can ask people what they make of the discussion thus far. Or you can nudge them towards conclusions in Socratic fashion by asking leading questions about the *implications* of their views. "If what you say is true, George, about the rocky road of political reform, and also what you say, Ann, about impatience for quick economic results, then isn't antidemocratic backlash a distinct possibility in countries that are breaking away from one-party rule?" Alternatively, you can ask people questions about their *assumptions*. "You seem to be saying, both of you, that socialism necessarily means that the government owns everything. How would you describe Sweden, where far more production is in private hands than in many other countries?" Drawing people out in this way sharpens their thinking not only when they are looking for closure but also when they are looking to expand their inquiries.[17]

Managing Emotions

The ability to read and manage individual and group emotions is a vital but often overlooked aspect of meeting leadership. The powerful role that emotions can play in meetings is captured in a story that author Milo Frank tells about a businessman and his exasperated associates.

Seven businesspeople met to decide whether to move from their current offices on the ground floor of an old building in a recently depressed neighborhood to the 34th floor of a new high-rise office building. The move required the approval of all seven people in the meeting. Six of them endorsed the move, but one man resisted. He took the position, "Why change a winning game? We're doing fine where we are. Why spend more money?"

No matter how hard his associates tried to persuade him, with logical arguments bolstered by facts and figures, that the move was a good one, he stubbornly refused to change his mind.

The man never revealed the real reason he resisted the move: As a child, he'd been stuck on the 20th floor of a high-rise hotel when a fire broke out. He'd been terrified by the smoke and flames. Worse, the elevator that was supposed to carry him to safety got stuck between floors, and "the nightmare seemed never to end."[18]

The moral of the story is that "logic loses to emotion."[19]

The message for meeting leaders: be conscious of the emotional agenda of participants as well as the written agenda of the meeting.

Researchers are discovering that emotions have a great impact on group productivity. "Emotions provide energy, motivation, commitment, and action," says Bob Bostrom, of the University of Georgia.[20] Bostrom believes that meetings should have the goal of "creating and maintaining positive emotions that promote working together effectively" as well as having a task objective.

That doesn't mean the meeting leader should ignore negative emotions. Instead, when a person expresses a negative feeling, "look for positive intent," Bostrom advises. For example, anger over a budget cut may be a legitimate expression of concern about whether the angry person can perform the extra work expected of him or her after the cut. By exploring the reasons behind the anger, the meeting leader can work with the group to address the problem productively.

Obvious displays of emotion are by definition easy to recognize, but meeting leaders also must be alert to subtle signs of emotional distress. "Use your own feelings as a guide," Bob Bostrom adds. When the leader feels uneasy, the group probably feels the same way. The leader should state his or her feelings and ask for feedback from the group. When in doubt about the group's emotions, it's best to take a poll.

Researchers are experimenting with group software systems that include "mood meters," which enable participants to give instant feedback about their feelings. At this stage relatively little is known about how to design and use mood meters, says Bostrom. But if nothing else, these devices could make groups more aware of their emotions, and the need to manage them.

Dealing with Latecomers

Antony Jay writes: "There is only one way to ensure that a meeting starts on time, and that is to start it on time."[21] How does the meeting leader handle the problem of late arrivals? Different experts have different ideas. Jay suggests listing the names of latecomers to call attention to them, on the theory that "people do not want that sort of information about themselves published too frequently."[22]

Willow Shire, corporate vice president at Digital Equipment Corporation (DEC), found an effective technique for getting people to show up at her bimonthly meetings on time. She decided to fine each straggler one dollar and donate the sum to St. Jude's Children's Cancer Research Hospital in Memphis.[23]

Latecomers don't mind the penalty, since they know it goes to a good cause. Typically, they smile, pay up, and get on with the meeting. The technique has been so successful in raising awareness about punctuality that other departments within DEC have adopted the practice.

Rewards may work as well as punishments. When employees in Hewlett-Packard's San Diego Printer Division started having daily meetings to identify production problems, the leader put out a large tin of chocolates five or ten minutes before the meeting to entice them to arrive on schedule.

"At start time, I closed the tin and began the meeting," says Kevin Bockman, engineering manager. Employees got used to the treat, and within a few days some were racing to get to the meeting before he snapped the lid shut.

"When I ran out of candy, I stopped putting it out," he says. "But by then, everyone was coming on time."

Anver Suleiman, president of the Marketing Federation in St. Petersburg Beach, Florida, suggests that in some cases, leaders should use the accommodation approach to deal with latecomers: start the meeting on time, but spend the first five or ten minutes giving noncritical information or a get-acquainted exercise.

"Accommodating stragglers in this way is really accommodating the group," says Suleiman. It prevents interruptions from latecomers who either ask questions about material covered in the first few minutes or fall asleep because they don't understand what's going on.

In some cases, making latecomers aware of the implications of their behavior is all that's needed to change it. "Coming late costs money and is a sign of disrespect," says Bernie DeKoven, director of the Institute for Better Meetings. If latecomers "make the connection," says DeKoven, "that should correct the behavior." In case it doesn't, the leader can use De-Koven's Meeting Meter® (described in Chap. 1) to tick off the dollars and cents being wasted waiting for latecomers to arrive.

Anver Suleiman suggests meeting leaders examine the value of punctuality in the organization's culture before devising techniques to deal with latecomers. For example, arriving fashionably late for a meeting may be an unspoken organizational norm. If so, it will take time to recondition people to arrive at meetings on time. The meeting leader must inform them that the old custom of fashionable tardiness is changing and consistently enforce the new custom of punctuality.

Fred Pryor, chairman of Fred Pryor Seminars, stresses the need to find out why certain people are habitual latecomers as a first step in solving the problem. For example, if some people are regularly arriving late to the 9 a.m. staff meeting, the leader might approach each latecomer in this way: "I've got a problem and I'd like your help. I started the meeting at 9:00 and you came in at 9:15. I missed your input, and that's important to me. Maybe you were putting out a fire, or maybe the meeting didn't seem important to you. Can you help me understand?"

Such a nonjudgmental approach can help leaders get to the root of the problem quickly. It may be that chronic latecomers do not belong in the meeting, or feel no commitment to the task, or think the meeting will accomplish nothing. "If people feel important and can anticipate achievement, they will be motivated to come on time," Pryor says.

Managing Conflict

When people with opposing views meet, some conflict is inevitable. This is not necessarily a bad thing. In fact, according to management consultant John Johnson, it's a mistake to discourage conflict, because it can boost the productivity of the group: "The best solutions and plans often develop from contrary points of view within the meeting group. If the expression of contrary points of view is discouraged, then the best solutions and plans are preempted."

Of course, not all conflict is productive. For example, when voicing of different opinions degenerates into personal attacks on other participants, productivity plummets. Whether a given conflict is constructive or destructive depends on how skillfully the meeting leader manages it.

One way to prevent conflict from spinning out of control is to set clear ground rules for interacting. The meeting leader must make it clear at the start of the meeting that it's fine to challenge ideas, but that personal attacks will not be allowed. And the rule must be strictly enforced.

Strategic seating arrangements can also help to prevent problems, according to Roger Mosvick. "If you have a garrulous individual who tends to dominate the discussion, the place to put him is next to you," Mosvick says. "This way you can avoid noticing him; he's not in your line of vision. And you can press his arm in a friendly fashion if he gets too domineering."[24]

If someone in the group becomes belligerent, silence is often the best remedy. Most people are quite uncomfortable with silence. If the meeting leader simply stops the proceedings, the group will generally take action to censure the obnoxious person to relieve their own discomfort (and the leader's). If an argument erupts among participants, the leader must forcefully remind the group of the agreed upon procedures to be followed.

Occasionally a participant will deliberately play devil's advocate, continually challenging everything the leader or other group members say. One effective way to handle such a participant is to give him or her an assignment—the bigger the better. For example, the leader might instruct the participant to develop a presentation on the subject on which he or she appears to be an expert and deliver it at the next meeting. In most cases, that will solve the problem.

Injecting Humor[25]

When all else fails, lighten up. One effective way to dissolve tension is to reframe a problem or conflict in a humorous light.

Here's an example: Shortly after the breakup of AT&T, the company fielded questions about the consequences of reorganization. A frequent hostile question from audiences was, "Why are long-distance rates going up?" One speaker gave this reply: "It's sort of a good news-bad news situation. It's true that long-distance rates are going up—that's the bad news. The good news is, the continents are drifting closer together."

Humor can be a valuable asset in many meeting situations. For example, it can be used to help put people at ease, make bad news easier to accept, or introduce a sensitive subject.

Humor has long been a staple of awards banquets and sales meetings, but it's rarely used in the typical business meeting because many managers think it wastes time. Maybe not, says Malcolm Kushner, a humor consultant in Santa Cruz, California and author of *The Light Touch: How to Use Humor for Business Success* (Simon & Schuster, 1990). "The real objective of meetings is to exchange information or solve a problem," he says. "If humor contributes to a free flow of information, then it can actually speed things up."

Humor is a rich source of productivity. Studies have shown that people with a sense of humor "tend to be more creative, less rigid, and more willing to consider and embrace new ideas," says Kushner. Not surprisingly, humor occurs naturally in brainstorming sessions. Brainstorming and problem solving "require a fresh perspective, looking at things from an offbeat angle. So does humor," says Kushner.

You don't have to be a comedian to use humor in meetings, according to Michael Iapoce, a humor consultant in San Anselmo, California, and author of *A Funny Thing Happened on the Way to the Boardroom: Using Humor in Business Speaking* (John Wiley & Sons, 1988). "Only professional comics need to get big laughs. If you can get people in a meeting to chuckle, they're grateful. And if your joke or one-liner doesn't get a laugh, just ignore it."

Personal anecdotes about funny, embarrassing, or ironic things that happened in school, on the job, on a first date, and the like, are a good source of humor. Personal anecdotes often work better than jokes, says Malcolm Kushner. The fact that they're real gives them added impact. The smart meeting leader keeps a file of personal anecdotes for use at the appropriate time.

Meeting leaders must be sure that their humor is relevant to the situation. Business people often make the mistake of "telling a joke just to get a laugh," says Iapoce. "Instead, you should use humor to make a point."

Here's an example: When David Kearns, then Chairman and CEO of Xerox Corporation, spoke at a management conference at the University of Chicago in 1986, he began this way:

> There's a story about a Frenchman, a Japanese, and an American who face a firing squad. Each gets one last request. The Frenchman asks to hear The Marseillaise. The Japanese asks to give a lecture on the art of management. The American says, "Shoot me first—I can't stand one more lecture on Japanese management."

Kearns went on to say he was not going to speak about Japanese management, but about what Japan might learn from America.[26]

In addition to using humor, it's important for the meeting leader to acknowledge others for the appropriate use of humor, and to discourage inappropriate jokes. That means taking the offending person aside and explaining why the joke is offensive (e.g., racist, ethnic, or sexist jokes)

and that it won't be tolerated. In some cases, it may mean taking discipli-
nary action.

The leader must also be careful to use appropriate humor. Even if a joke
is not offensive, it may be inappropriate for the audience. For example, it's
not wise to joke about declining literacy rates of American students when
you're meeting with a group of teachers.

"Sometimes people are not sure whether a joke is appropriate for a certain
group, but they tell it anyway," says Kushner. "That's like saying, 'I'm not
sure if this gun is loaded, but I'll fire it anyway.'" Rule of thumb: When in
doubt, leave it out.

Knowing the audience is vital to choosing appropriate humor. One 3M
manager (who requested anonymity) recalls:

> I spent a great deal of my career in Minnesota and surrounding areas,
> and people would pick up the Texas inflection in my voice. When I
> was doing a speech to any large group I could make a joke about
> Texans or Texas accents as a little opener to warm up, give them a
> feel for my personality and a little bit of my background. And it
> always went really well.
>
> I made a speech in Dallas once to about 600 people with the same
> opening, and I died. I could not recover ... That was one of those things
> you have to learn the hard way.

Ending the Meeting

"Very few things are as irritating as leaving a meeting knowing that nothing
was accomplished and time was wasted," writes Ann Depta. "The meeting
leader must manage the process to avoid that situation."[27]

When all items on the agenda have been covered, or the group has gone
as far as it can without gathering more information, it's time to bring the
meeting to a close, whether or not the scheduled time has run out. If the
leader does not end the meeting at this point, participants may tend to
rehash decisions that have already been made or reintroduce problems that
have already been addressed. This is a waste of everyone's time.

In closing the meeting, the leader should sum up what has been accomplished and what is left to do. He or she should recap what action is
expected of each participant. If another meeting on the subject is to be
scheduled, the leader should set a tentative date and time.

It's a good idea to close on a positive note. Even if the group hasn't
reached an agreement, solved a problem, or met some other objective,
the meeting leader can acknowledge any progress that has been made.
This sets a positive tone for future meetings and helps to impart a feeling
of control.

The Seven Deadly Sins of Meeting Leadership

1. *Resenting questions.* Questions signal interest in the subject. If you don't have the answer, assure the questioner you will find it.

2. *Monopolizing the meeting.* Meetings are a group effort. The leader's responsibility is to guide the group, not dominate it.

3. *Playing the role of comic.* A little humor is welcome in most meetings, but the leader who plays the role of comic loses respect and diverts the attention of the group to the work at hand.

4. *Publicly chastising participants.* Never criticize someone in front of the group, even if the person has been hostile to you. If you embarrass one person, other group members will stifle their contributions for fear of being the next target.

5. *Allowing interruptions.* Don't allow latecomers, noise or other distractions to ruin your meeting. Prepare in advance for phone messages to be posted outside the meeting room, and to avoid other interruptions.

6. *Losing control.* Do not allow participants to stray from the agenda, engage in side conversations, get into an argument, or otherwise take control of the meeting away from you. Use your agenda as a control tool.

7. *Being unprepared.* This is the deadliest sin, and the most common. Don't think you can "wing it" when it comes to meeting leadership. Participants will sense instantly whether or not you are prepared. If you are not, you will lose your respect and will have difficulty controlling the meeting. If there's no time to prepare, postpone the meeting.

Figure 4.2.

The Role of the Facilitator

In the past two decades organizations have increasingly turned to facilitators to guide groups in complex tasks such as setting goals, defining problems, and resolving conflicts. The facilitator works in tandem with the meeting leader. While the leader deals with the content of the meeting, the facilitator manages the process. Among other things, facilitators make sure that procedures are followed and rules enforced. And they ensure that all group members feel free to communicate openly and honestly.

"People should be able to say everything on their minds about the subject at hand," says Deborah Nicklaus, an organizational development consultant at Eastman Kodak who trains managers and internal consultants to be group facilitators. "You want to be sure they share what they're thinking in the conference room and not in the hallway," she adds.[28]

Facilitators usually have a working knowledge of meeting procedures, and a good understanding of group dynamics. A growing number of facilitators also are adept at using electronic meeting tools such as keypad voting systems and computerized group decision support systems, which automate brainstorming and other meeting procedures. (We'll discuss meeting technology in depth in Chap. 5.)

Neutral Third Party

The facilitator should be someone who is not central to the content being discussed. John Johnson explains why: "If a research scientist is presiding at the meeting at which her research project is being reported and evaluated, she is not the most able to manage the pros and cons discussion and decision making regarding that project. Her own biases and deep feelings of ownership of the content of the project get in the way of open review and deliberation on the subject. It's a little bit like having one of the prize fighters in a boxing match serve also as the referee."

A good facilitator "is mature enough to leave the ownership of success where it belongs—in the participants," says Chris McGoff, president of Group Decision Support Systems, Inc. of Washington, D.C.[29] This is the quality that distinguishes master facilitators from good facilitators, McGoff believes. "The master facilitators derive reward from within. They are self-actualized enough to obtain satisfaction from doing a good job without needing other people to tell them so. They're not motivated to be heroes."

McGoff adds, "There are a ton of good facilitators, but damn few master facilitators."[30]

Other Benefits of Facilitation

Because they are content-neutral, facilitators can pay close attention to interaction problems and help the group to overcome them. The expertise and neutrality of a facilitator "can help a group develop more rapidly or overcome interpersonal obstacles to working effectively," according to Rob Anson, a management professor at Boise State University.[31]

Anson headed a 1990 study commissioned by the 3M Meeting Management Institute regarding the effects of facilitators and computerized group support systems on meeting productivity. The study found that facilitators enhance the development of group cohesion and counteract group process problems. For example, they help groups to avoid the use of incomplete or biased information, unwarranted inferences, or stereotyped thinking.[32]

Facilitators are useful in situations in which a group is stuck and can't progress beyond a certain point without the help of an outsider. A facilitator can prove especially valuable when conflict exists among group members. The skillful facilitator can help turn conflict into constructive discussion.

Facilitators can also be useful for organizations in the midst of a major transformation. The facilitator can help members to recognize and reshape deeply rooted assumptions that stand in the way of change.

The 16 Functions of an Effective Facilitator

In a recent research effort, Victoria Clawson, a St. Louis management consultant, and Bob Bostrom of the University of Georgia identified 16 key functions of effective facilitators, based on the input of 50 experienced

---

16 Key Functions of Effective Facilitators

1. Plans and designs the meeting process.

2. Listens to, clarifies, and integrates information.

3. Demonstrates flexibility and adaptability.

4. Keeps the group focused on the outcome or task.

5. Creates an open, positive, and participative environment.

6. Selects and prepares appropriate technology, based on the outcome and the group.

7. Directs and manages the meeting.

8. Develops and asks the right questions.

9. Helps the group own and take responsibility for the meeting out comes.

10. Actively builds rapport and relationship among the group members.

11. Demonstrates self-awareness and self-expression.

12. Manages conflict and negative emotions constructively.

13. Encourages and supports multiple perspectives.

14. Understands the technology and its capabilities.

15. Explains the technology and creates comfort with it.

16. Presents information clearly.

Figure 4.3. (*Source: Victoria K. Clawson and Robert P. Bostrom,* The Role of the Facilitator in Computer-Supported Meetings. *University of Georgia, 1993.*)

facilitators who participated in the study.[33] (See Fig. 4.3.) Although the study focused on computer-supported meetings, 13 of the 16 functions apply equally to traditional meetings.

Following, in order of importance, are the 16 functions that an effective facilitator performs:[34]

1. *Plans and designs the meeting process.* The facilitator involves the meeting leader in planning; develops clear meeting outcomes; designs an agenda and selects group processes designed to achieve those outcomes; clarifies the ground rules of the meeting; learns about the group members ahead of time; and incorporates the use of appropriate tools, such as visual aids and meeting software.

2. *Listens to, clarifies, and integrates information.* The facilitator listens carefully to what the group is saying and makes an effort to make sense out of it. He or she clarifies goals, terms, and definitions; "backtracks" participant responses, that is, summarizes what the participant says, so that the person knows he or she has been heard and understood; remembers previous comments to reconnect information; gathers and integrates information; and helps organize information into themes.

3. *Demonstrates flexibility.* The facilitator adapts the agenda or meeting activities on the spot as needed; handles multiple tasks smoothly; adapts his or her personal style to the group; tries new things; and is willing to do something different than originally planned, if the situation calls for it.

4. *Keeps the group focused on the outcome or task.* The facilitator has a definite direction and knows where to go next; clearly communicates expected outcomes to the group at the start of the meeting; keeps the group's comments relevant to the outcome; and demonstrates concern for the group's outcome.

5. *Creates an open environment.* The facilitator draws out individuals by asking questions; uses activities and technology to get people involved early in the meeting; manages dominant group members to ensure equal participation; provides anonymity and confidentiality when needed; acknowledges and is open to the group's contributions; creates and reinforces positive energy in the group; and uses humor, games, music, and play to enhance an open, positive environment.

6. *Selects and prepares technology.* The facilitator appropriately matches computer-based tools to the tasks and outcomes the group wants to accomplish; selects tools that fit the group make-up; uses technology as a tool, not an end in itself; prepares and tests the technology ahead of time; and prepares a back-up plan in case of technology failure.

7. *Directs and manages the meeting.* The facilitator leads the group through the meeting process; uses the agenda to guide the group; uses technology

effectively to manage the group; sets the stage for the meeting and each activity; restricts the meeting process appropriately, by setting time limits, enforcing roles and ground rules, limiting choices, and so on; provides models, frameworks, and processes to guide the group; uses breaks effectively; and checks progress and reactions with the meeting leader and group.

8. *Develops and asks the right questions.* The facilitator considers how to word and ask the best questions; asks questions that encourage thought and participation; develops thoughtful questions on the fly; and carefully phrases all questions to ensure that the most relevant information is elicited from the group.

9. *Promotes ownership and group responsibility.* The facilitator helps the group take responsibility for and ownership of meeting outcomes; helps the group create follow-up plans; turns the floor over to others; permits the group to call its own breaks; and encourages the group to evaluate the process and the technology.

10. *Actively builds rapport and relationship.* The facilitator demonstrates responsiveness and respect for people; is sensitive to emotions; regularly "reads" the group; watches and responds to nonverbal signals; empathizes with people with special needs; helps develop constructive relationships with and among members; puts the group at ease; greets and mingles with the group; uses the group's own words and symbols; moves about in the group.

11. *Demonstrates self-awareness.* The facilitator recognizes and deals with his or her own behavior and feelings; is comfortable with himself or herself; responds in an emotionally appropriate way—for example, exhibits calm under pressure; pays attention to and acts on gut reactions; behaves confidently; behaves honestly, openly admitting mistakes and lack of knowledge; shows enthusiasm and human spirit; and keeps personal ego out of the way of the group.

12. *Manages conflict and negative emotions.* The facilitator encourages the group to handle conflict constructively; provides techniques to help the group deal with conflict; uses technology to gather and check group opinions and agreement level in disputes; helps the group gain agreement and consensus on issues; and allows the group to vent negative emotions constructively.

13. *Encourages and supports multiple perspectives.* The facilitator encourages the group to look at issues from different points of view; uses techniques, metaphors, stories, and examples to get the group to consider different frames of reference; and uses meeting technology to explore diversity and multiple perspectives.

14. *Understands meeting technology.* The facilitator has a good conceptual understanding of meeting technology and knows how to operate it; clearly

understands individual technology tools and their functions and capabilities; identifies and solves common technical difficulties; and identifies and uses other sources of technical expertise as needed.

15. *Creates comfort with technology.* The facilitator carefully introduces and explains meeting technology to the group; directly addresses negative comments and inconveniences caused by the technology; helps the group interpret screens and graphs; paces the review of computer results to keep the group from experiencing information overload.

16. *Presents information clearly.* The facilitator gives explicit instructions; uses clear, concise language in presenting ideas; gives the group written information such as handouts and printouts; provides research and background information; presents models and framework clearly; and makes sure important information is visible to the group at all times—for example, by displaying outcomes on flip charts or overhead transparencies.

Organizations can use this list of 16 functions as a set of criteria for selecting facilitators and judging their performance. The list also provides a basis for training facilitators—something an increasing number of organizations are doing.

Graphic Facilitation[35]

Lois walks into the conference room one morning to begin a three-day planning meeting and stops short. Plastered along one wall are butcher paper sheets with six-inch lettering and symbols.

"It's the agenda," she realizes. Her eyes quickly scan the major events, which is easy since each activity appears in its own box. She immediately picks out the brainstorming session, illustrated with a light bulb, and the mealtimes, depicted with a plate and fork. Her eyes follow a large arrow to the right, pointing to the list of outcomes the meeting is expected to produce.

In a matter of seconds, she has grasped the meeting's purpose and the proposed flow of events. Even though she had earlier received a traditional printed agenda, seeing this graphic wall chart helps her feel more focused, confident, and eager to begin.

Graphics provide a way not only to post the agenda but also to help participants work interactively through a meeting. In project planning, for example, participants might draw a time line and flow chart with symbols and arrows showing what has to be done by when. The group's secretary or recorder might keep minutes on a flip chart, using stars or other symbols to mark key decisions. Post-It® easel pads can be used in place of flip charts. The pads are similar to flip charts, but the sheets can be peeled off if desired and stuck to most walls without damaging them. This enables the recorder to display more than one sheet at a time.

"It's a visual way of getting people to understand complex information and think about it as a group," says Suzanne Bailey, an organization and management consultant in Vacaville, California.

"Graphic facilitation" has emerged as a new field, largely through the pioneering efforts of David Sibbet, a graphic designer who has conducted workshops on the topic since the early 1970s.

Generally the graphic facilitator works with the meeting sponsor or leader in advance to plan the environment and arrange for equipment. For a meeting of 100 people, for example, the facilitator might set up three overhead projection screens and write or draw on blank acetate sheets with special overhead pens. A convention of 2000 people might require a movie-size projection screen and roving microphones in the audience.

After considering the task the group needs to perform and the kind of information to be presented, the facilitator chooses appropriate graphic formats to use during the meeting. If people need to analyze how price relates to product demand, for example, the facilitator may choose a matrix format.

As the meeting begins, the facilitator describes the group process and the common graphic devices to be used to record input and action. For example, bullets (large black dots) may be used for items in a list, straight lines for borders, and arrows for direction. Circles may represent whole units, and triangles may depict options.

In addition, the facilitator urges the group to agree on a set of pictographs and ideographs they will use. A *pictograph* is a stylized picture of the real thing—a stick figure for a person, for example. By contrast, an *ideograph* is a picture that stands for something else—a lightning bolt for a problem, or a handshake for an agreement.

The facilitator may draw the visual images spontaneously while guiding the meeting or add them at the break. Or the group's secretary or recorder may do so. However, Bailey believes that everyone in the meeting should be encouraged to participate in the graphics, to "doodle in public."

In a large group such as a convention, drawing by individual participants may not be feasible. If so, graphic symbols can be prepared beforehand for participants to paste or tape on a wall chart.

Developing Facilitation Skills

It would be prohibitively expensive for organizations to hire outsiders to facilitate all or even most of their meetings. As they discover the value of facilitation, organizations are increasingly training their own managers to be facilitators.

The transition from manager to facilitator is not an easy one. Management consultant Ann Depta points out that other roles managers play "call for decisiveness, quick problem solving, being the person with the answers. As a result, many managers do not know how to back off, listen, and allow others to work through a process such as a meeting."[36] With time and practice, though, these skills can easily be learned.

Groups must also learn to accept the value of facilitation. The newly trained manager/facilitator often encounters resistance from group members whose unspoken attitude is "just tell me what to do and I'll do it." Once people experience the benefits of facilitation firsthand, they become its biggest supporters.

To speed acceptance of the process, it's wise to practice cross facilitation—that is, to have someone from one department within an organization serve as facilitator for another department. It's easier for groups to accept guidance from an outsider—even if the outsider works for the same organization.

Active Participation

A meeting should not be a spectator sport. Meetings require the active participation of everyone present, if they are to be effective. Active participation involves the ability to listen well and communicate accountably, and the willingness to take risks.

Empathic Listening[37]

Meeting participants must develop the ability to listen well if they are to perform their roles effectively. Most people are not good listeners, according to Stephen Covey, Chairman of Covey Leadership Center, Inc., based in Provo, Utah and the author of the best-selling book, *The Seven Habits of Highly Effective People* (Simon & Schuster, 1989). Typically, when people meet to solve a problem, set goals, share ideas, or negotiate a deal, he says, "they're either speaking or preparing to speak."

"Most people do not listen with the intent to understand," says Covey. "They listen with the intent to reply." Consequently, meeting discussions often become collective monologues.

Listening generally occurs at one of four levels: (1) ignoring—not listening at all; (2) pretending to listen—nodding the head, responding "yeah" or "un-huh" every few minutes; (3) selective listening—tuning in to parts of what is being said, tuning out others; and (4) attentive listening—paying attention only to the speaker's words.

Covey suggests that meeting participants develop a higher-level skill he terms "empathic listening." "Empathic listening means getting inside a

How to Get More out of Meetings

1. Set *goals*. Develop a list of three to six overall goals. It will start you thinking properly. These goals generally are oriented toward quality, sales, cost reduction, and profits.

2. Think about *specific questions* you want answered. Develop a list of 10 to 50 pointed questions.

3. *Meet everyone* at the program. Talk to them. Each attendee has a specific area of expertise. Make a note of it. Start your own network. Exchange cards. Go to breakfast, lunch, and dinner with someone with whom you can share information.

4. Develop an *action plan* and/or use the format provided in your workbook. Make a list of anything you want to consider *doing differently* when you get back on the job. This will take the fuzziness out of your thinking and give you *tangible benefits*.

5. *Participate!* Ask questions. Make contributions. Comment. Be visible. You'll benefit in two ways. First, your mind will almost magically start working on information, problems, solutions. Second, the speaker and attendees will also contribute to finding answers for you. (Don't overdo it. Be relevant and don't hog time.)

6. Make contact with the speakers *personally* (and early). They will think more of and about you. And it will be easier to follow up with questions and problems after the program.

7. Take clear *detailed notes*. Not only will this be helpful for future reference, but the very act of taking good notes and organizing your thoughts will keep you more involved. Do them right the first time. Forget about rewriting them when you get back. You'll never do it!

8. Write a *brief report* based on your action plan and notes—one to three pages. And circulate it to anyone who might be interested. It helps them and you. Give them an opportunity to write back in a section entitled, "Your Comments."

9. Hold a *staff briefing* with key personnel when you get back. Refine your action plan and put all that good stuff to work immediately.

10. *Enjoy yourself.* You learn more when you're having a good time!

Figure 4.4. (*Source: Anver S. Suleiman, president, The Marketing Federation, St. Petersburg Beach, Fla. Reprinted with permission.*)

person's frame of reference, seeing the world as that person sees it, feeling the person's feelings," says Covey.

"Empathy is not sympathy," he points out. "Sympathy means you agree with them or judge them in some way, and sometimes that is appropriate. But the essence of empathic listening is that you fully, deeply understand that person, emotionally as well as intellectually."

When Covey asks his seminar participants to try empathic listening, they often cannot do it at first. "Our natural tendency is to listen autobiographically, from our own frame of reference, and respond accordingly," says Covey.

Suppose a person says, "I don't like the way this project is going." As listeners, we tend to respond in the following ways:

- We evaluate—we agree or disagree. "I don't like the way this project is going either."

- We probe—we ask questions, we approach the person logically. "What don't you like about the project?"

- We advise—we give well-intentioned counsel. "Stay with it another couple of weeks; things will get better."

- We interpret—we try to figure out the person's motives and behavior. "You're a perfectionist; you're expecting too much from this project."

These responses may be appropriate in some situations, but they are not empathic listening. A more empathic response might be: "You seem to be feeling uneasy." This response shows that the listener is trying to put himself in the shoes of the speaker.

"In empathic listening, you listen with your ears, but more importantly, you listen with your eyes and with your heart," Covey says. That means watching a person's behavior, not just listening to the person's words. According to experts, 60 percent of what we say is communicated by body language, 30 percent by sounds, and only 10 percent by words.

"The next time you're in a meeting, cover your ears for a few minutes and just watch," Covey suggests. "See if you can sense what people are trying to say without knowing the words they use." In other words, try to listen with your eyes.

Listening with your heart means listening for feelings. Most of us think of business discussions as objective and impersonal, but they're often highly subjective and full of emotions, ranging from fear, doubt, and anger to joy, excitement, and pride. Listening with the heart, trying to pick up on those emotions, gives you "accurate data to work with," says Covey.

To illustrate the concept of empathic listening, Covey cited a seminar participant in Chicago who realized he was about to lose a big commercial real estate deal. In a meeting with the principals, the man decided to try Covey's approach. He said to the principal: "Let me see if I really understand what your concerns are. When you feel I understand them, we'll see whether my proposal has any relevance." The more he expressed the things the principals were worried about, the more they opened up. By the end of the meeting, he closed the deal.

Empathic listening is for meeting leaders as well as participants. Covey suggests that in advance of meetings, leaders meet individually with participants and listen empathically to what they have to say. Participants will feel valued and appreciated, and the meeting can proceed in a climate of trust.

As with any other skill, it takes time and effort to become an empathic listener, but the rewards are worth it. As Stephen Covey points out: "When we really, deeply understand each other, we open the door to creative solutions." By helping groups to overcome communication blocks that inhibit performance, empathic listening points the way to greater meeting productivity.

Communicating Accountably[38]

In addition to listening empathically, meeting participants must learn how to communicate accountably. That's the view of Leonard Hawes, professor of communication at the University of Utah. Hawes says that meetings improve when they include rules that make participants responsible for what they say. That means "each person has to speak for themselves and from their experience. It also means that the pronoun 'I' gets used almost exclusively. 'We' and 'you' get used practically not at all. That's the opposite of most meetings."

Instead of saying things like "we all know that ..." or "I think I can speak for all of us when I say that ...," meeting participants who communicate accountably focus only on what they think or feel: "I like this," "I don't like that," "I'm afraid of your approach ...," and the like. When people begin to speak only for themselves and not the rest of the group, "it becomes real clear who stands for what," says Hawes.

The technique sounds simple, but it's a radical idea for companies in which managers aren't used to "laying themselves on the line" and meetings become convenient places to hide. "The costs are that each individual becomes responsible for his or her ideas or suggestions," Hawes says. "So the individual stakes go up. But so does the quality of the communication."

Risk Taking[39]

Communicating accountably requires taking risks—another vital skill for meeting participants to develop. "Too many people are afraid to be assertive in meetings. They fear being seen as obnoxious and aggressive," says management consultant Dick Byrd. "The result is they are seen as jellyfish—compliant, easily manipulated, and taken for granted."

Byrd is a pioneering advocate of personal risk taking in organizations. He notes that people who avoid taking risks usually are acting out of fear—fear of failure, fear of what people might think, fear of change. While such fears are natural, people who consistently stave off risks may damage the organization as well as deprive themselves of recognition, promotion, and self-fulfillment.

People who regularly take risks, on the other hand, may be motivated by excitement, by the adrenalin rush that results from toying with danger. Addicted risk takers, says Byrd, may lead the organization and themselves to ruin.

Both obsessively high- and low-risk takers are neurotic, according to Byrd. They venture the same personal risk in every situation. By contrast, creative risk takers—the type that Byrd advocates—choose a different level of risk based on circumstances, rewards, punishments, and odds.

"Creative risk takers are not gamblers," says Byrd. "They take risks only when they have some control over the outcome, when they can use their talent, skill, judgment, and experience in reaching for something beyond their grasp."

Byrd points out that individuals vary in their perception of risk. Suppose that in a group on the verge of making a decision, someone says, "I don't think we're really in agreement; we're just pretending to agree." The person who made the statement may view it as a safe, natural comment, while someone else in the group may see it as incredibly risky.

Byrd notes that there's often "a gap between what interpersonal risks we think we can take and still be accepted and valued and the actual acceptable limits." He offers three rules to follow in determining how much risk to take in any given situation:

1. *Never risk more than you can afford to lose.* If your boss is known for firing people who challenge him in meetings, think twice about doing so unless you can afford to lose your job.

2. *Don't risk a lot for a little.* Don't put a cherished promotion in jeopardy by refusing to budge on a trivial issue—say, the typeface to be used in your committee's final report.

3. *Consider how much control you have over the odds.* If your father is chairman of the board, you own a third of the company stock, or the firm will

collapse without your knowledge about widgets, you can probably speak freely in meetings, without fearing the consequences. The more control you have, the more risk you can take.

To those who aren't used to taking risks in meetings, doing so may seem like a career-threatening strategy. In fact, the opposite may be true. Dick Byrd points out that people who remain silent in meetings to protect themselves lose out if their organization is looking for somebody who stands out. "You take a risk in risking," says Byrd, "but you also take a risk in not risking."

5
The Rise of Electronic Meetings

Chris McGoff, president of Group Decision Support Systems, Inc. and an expert on technology to support work groups, envisions a meeting of the future:

> You will exchange cordials and then take a seat at a semi-circular, arched table. The open ends are pushed up against what appears to be a window. The lights dim and the front glass produces an image of two other curved tables that, when viewed along with the table physically in front of you, complete a circle. By simply looking at the image, it is hard to recognize that two-thirds of the people sitting at this "table" are physically located in Germany and China.[1]

If technology trends continue, meetings in the year 2000 and beyond will take on a new look and feel. Not all meetings will have the "virtual" quality of the one McGoff describes. But technology will play at least a modest role in most meetings. Participants may scribble notes on a laptop or even a "palmtop" computer that can recognize their handwriting. Ideas and comments may be recorded on an electronic whiteboard. Groups that meet to solve problems or make decisions will likely use computerized group decision support systems to speed the process. A team in Toledo might bring in an expert from Tokyo, at the touch of a computer key.

The Growth of Meeting Technology

Much of the technology to support such scenarios is already on the market, and a growing number of organizations are implementing it in meeting rooms around the world. Why the accelerating growth of meeting technology? One of the biggest factors is global competition, which has increased the pressure on companies to cut costs and to make better, faster decisions. One way to do that is by forming flexible teams—many of them composed of people who work in different locations.

"There's tremendous enthusiasm for teams right now," says Bob Johansen, senior research fellow at the Institute for the Future in Menlo Park, California. "The idea of small, cross organizational, ad hoc, time-driven, task-driven work teams has become so common that it's assumed that's going to be one of the primary units of measure in the organization of the future."[2]

The emergence of cross-organizational teams and other alliances guarantees that "the people you need are never in the same place."[3] The group's only option is to meet electronically.

The growing numbers of cross-national teams are even more reliant on electronic links. To be competitive in a global economy of 24 different time zones, organizations must be capable of holding asynchronous computer conferences, with participants across the hallway or around the world logging on and off at different hours, day and night. "Ultimately, in the business environment of the future, we are going to want meetings that can occur any time, any place," Johansen says.[4]

Time/Place Dimensions of Meetings

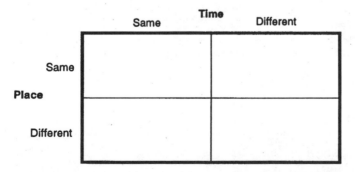

Figure 5.1. (*Reprinted with the permission of Macmillan College Publishing Company from* Group Support Systems: New Perspectives *by Leonard M. Jessup and Joseph S. Valacich, eds. Copyright 1993 by Macmillan College Publishing Company, Inc.*)

If We Build It, They Will Come ...

Janet Fulk, associate professor of communication at the University of Southern California, agrees that competition is a primary factor in the growth of electronic meetings. But she believes that technology itself is accelerating the trend: "Advancements in communication and computing technologies have fueled the technological possibilities," according to Fulk, who headed a 3M-sponsored research review on the subject of electronic meetings. "Digital compression techniques have made high quality video conference signals more available and affordable. The growth of PCs and workstations, quick developments in networking technology, have made electronic meetings possible for a broad range of organizations." Fulk continues: "Plus the development of computing and communications technology that makes it possible for teams to do more types of work electronically."[5] In other words, one reason groups use technology in the meeting room is that they *can*.

Audioconferencing[6]

The simplest, and most underrated, form of electronic meeting is the audioconference, in which two or more people confer by telephone. "Many face-to-face meetings should not take place," says George Silverman, president of Market Navigation, Inc. of Orangeburg, New York and a veteran of audioconferencing. "The telephone works equally well—and sometimes better—for many kinds of meetings."

Audioconferencing is a useful vehicle for crisis management (e.g., when an accident occurs or a rumor needs to be squelched). It also works well for external communications such as press conferences, allowing reporters at distant sites to interview hard-to-reach executives or celebrities.

In general, audioconferencing is effective when the information to be communicated is straightforward, according to Janet Fulk. But some tasks that may seem too complex for the telephone are not, including certain kinds of training.

For example, George Silverman recalls working with a company that needed to install modems on the computers at its field offices. The company couldn't afford to send technicians to each site or to have all the employees travel to a central training meeting, so the decision was made to conduct the training by phone. At the appointed hour, an instructor came on line with the 10 field sites and began giving directions: "Open the box ..." The instructor walked the field-office staffs through the entire installation this way, pausing now and then to answer questions. The job was completed in less than an hour.

The Power of Verbal Cues

Isn't it important to see the person on the other end of the telephone line? Not necessarily. "Yes, people are very visually oriented, but on the other hand when they can't see each other, they're often not as intimidated as they might be," says George Silverman. And, he notes, "you can pick up a lot over the telephone—energy, hesitation, laughter, tone."

Research supports his claim. Studies comparing audio and video communication to the written word show that most of the improvement in quality comes from vocal, not visual, information. A number of studies indicate that people interpret voice cues better than facial expressions. "Studies of deception show that accuracy in identifying liars is higher when listening to a speaker's voice than watching the person's face," Janet Fulk notes.

It also may be easier to detect alliances when the people involved cannot be seen, according to meeting expert Clyde Burleson. "Not being able to see the participants actually seems to help when trying to sort out who is joining whom, or how factions are aligned," Burleson writes. "Leaders of these factions are more easily recognized, too, as the others tend to hold back and let the leader speak. With no facial expressions or body language to distract, it's much easier to recognize a leader's tone."[7]

Of course, audioconferencing doesn't preclude the use of visual aids. In a well-planned audioconference, participants are sent an agenda, background materials, videotapes, or other visual information they need to prepare for or reference during the meeting. Additional materials can be sent back and forth on meeting day through the facsimile machine.

The Price Is Right

The biggest advantage of audioconferencing is its relatively low price, compared to videoconferencing. The ability to meet at any location that has a telephone is another obvious advantage of audio meetings. People who wouldn't have the time or travel budgets to meet face-to-face are far more accessible by phone.

Some people refer to the audio medium as the "horse and buggy" of teleconferencing. But that characterization may be unfair. Recent technological advances, such as the installation of fiber-optic cable between major U.S. cities and the conversion from analog to digital transmission, have improved the quality of telecommunications. The following innovations have been particularly useful:

- Bridging equipment, which allows 500 or more people to come on the line without a loss in sound quality and enables a facilitator to divide a large group into smaller ones for breakout discussions, or to place some participants on listen only.

- Polling or voting devices, which enable participants at remote sites to indicate to the meeting facilitator that they have questions or views to express.

- Improved speaker phones, which allow everyone within 12 to 15 feet in a conference room to hear and be heard by participants at other sites.

- Recording capability, which allows the facilitator to provide instant replay of discussions and to create audiocassette transcripts of meetings.

Potential Drawbacks

Audioconferencing does have potential drawbacks. For example: It's more difficult to establish rapport with people you can't see, unless you've met them beforehand. It's more awkward to begin a spontaneous discussion by phone than in person. Most people find it taxing to listen for a long period of time without becoming distracted. And it's harder to identify cues for taking turns in the discussion.

But such barriers can be overcome or at least minimized. It may be possible for participants to meet each other before the audioconference. An effective meeting leader can minimize the awkwardness of starting a conversation, and can prevent distractions by keeping participants involved in the discussion. And rules for taking turns can (and should) be established at the beginning of the meeting.

How to Plan an Audioconference

In planning an audioconference, experts offer the following suggestions:

- Make sure you have the right equipment. If there will be five or more participants and you require long-distance lines, consider using an audioconferencing service that can ensure volume and clarity, unless you're certain that your telephone system has bridging capabilities.

- Carefully plan the agenda, and be clear about your objectives.

- Give each agenda item a time slot, just as you would for a face-to-face meeting.

- Identify procedures to be used for each agenda item. Participants should know that they will first give feedback on customer reactions and then brainstorm ideas, for example.

- In some cases it may be helpful to hire a professional facilitator who has audioconferencing experience, to run the meeting.

- If visual materials are required, mail them well in advance of the meeting. Make sure fax machines are available at each meeting site. And don't go too long without checking in with participants, to ensure that everyone stays awake and on track.

- Assign numerals or symbols to paragraphs, so you can refer to them easily, since you can't point to them on a flip chart or slide. Transform information in written reports and spreadsheets into charts and graphs that you send in advance.

- Consider ways to "humanize" participants. If an executive team is going to talk to employees through the use of a speaker phone, display a photographic slide of the team on a screen, or give everyone photographs, particularly if employees have never seen the executives before.

- Begin the meeting by having participants introduce themselves. If all members of the group know one another, a simple roll call will do. If they don't, longer introductions may be required, and it might be a good idea to spend the first few minutes of the meeting socializing.

- Since participants can't see each other, they must have other signals for communicating. Before speaking, participants should identify themselves: "This is Joe, and I think...."

  After a person speaks, participants should ask clarifying questions such as "This is Mary. Did you mean...?" or rephrase the speaker's ideas, "Tom here. Let me see if I can summarize what you said...."

Advice for Participants

Two additional pieces of advice for audioconference participants: speak slowly and listen carefully. Participants in an audioconference should speak slightly more slowly than they would in a face-to-face meeting. Without a visual link, it takes a fraction of a second longer for listeners to absorb the spoken word.

Listening carefully is equally important. Clyde Burleson observes:

> If it is important to listen in face-to-face meetings, then the need to listen in telemeetings cannot be overstressed. Remember: The telephone only takes one of your senses, that of hearing, but you still have to receive and retain the message with the same alacrity, as if all your senses were in play. Face-to-face, you use vision and hearing, and, probably, although psychologists are not in agreement on this, smell. Sometimes, there is even physical contact, adding touch. That's a great deal more sense input than merely hearing another's

voice. Yet you are expected to understand and retain, so you can contribute and help reach a decision.[8]

Taking notes can help. "There is no need to take down every word, but there is demonstrable need to make clear notes on who is saying what," Burleson maintains, "to help you follow the group's action. You hear it, you think it, you write it, and you see it. That's closer to the same level of sense stimulation you would experience in a face-to-face meeting."[9]

Videoconferencing[10]

A growing number of organizations are turning to videoconferencing as a way to communicate vital information quickly and uniformly to remote locations, and to interact with colleagues around the globe. *Videoconferencing*, as the term is defined by the International Teleconferencing Association, refers to a telecommunications system that combines audio and video media to provide both voice communication and motion video images. The video channel may broadcast a single image that is updated periodically (freeze-frame) or transmit full-motion, real-time imagery, either by a satellite or over telephone lines. Images transmitted over phone lines are not as sharp as those broadcast by satellite, but the cost is far lower (more on that later in the chapter).

Like audio meetings, videoconferences save time and travel costs and enable groups to bring employees or outside experts into a meeting from anywhere in the world. The added visual component makes a videoconference more like a face-to-face meeting.

Videoconference Applications

Like its audio counterpart, videoconferencing is more effective for meetings that involve straightforward communication, and less effective for complex tasks such as bargaining and negotiation (although it is more effective for these tasks than is audioconferencing). Videoconferencing is particularly suitable when the message contains some visual element. For example, it's ideal for introducing products. The speaker can demonstrate the new product, and the camera can zoom in to show its features.

"If you can see it or show it on television, you don't need to gather people in a room," says Connie Julius, owner of Teleserv Inc., a Michigan consulting firm that helps companies set up telecommunications networks. Another advantage of videoconferencing is that "everyone gets the same information at the same time," she says. Uniformity can be critical when

Figure 5.2. Videoconference. (*Courtesy Compression Labs, Incorporated, San Jose, California.*)

introducing a new product, explaining changes in policy, managing a crisis, or training employees—all potential applications for videoconferencing.

One-Way Video

There are two basic formats for videoconferencing: one-way video with a one- or two-way audio link, and two-way video and audio transmissions. A one-way videoconference, broadcast to multiple locations by satellite, with two-way audio, is also known as *business television*. The audience is able to see and hear the speaker. The speaker can hear the audience, but cannot see them.

One-way videoconferencing with one-way audio is usually reserved for special events, such as annual meetings or new product introductions. It's appropriate for any occasion when a speaker at a remote site must address a group, but the group doesn't need to interact with the speaker. For example, the Independent Insurance Agents of Texas (IIAT) arranged a one-way videoconference to broadcast a message from state officials to 1600 agents in 17 cities regarding changes in workers' compensation laws.

"We probably could have done it more cheaply by holding traditional conferences throughout the state over a month," says David VanDelinder,

IIAT's education director, "but we wanted the experts, the top managers of the various commissions and boards charged with implementing the new laws. They could take one afternoon out of their busy schedules, but not a month on the road."

Two-Way Video

With two-way videoconferencing (also known as interactive videoconferencing) each site has full video and audio transmission and reception capabilities. This format is appropriate for meetings between groups that are separated by geography but must interact in order to achieve their goals. For example, TRW has used two-way videoconferencing to link strategic planning groups on opposite coasts in a quarterly forecast meeting.[11]

Producing a Videoconference

An organization can produce a videoconference on an ad hoc basis by renting video rooms from a long-distance telephone company, renting self-contained videoconferencing equipment that can be brought on site, or using the services of business television firms such as Chanticleer, which use rented studios and meeting rooms equipped with satellite antennas, TV monitors, and telephone lines.

The costs are especially high for broadcast videoconferences because of the satellite component. The going rate for satellite transmission as of the end of 1993 was roughly $4000 per hour, and if the meeting goes overtime by even one minute, the company is charged for a full additional hour.

Some companies buy their own videoconferencing equipment. The least expensive systems can be bought for around $40,000, and costs are continuing to decline somewhat. But the cost of even the least expensive systems is still outside the range of small businesses, most of whom rent an outside facility for their conferences.

As videoconferencing becomes more popular, a growing number of large organizations are establishing private television networks. Hewlett-Packard installed the nation's first direct broadcast network in 1983 so it could communicate more efficiently with its field locations in North America and Europe—more than 100 in all. Since then, more than 50 companies, including Eastman Kodak, Coca-Cola, CitiBank, Digital Equipment Corporation, AT&T, American Express, and 3M have installed their own networks.[12]

It's expensive to build an in-house videoconference facility, and costly to maintain it—especially if the state of the art changes frequently. But many companies have helped to defray the cost by marketing their facilities to outsiders.[13]

Those who manage on-site facilities claim that organizations are more likely to use videoconferencing if they have in-house capabilities. They also feel that the quality of the conferences is higher because participants can go down the hall and rehearse. If security is an issue, an in-house facility may be a better choice because it eliminates the need to deal with outside technical people who might be exposed to sensitive or proprietary information.[14]

In addition to the basic cost of equipment or facility rental, and telephone or satellite transmission, there are the costs of producing the material for the videoconference. "Because each videoconference is custom-crafted for the client," the total outlay can vary "tremendously," according to Bill Jackson, president of Chanticleer Communications, which produced the IIAT videoconference.

The IIAT conference was straightforward and relatively low-cost. It started with a simple slide featuring the company logo. This was followed by a lecture and chart presentations by David VanDelinder (with occasional shots of the studio audience). The conference ended with a panel of experts answering phone-in questions.

"The tone was informal, the same kind of atmosphere you find in an ordinary meeting," Bill Jackson says. "We wanted it to seem like a class," David VanDelinder adds.

When United Technologies Corporation (UTC) set out to develop its annual Positive Employee Relations Leadership Conference in video form, it had a more ambitious presentation in mind. The UTC videoconference, produced by Chanticleer and broadcast from two sites to 3000 employees in the United States and Canada, was a made for television production. It started with music and animated graphics, was hosted by a professional narrator (Doug Ramsey, managing editor of Financial News Network), and used television production techniques such as a split screen showing two vice presidents fielding phone-in questions from participants.

Neither format is better or worse. The choice of format depends in part on the purpose of the meeting. UTC wanted to "build momentum, enthusiasm, and excitement," according to Harold Phair, director of positive employee relations. Hence the slick, expensive production, which would have been harder to justify for a meeting designed to inform insurance agents of changes in state law.

Tips for Success

In considering whether to hold a videoconference, meeting managers should think carefully about what they want to accomplish. To help them focus on their objectives, Connie Julius asks potential clients such questions as: "What information do you need to get out right away? What are your 'hot spots'? Can you use another telecommunications method just as effectively?" In some cases, it's equally effective (and far cheaper) to send participants a videotape with the instruction, "Watch this tape, and be prepared to discuss it in a telephone conference call at 2 p.m. on Thursday."

Janet Fulk recommends that videoconferences be restricted to groups of people who know each other or have at least had some contact before the meeting, and who are not in conflict with one another.[15] She also offers the following suggestions for ensuring a successful videoconference:[16]

- Send visual aids to all participants prior to the conference. Make sure that conference rooms are equipped with overhead projectors, VCRs, whiteboards, and flipcharts, as appropriate.
- Develop and distribute an agenda prior to the meeting.
- Prepare inexperienced participants for the video medium by giving them a brief orientation.

This last point is particularly important. Most people feel uncomfortable the first time they participate in a videoconference. Bill Jackson of Chanticleer recommends that novices receive coaching in how to perform effectively before the camera. It also may be a good idea to hide the camera and microphone as a way of making presenters feel more comfortable.[17]

Room design can also help to raise participants' comfort level. Communications consultants Marya Holcombe and Judith Stein note that "participants feel more relaxed when they see the entire room at the other location than when they see only a close-up shot of the person talking, as is the case in a freeze-frame videoconference. It is even better when the two rooms are similar enough to look like extensions of each other."[18]

All of these suggestions can improve the quality of a videoconference, but keep in mind that no amount of production savvy can overcome a poorly conceived video meeting. Even Bill Jackson admits: "If the content is boring, it will be boring on satellite."

The Future of Videoconferencing

Videoconferencing is not yet used extensively in most organizations. But it is quickly gaining in popularity, partly because prices are decreasing and technology is advancing. Already we are seeing the emergence of desktop-to-desktop videoconferencing, and while the price tag is still high, it's likely to decline over the coming decade.

Right now telephone companies, cable television operators, and computer manufacturers are lobbying Congress for the right to transmit multiple signals—voice, video, and data. "The marriage of all TV transmission, voice and computer facilities is going on right now at breakneck speed," says Jerry Tapley, marketing communications manager for 3M's Visual Systems Division. If federal legislation paves the way for these industries to compete on equal footing, it will open up a host of new possibilities. Videoconferencing equipment may then come in a staggering variety of forms, from television sets to notebook computers to cellular telephones. If that happens, we can expect to see "zillions of trademarks," says Tapley.

Another reason for expanding interest in videoconferencing: the growing problem of gridlock. "Now and even more in the future, we will not be able to move people," says Connie Julius. "We will have to move information." Videoconferencing is quickly becoming a viable route.

Computer Conferencing

The "Interpersonal" Computer

The personal computer, which has radically altered the way people work, is rapidly changing the way people meet. "The personal computer is often *too* personal," writes Bob Johansen of the Institute for the Future. "In fact, much office work occurs in groups: teams, projects, meetings, committees, task forces, and so on. Group work is in fact a natural way of doing business and computers are just catching up to that fact." Johansen adds that "many office workers have personal computers (PCs) on their desks, people are beginning to ask about connections to other people with whom they work closely. The personal computer is gradually becoming the interpersonal computer."[19]

The "interpersonal computer" makes it possible for people to meet electronically without hearing or seeing one another (although audio and visual support can be added). Bob Johansen calls computer conferencing the "group version of electronic mail."[20] E-mail allows a single person to communicate electronically with an individual or a group; computer conferencing enables a group of people to interact electronically with other groups of people.

In a simple computer conference, participants log on to a central conference database as they would to send or receive electronic mail. The database can be customized to allow users to exchange private messages, to restrict access to certain individuals, or to meet some other need of the group. For example, engineers in scattered locations throughout Procter & Gamble use computer conferences to share ideas for research and development. The central database is divided into partitions, and engineers are assigned varying levels of access.[21]

Computer meetings can take place in real time, or they can be held "asynchronously," with participants contributing to the on-line conference database at different times, depending on their schedules and/or locations. Asynchronous meetings may go on for weeks or even months, depending on their nature and purpose.[22]

A Flexible Tool

Because it enables people to meet across time as well as space, computer conferencing is a far more flexible tool than audio- or videoconferencing. A side benefit is that participants who meet at different times have the chance to think before they speak. According to Scott Poole of the University of Minnesota, "members of asynchronous conferences often report being able to mull over their comments before entering them, resulting in deeper and more thoughtful discussions."[23] Another advantage of meeting by computer is that participants can directly access databases and electronic tools to help them with modeling and analysis.[24]

Computer conferencing is relatively easy to implement in most sizeable organizations because they already have the essential equipment and communications technology: personal computers and local area networks. By contrast, relatively few organizations have the equipment and facilities needed to hold a videoconference.

As with all forms of electronic meetings, computer conferencing has weaknesses as well as strengths. For one thing, some people view computer meetings as impersonal. For another, it takes longer to type a thought than to speak it (depending on the participant's skill level, it can take *a lot* longer). And not everyone—including skillful typists—feels comfortable in dealing with computer technology. But comfort levels will likely increase as more people experience firsthand the advantages of meeting on-line and as meeting technology becomes more user-friendly.

Groupware

There is a broad range of computer hardware and software designed to support group work. These computer tools are known by a variety of names, including group decision support systems, collaborative systems, computer-supported collaborative work, shared systems, work group computing, coordination technology, and *groupware*—the term we will use. We define groupware as *software and hardware that meeting participants use at workstations to perform group tasks* such as brainstorming, problem solving, and decision making.

In a typical meeting in which groupware is used, each participant sits at a computer terminal. The leader begins the meeting by telling participants what problem they need to solve or decision they need to make. Then each participant begins to input ideas and cast votes on their individual computer screens which are integrated by the groupware and shown on a public screen at the front of the room. The content of the meeting is automatically documented and hard copies are made available to participants at the end of the session.

Groupware meetings can be face-to-face, in which case members may converse directly as well as by computer. Or they may be held across two or more sites, with a voice or video link added if necessary.

Groupware is effective for brainstorming, planning, problem solving, product development, and other complex, unstructured tasks, including those that involve negotiation or that require creativity and have no right answers.[25]

A Sampling of Groupware Products

Groupware comes in two basic varieties: keypad systems, which take and tally votes, and keyboard systems, which allow participants to type words or narrative, not just a number. Following is a sampling of groupware products, to show the range of technology available. OptionFinder® is an example of a keypad system. Lotus Notes® and GroupSystems V® are keyboard systems.

OptionFinder[26]

OptionFinder is a product of Option Technologies, Inc., of Mendota Heights, Minnesota. In a meeting using OptionFinder, each participant is given a 10-digit keypad wired to an IBM-compatible personal computer. The system can support more than 100 keypads (see Fig. 5.3).

At critical points in the meeting, the leader asks participants questions, such as "On a scale of 1 to 10, how satisfied are you with our liability coverage?" or "Of the eight names given, which do you prefer for our new product?"

Participants register their votes by pushing buttons on the keypad that correspond to their opinions or choices. OptionFinder provides four forms

Figure 5.3. *Top:* Group using OptionFinder. *Bottom:* OptionFinder keypad. (*Courtesy Option Technologies, Inc., Mendota Heights, Minn.*)

of voting: forced-choice paired comparison, or rating using a Likert, discrete, or nominal scale.

When the voting is complete, the computer processes the responses and displays them on an overhead projector equipped with a liquid crystal display (LCD) panel (discussed in Chap. 6). The system can display the results of one vote or show a comparison of the outcomes of two votes.

As participants view the group votes on the screen, they explain or clarify their opinions, compare them with others, offer new ideas, discuss areas of disagreement, and ultimately reach a decision. Responses are stored on disk and can be printed later for minutes or reports.

OptionFinder is mainly used for planning/designing and opinion gathering meetings (e.g., a focus group or employee attitude survey), or for making a decision (e.g., selecting a new employee). Fast feedback of voting is considered the most important contributor to its success. Anonymity is another contributing factor. Participants in an OptionFinder session are less likely to be influenced by the opinions of the boss and more likely to give candid, useful responses.

OptionFinder is portable enough to take to a client's office or hotel; the meeting leader can carry 15 keypads, computer, and accessories in a traveling case that fits in the overhead compartment of an airplane. One drawback: It can only be used in same time/same place settings.

Strategic Planning Using OptionFinder

The senior management of Round Pipe Company met to develop plans for long-term plant investment and strategy in the waterworks business, and to focus on short-range strategies to keep the overall business afloat during the current recession.

The first task of the STRAT group, as senior management was called, was to determine what had to happen to make the company successful now and in the long run. To do this, the group identified the eight Critical Success Factors (CSFs) shown in Fig. 5.4.

Critical Success Factors

A. Know cost of products.
B. Produce high-quality and specialty products.
C. Make pipe at a low cost.
D. Develop and influence the market.
E. Handle all paper transactions smoothly.
F. Smooth out the "peaks and valleys."
G. Formalize the plan for the RW business.
H. Optimize the delivery system.

Figure 5.4. Critical success factors.   (*Continued on next page.*)

Processes/tasks	A	C	B	D	H	E	G	F	Impacts
A. Dev. cost sftwr	X	X	X						3
B. Use cost info	X	X	X						3
C. Detrm how to make pipe in 5 yrs	X	X	X						3
D. Plan new manuf mths		X	X						2
E. Get engnr onboard			X	X					2
F. Dev. trained QA staff			X	X					2
G. Auto/smooth pint flw	X								1
H. Dev. good MRP prog.	X								1
I. Buy wire makng mach	X						X		2
J. Focus on 2" pipe	X	X	X						3
K. Neg. gv/bks w/ union	X								1
L. Dev. low cost supplrs	X								1
M. Reduc reqm't in prods	X								1
N. Dev/dist prods catlg			X	X					2
O. Engage in advertising			X	X					2
P. Create adv proj rev	X		X	X					3
Q. Maintain Ass'n invlv			X	X					2
R. Dev ord entry softwr			X	X			X		3
S. Expit RW advantages			X	X					2
T. Finish RW budget proc				X					1
U. Dev. dispatch softwr	X				X	X			3
V. Imprv wrk/sis ord acc	X	X			X	X			4
W. Asgn champ fleet mgt		X			X				2
X. Lm mr about fleet mgt	X				X	X			3
Y. Dev smir fulltm pk stf							X		1
Z. Asgn champ to dis pr	X	X		X			X	X	5

Figure 5.5. Process/task matrix.

The CSFs were entered into OptionFinder. Using the keypads, members of the STRAT group first compared each CSF to all the others to produce a prioritized ranking, then used a 5-point Likert scale to rate their current efforts in making the factor happen, where 1 = embryonic; 3 = fair; and 5 = excellent. The results of the session were immediately displayed to the group (Fig. 5.5).

In reviewing the display, the STRAT group concluded that CSFs A, B, C, and D were the most important and that their efforts were fair to good; H was of medium importance and efforts E, F, and G were of lowest importance and effort (see Fig. 5.6).

Now the group used storyboarding to develop a list of specific processes/tasks that would contribute to each CSF. Figure 5.6 shows each process/task along with the number of other CSFs that would be affected.

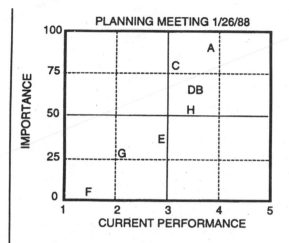

Figure 5.6. Prioritized ranking of CSFs.

The list was then entered into OptionFinder. The group was asked to rate each item on the list on two dimensions, performance (how well the task/process was currently being performed), and timing (in what time frame the task/process should be tackled). The results are shown in Fig. 5.7.

Review of these results helped the STRAT group to focus on what needed to be done during the next 100 days. With this information, the group was able to assign individual responsibility for various tasks/processes, focusing on those which were weakest in terms of performance and had to be addressed the soonest. Review of Figs. 5.7 and 5.8 shows that the highest priorities were P, Z, V, B, and X.

The entire process took two days to complete. The first day focused on the CSFs and the second on action planning.

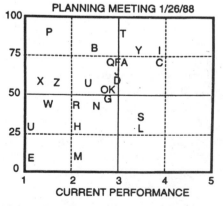

Figure 5.7. Rating of elements on two dimensions.   *(Continued on next page.)*

	Processes/tasks	Impacts	Resp/assgn
P.	Create adv proj rev	3	Ned: < 3/14
Z.	Asgn champ to dis pr	5	Rob: by 6/1
V.	Imprv wrk/sis ord acc	4	Geo: by 2/5
B.	Use cost info	3	Sue: by 2/12
X.	Lm mr about fleet mgt	3	Geo: by 2/3
A.	Dev cost software	3	Sue: by 2/3
J.	Focus on 2" pipe	3	Ken: how to $; mkt surv by 4/1
Q.	Maintain ass'n invlv	2	Jan: pln by 3/5
F.	Dev trained QA staff	2	Jim: rpt by 2/3
D.	Plan new manuf mths	2	Jim: rpt by 2/17
O.	Engage in advertising	2	Ned: $$/pln 5/1
T.	Finish RW budget	1	Rob: by 2/3
K.	Neg gv/bks w/ union	1	Sue: ongoing
C.	Detrm how to make pipe in 5 yrs	3	Geo: dec-2/3
I.	Buy wire machine	2	Jim: dec-2/15

Figure 5.8. Prioritized ranking of processes/tasks.

Lotus Notes

Lotus Development Corporation introduced a groupware product called Notes in late 1989. Notes is a highly flexible software program that enables its users to organize, access, share, and track information through the use of databases which they create, access, and manipulate. Notes also includes E- mail capabilities, electronic bulletin boards, text editing, document management, and various applications development tools. Documents produced in Notes can incorporate spreadsheets, text from word processing applications, graphics, photos, and a video or audio track. A menu-based interface makes it easy to use, even for computer novices.

Bob Johansen calls Notes "the bellwether groupware product out there."[27] Tim Deagan, manager of the services tools development group at Dell Computer, refers to it as the "Swiss Army knife of tools." Deagan was in the R&D group when it began using Notes—the first department within Dell to adopt the product.

Users can enter a Notes database and search for information sorted in a variety of ways—such as by client, product type, or industry classification. In addition to standard categories, users can create their own customized views of the database, depending on their information needs.

Notes has a broad range of potential applications. For example, a product development team could meet through Notes and use the system to track the progress of the project, analyze problems, and identify bottlenecks.

One of the most powerful advantages of Notes is that its users can pose a question or ask for information without knowing who might have the answer or the data. Anyone within the Notes network, which may include thousands of users, can respond. A typical Notes conversation in a large organization might include a dozen people from half a dozen cities around the globe.

Information added to Notes databases is automatically updated whenever a user adds a comment or otherwise edits a file. By using a simple command, individual users can tell which documents in the database they've already read and which are still to be reviewed. As with other groupware products, access to Notes databases can be controlled.

Notes can link almost any desktop or mobile user of Windows, Macintosh, OS/2, or UNIX into a common set of applications. From a single local area network, it can be expanded to serve thousands of users around the world. (Price Waterhouse, which was the first customer to buy Lotus Notes, now has more than 9000 employees linked to the system, making it the world's largest user of the product.)

Sheldon Laube, national director of information and technology, was responsible for the selection and implementation of Lotus Notes throughout Price Waterhouse. He says that Notes is used for all of the company's core applications, from developing proposals to drafting elaborate reports for clients.

Says Laube: "In a business like ours, the key is accessing knowledge, getting expertise from where it is to where it needs to be. Notes provides a mechanism for doing that. Notes is all about capturing knowledge, using it, maintaining and distributing it."[29]

A business magazine described how Price Waterhouse had bested a competitor for a multimillion dollar contract by drafting a winning proposal in a matter of a few days, with the help of Notes. The proposal was developed by three executives in three separate locations. The company's competitors had been developing their bids for weeks.

Laube commented: "That's a standard day-to-day use of Notes. It's a nice example, but not unique." He added: "We believe that Notes is a dramatic factor in our competitiveness as an organization."[30]

The tremendous flexibility of Notes is one of its major strengths. It may also be its biggest weakness, especially to novice users. "Precisely because Notes is so general, it is often hard to understand at first what it is useful for," says Thomas Malone, director of the MIT Center for Coordination Science.[31]

Says Tim Deagan of Dell Computers: "You have to lure people to Notes." At first, he recalls, department managers were hesitant to spend money on a product that seemed to have no clear mission. But the product gradually gained acceptance, and now it's used widely within Dell for applications as diverse as database development, training, and quality control.[32]

GroupSystems V

A team led by Jay Nunamaker developed GroupSystems at the University of Arizona in the early 1980s. Nunamaker went on to found Ventana, a Tucson-based company that now markets the software. An early version of GroupSystems was licensed to IBM, which sold it under the TeamFocus brand name. Ventana and IBM are both marketing the most recent version of the product, GroupSystems V.

The basic package includes features that enable groups to plan meetings; evaluate alternatives; vote on issues in seven different, quantifiable ways (with anonymity guaranteed); generate ideas, using a structured or un-structured format; and develop policies through an iterative process of reviewing and revising policy statements. There's also a set of utilities, such as a calendar, electronic notepad, and even a mood meter, that group members can access electronically during a GroupSystems session. A Windows version of the product adds graphic capabilities, including a People feature that provides information about meeting participants, a diagram of the room, office building, the part of the world where they are located, short biographical descriptions, and even graphical portraits.

GroupSystems V can be used in face-to-face, real-time meetings and for asynchronous conferences. In each case, participants are linked through a network of personal computers (see Fig. 5.9).

GroupSystems V sessions may be coordinated by any member of the group. They are usually managed by a facilitator, but not always in the traditional sense of the term. The GroupSystems "facilitator" is simply the person who has overall responsibility for the meeting, whether it's a one-hour session held in real time or an asynchronous meeting held over a period of weeks or months.

But Does It Work?

Key Advantages

Most research suggests that groupware does improve the quality of meetings.[33] And there's no shortage of anecdotal evidence about the productivity gains that come from using groupware products. Two typical examples: IBM cut meeting time at its manufacturing and development facility in Owego, New York by 56 percent with the help of TeamFocus groupware.[34] And the Software Technology Branch of the Army Research Laboratory got "4-6 weeks of work done in 3½ days" as a result of using GroupSystems, according to James Gantt, director of groupware research for the Laboratory.

Figure 5.9. GroupSystems V® session in progress. (*Photo courtesy Ventana Corporation, Tuscon, Arizona.*)

As these examples show, the time savings that accrue from using groupware can be substantial. Because people read much faster than they listen, they're able to deal with much more material during a given time period, so more gets done. Jay Nunamaker notes: "In a typical hour-long meeting of 15 people, everybody's got an average of only four minutes of air time. With computer support, everybody's got the potential to talk for 60 minutes. That's a big increase in productivity."[35]

The fact that groupware enables people to offer their ideas anonymously encourages participation and provides another spur to productivity. And it can help groups with a diverse mix of members to become more cohesive and work together more effectively. As Carl Di Pietro, formerly a human resources executive at Marriott Corporation, notes: "It's a room of nondiscrimination. You don't know if that idea you're reading comes from a woman or a man, part of the minority or majority, or a senior or junior person. People begin to say, 'Hey, we've got a lot in common with each other.'"[36]

The promise of anonymity can also elicit valuable negative information that otherwise might not surface. For example, during one groupware session at the Phoenician Resort in Scottsdale, Arizona, a pharmaceutical company asked the audience of physicians a series of questions about the drugs they would recommend to patients for various illnesses.

In response to one question, almost everyone in the audience chose a competitor's drug. One of the pharmaceutical company reps, obviously surprised by the answer, stopped the meeting and asked the doctors why. They told him they wanted the drug in suppository form but his company only sold it as caplets. The company quickly produced a suppository version of the drug.[37]

Groupware can also help to build consensus, even among those accustomed to conflict. In early 1992, the U.S. Army Research Laboratory tested groupware among a broad mix of users, including experts and novices. Research director James Gantt and staff member Catherine Beise recall: "One of our more interesting sessions involved members of an academic department with a reputation for raucous meetings. At the end of their test, they were amazed: They had reached a consensus on a touchy curriculum issue with everyone participating but with no one yelling in anger."[38]

Another strength of groupware is that it can automate important but often neglected aspects of meetings, such as procedures. "Groups may be reluctant to use procedures because they don't have the experience and don't want to spend the time to become knowledgeable about procedures," Scott Poole notes. Groupware can help, he adds, by guiding the uninitiated through meeting procedures.[39]

In addition to automating procedures, groupware can help with housekeeping chores, such as recording ideas and votes, producing minutes, planning future activities with the help of an electronic calendar, and performing other necessary tasks that groups might neglect "because they seem to be too much trouble."[40]

Finally, according to Michael Schrage, author of *Shared Minds: The New Technology of Collaboration*, one of the key strengths of meeting technology is that it enables a group to create a tangible product:

> Most significant, perhaps, is that what's displayed [on computer monitors] can be physically printed out, copied, and distributed to all the group members and any other relevant parties. I can't overemphasize how significant this is. It transforms the traditional meeting ecology—to discuss a topic, come to a conclusion, or make a decision—into an *act of shared creation*. The ability to create a tangible product completely revolutionizes what a meeting is. The meeting becomes a group process to create a group product. It's the difference between talking about what you'll have for dinner and actually cooking the meal. The focus shifts from planning and reviewing work to actually *doing work*. That people can end a meeting and then literally grasp a document that captures what the meeting was about and what the group's priorities are transforms the entire experience. Note that the hard copy can appear literally moments after the meeting concludes. There's no need for delay or

dissonance. The immediacy reinforces the idea that the meeting is a genuine act of creation.[41]

Potential Drawbacks

Groupware doesn't automatically make meetings more productive. Some of the features of groupware that are designed to enhance productivity can also inhibit it. For example, anonymity encourages participation, which might improve productivity. But it might not, says Andy Whinston, a professor in the graduate school of business at the University of Texas at Austin. Because no one knows who is contributing a given idea, participants may not be as careful in formulating their ideas. Says Whinston: "Anonymity shields people who haven't thought through their views carefully."[42]

Anonymous input can also lead to confusion. If participants have questions about an issue that's raised in an anonymous groupware session, they don't know whom to ask for clarification. Furthermore, in some situations, it's important to know who said what. "If we're discussing a marketing effort in China and we have the world's leading expert on Asian marketing in the room, I want to know that person's view," Whinston says.[43]

Anonymity has another dark side. Consultant Mark Tebbe, president of Lante Corporation, began using groupware every other week with his 10-member management team. Over time, he realized that one meeting participant—a fast typist—was pretending to be more than one person when he vehemently agreed or disagreed with an idea being discussed. "He'd type 'Oh, I agree,' and then 'Ditto, ditto' or 'What a great idea' all in quick succession, using different variations of upper-case and lower-case letters and punctuation," Tebbe recalls. "He tried to make it seem like a lot of people were concurring, but it was just him." Tebbe discovered the ploy when the person sitting next to him got suspicious and began watching his screen.[44]

There are other drawbacks in addition to those associated with anonymous input. For example, groupware is rightfully credited with encouraging introverts to participate in meetings. But it can also discourage extroverts from participating, because they no longer have the chance to display their verbal skills.

Groupware can speed things up, and that's a plus—unless the goal is to solve a problem or reach consensus, in which case "speed is not a particularly good way of doing things," says Whinston. "The more subtle question is the quality of the conclusions drawn."[45] Groupware can become a victim of its own success, by making it easy for groups to generate a large volume of ideas—perhaps too large a volume. Walking away from a meeting with a long list of product concepts or marketing strategies sounds wonderful, but "maybe that's terrible," Whinston argues. Instead of 100 ideas," perhaps it's better to have 10 that have been carefully distilled."[46]

Getting the Most Out of Groupware

Whether or not a particular aspect of meeting technology is a strength or a weakness largely depends on how it is used. "You can't just throw technology into a meeting," says Rick Watson, assistant professor of management at the University of Georgia. "You have to understand where it fits in the process."[47]

For example, anonymous voting is a powerful feature of groupware systems, but one that should be used with discretion. Says technology guru Jerry Wagner: "I've always felt anonymity is useful in getting someone started with the technology. If it becomes part of the organization's infrastructure, then something's wrong with the organization."[48]

Nor will technology by itself help a group to overcome its bad habits. The results of 3M-sponsored research show that groups who get computer support suffer from "many of the same process problems" that all groups normally encounter, such as discussing irrelevant issues, failing to consider all the available alternatives, and dealing with issues in an unsystematic fashion.[49]

Technology cannot substitute for sound meeting management, as Clyde Burleson reminds us: "A meeting is a meeting whether electronic or face-to-face. The same concepts ... still apply. If it is difficult to hold a productive meeting with everyone in the same room without an agenda, it is far more difficult to do this in an electronic conference." Burleson advises meeting managers: "Stay with the principles that work. Deserting them will not result in better electronic meetings. The result of shortcuts in these areas is chaos."[50]

Most importantly, unless the people who use it have good intentions, groupware won't produce good results. "Groupware is not inherently democratic or authoritarian," says Bob Johansen, "it allows increased options in both directions. It is possible to design a groupware system that facilitates high individual participation in all decisions, but it is also possible to design group systems to channel people in a very manipulative fashion toward a particular direction."[51]

Bernie DeKoven "ruefully recalls one chief executive of a small company who half-jokingly suggested that the shared space be reapportioned on the basis of rank. Because he was the CEO, this CEO argued, his vote should have a greater weight than the votes of his colleagues. That way, the ideas the CEO wanted could 'win' the approval of the group."[52]

"As long as there are incentives for competition and control, people will use groupware only to further their individual goals," says management consultant Bernie DeKoven.[53] For example, some bosses defeat the purpose of groupware by "walking around the room glaring at people's terminals or loudly bullying everyone to put in ideas that resemble their own," says Geraldine DeSanctis, a professor of information systems at the University of Minnesota. "The group has to decide it wants to get more out of meetings" if the technology is to be applied successfully, she says. "It's like an alcoholic has to want to stop drinking."[54]

The Future of Groupware

Whether or not it is used effectively, groupware is likely to experience continued growth as teams become more dominant in organizational life. According to Bob Johansen: "Business teams are here to stay and they need tools to help get their jobs done, whether or not the computer and telecommunications industries choose to help them. While the process of introducing this perspective is likely to take a while, there are real opportunities that are not to be denied."[55]

In the future we can expect to see a variety of new forms of groupware. Researchers, including Jay Nunamaker, are already developing ways to conduct "virtual meetings," such as the scenario described in the chapter opening.[56] The development of lightweight, inexpensive computers that may be small enough to fit in a vestpocket will make it possible in the future to hold electronic meetings any time, any place.

Intelligent telephones that can accept messages and alert the recipient already are being foretold through cellular telephones, pagers, and voicemail. "There is one now where if you don't pick up your voicemail in one hour, a pager is triggered," Robert Johansen says. "The technology of ultralight portables is becoming very, very good and we're also seeing ultralights which are dockable in your office so you can unplug it and take it home in your briefcase," he adds.[57]

Other meeting technology on the horizon: cross-cultural, Total Quality and market research groupware, and virtual "skunkworks" that use different time/different place groupware to coordinate global projects and operations.[58] Finally, over the next decade we can expect to see the emergence of "softer software" that is easier to use and more powerful than the technology available today, thanks in part to advances in artificial intelligence research.[59]

Not even the experts know precisely what the ramifications of the emerging technology will be. Leonard Jessup and Joseph S. Valacich write:

Our expectations of what we will do with these systems are inherently simplistic and constrained. Our forecasts are inevitably constrained by traditional notions of what we did previously in similar situations without the technology. For example, with the introduction of a new computer-based loan application data base, loan processors or loan officers can easily see that the new system will enable them to process loan applications faster. It is not as easy for them to see that the new system might enable them to do the process better, with better control over information, with enhanced security capabilities, and with greater probability of accepting sound applicants and rejecting risky applications. The new system may also enable them to better understand the cycles and patterns of their work processes so that they can, perhaps, better monitor, control, or even completely change the process in ways that enable them to do their jobs better.[60]

In his book, *Connected Executives*, Bernie DeKoven describes a new type of manager whose workspace inside and outside of the office are linked by technology:

Connected executives are those who are as computer literate as they are socially literate. They use every communication or information technology they can find to become more informed and to communicate more productively. They use phone and fax, e-mail and electronic bulletin boards, whatever they have available to increase the speed and efficiency of communication. "Connecting" their offices, they redefine the very concept of "executive office." Connecting their personal workstation to their network computer, to their home computer, to their personal laptops, they control a personal workspace that has no physical boundaries.[61]

Ultimately, technological advances may change our thinking about the very nature of meetings. "My Webster's dictionary defines a meeting as 'an act or process of coming together,'" says Gary Tritle, manager of technical planning for the Information, Imaging and Electronics Sector of 3M. "But we may need to think of a meeting in broader terms, such as 'communication, coordination, and collaboration of group activities,'"—a definition put forward by Skip Ellis, formerly a senior technical staff member with the Microelectronics and Computer Technology Corporation.[62]

The Limits of Technology

The transformation in our thinking about meetings will occur only gradually, as people become more comfortable with meeting technology. Bob Johansen writes:

> Groupware will become a major user application area, but probably neither quickly nor simply ... Many people are still becoming accustomed to the idea of having a PC on their desks or within easy access. Many have not yet become comfortable with the concept of using it for assistance in work tasks. And a very few have integrated the PC into their work activities as a regular tool. Until a large share of the potential user base has reached this level of comfort, a product based on the PC is unlikely to achieve mass acceptability.[63]

Gary Tritle agrees that comfort with technology is a limiting factor in the growth of computer-supported meetings: "Most people rate giving speeches as a major fearful event," he notes. "A speaker using a multimedia computer not only has to overcome that fear but also gauge audience response and think about which keys to press and what to do next."[64] Not everyone is up to the task—at least not yet.

Even those who use technology effectively may not feel entirely comfortable with it. For example, three-fourths of the facilitators in the 3M-Boise State University study achieved better results when they used computer support, but most preferred to work without it. Their comments suggested they felt uncertain and uncomfortable. Some felt that computer support was contrived and unnatural.

But there is nothing inherently unnatural about using technology to communicate. Tom Peters remembers: "When I was a kid, pen pals developed friendships without meeting." He calls the pen pal craze the "precursor to electronic meetings." And, he notes, the growing popularity of on-line friendships among users of services like Prodigy proves that it's possible to create "familiarity and intimacy over the airwaves."[66]

In some cases, discomfort with technology is simply a function of age and inexperience. In others, the comfort problem masks a deeper attitude problem. For example, Jay Nunamaker notes that executives often "won't use a keyboard. [Typing] is considered mundane work, not executives' work."[67]

But it's possible for the technology-averse to make an attitude adjustment, and peer pressure can sometimes help. Nunamaker recalls one senior manager who brought his secretary to a groupware session, to do his inputting. He was so ridiculed by his peers that he never did it again.[68]

More often the problem resolves itself in the course of the meeting. "We will start a group with a very sensitive issue, and people dive in and forget they're using a keyboard," says Nunamaker. "There's so much emotion that people want to get their two cents in."[69]

Much of the resistance to meeting technology will inevitably dissolve as the Nintendo generation moves into the conference room. Still, there are limits to what technology can bring to the meeting room. "I'm fully confident that electronics will enhance aspects of certain types of meetings, but I'm equally confident that we're not going to switch totally to electronic meetings," says Gary Tritle. "Meetings have many dimensions. Sometimes they involve information and data exchange, and computers can do an excellent job at that. In other meetings," says Tritle, "personality, politics and posturing are very dominant and computers are not capable of handling that situation at this point."

No matter how sophisticated electronic technology becomes, there will always be room for the traditional face-to-face meeting in which people mingle over coffee and mull over decisions. "As human beings, we have a social need to be with people, and meetings help fill that need," Gary Tritle reminds us, echoing a theme introduced in Chap. 1.[70]

Tom Peters agrees. While he acknowledges the "fabulous potential" of emerging meeting technology, he scoffs at the notion that technology will magically transform organizational life. "Technology is not a panacea," he warns. "It offers a terrific avenue for changing the nature of meetings. But to imagine that technology can fully supplant face-to-face meetings is nonsense!"[71] Sometimes a pen pal just isn't enough.

6

How to Develop and Deliver Powerful Presentations

Veteran speaker and trainer David Peoples recalls one of the most powerful presentations he ever attended:

> I was going through jet fighter pilot training. Before they strap the stove pipe on you, you have to go to ground school to learn the electrical system, the fuel system, and so on. One day the instructor walked into class and held up a red ribbon with a pin at the end. He said, "Gentlemen, do you know what this is?" Well, of course we didn't know what it was.
>
> He explained that this was the safety pin from the ejection seat of an F-86 Saber Jet, and that for the next hour he was going to lecture to us on how to eject from an F-86 Saber Jet and survive. Then when we finished the lecture we were going out that door to the parade grounds where there was an actual ejection seat mounted on a vertical railroad track. And, one at a time we were each going to be strapped into that seat. We would pull down our visors, pull up the left arm rest, pull up the right arm rest, then pull the trigger underneath the right arm rest—and when we did, a live 20 millimeter cannon shell was going to explode under our you-know-what, and we were going to be shot straight up.
>
> Do you think he had our attention? Let me tell you, every man in that room could have given that lecture.[1]

Unfortunately, not all presentations are as riveting as the one Peoples describes. Too many are poorly conceived, carelessly crafted, or badly delivered—usually because the presenter has not mastered a few simple techniques.

In this chapter we'll cover the fundamentals of developing and delivering a powerful presentation, from drafting an outline to creating visuals to managing nervousness to evaluating and improving performance. We cannot cover all of the territory of presentations in a single chapter, but we'll give you a solid overview of the terrain.

The Effective Presentation

What makes a presentation effective? To find the answer to that question, Genesis Training Solutions, a training and development firm in Montgomery, Texas surveyed a group of senior executives in seven East Coast companies. Some of the key findings:[2]

- Brief is beautiful. Two-thirds of the executives polled said that presenters should get their points across in 30 minutes; one-fifth said 15 minutes is better. This jibes with the views of psychologists, who observe that an audience's attention span declines steadily to a low point over 20 minutes, and doesn't rise again until it's clear that the presentation is about to end.

- Effective presenters don't flood the audience with facts or drown them in detail; instead, they communicate the big picture. The best presentations are "effective and efficient," says Raymond Slesinski, president of Genesis. "They are effective in that they cover top priority areas, and they are efficient in that they convey a solid, complete message with minimal words."

  Survey respondents complained that too many speakers try to "data dump" them with too much technical or financial information, or too much information overall. Effective presenters distill the data into key nuggets of information the audience needs to know to make a decision or take action.

- Visual aids enhance the overall effectiveness of a presentation. Of the executives surveyed, 89 percent said visual aids are either very important or important in conveying ideas.

- When asked to choose the five most important traits of a speaker, the survey respondents selected these, in this order: (1) subject knowledge, (2) organization, (3) logic, (4) confidence, and (5) thoroughness.

In the following pages we'll revisit all of these themes as we explore the mechanics of developing and delivering a presentation.

Developing an Effective Presentation

Analyzing Your Audience

One aspect of thoroughness that presenters often overlook is researching the audience. The first step in developing an effective presentation is to learn all you can about those who will be attending. What is their educational background? What is their level of expertise? What is their interest in the subject matter? What are their biases? Will they be required to attend? What is the average age of the group? What is the gender and ethnic makeup of the group? How does the group feel about you? Answering such questions will help you to shape the content and determine the appropriate style, language, and technical level of your presentation.

If you are presenting to an outside organization, you must also learn about its culture and circumstances. Is the organization formal or informal? Aggressive or conservative? Is the company growing, stable, or declining? Is morale high or low? Knowing this information will enable you to tailor your presentation to address the unique needs of your audience.

Developing a Structure

Once you have analyzed your audience, you can begin to organize your presentation. There are a number of ways to do so. Claudyne Wilder, president of Wilder Management Services, a management consulting firm in Boston, suggests the following general format:[3]

1. State the objective of your presentation.
2. State the three or four major points you are going to make.
3. Explain each of these key points.
4. Include examples or anecdotes to add interest.
5. Restate your major points.
6. Recommend any next steps that you or the audience needs to take.

One advantage of this format, according to Wilder, is that people retain information better if a general structure is outlined first, with the details given later.

There are many other ways to organize a presentation. In her book, *The Presentations Kit*,[4] Wilder suggests nine other formats that vary according to the presenter's objective (see Fig. 6.1).

The General Format	Recommend a Strategy	Share Information
1. Make an opening statement. 2. State the three or four key headings of the talk. 3. Give the detail under each of the headings. 4. Put in an example or anecdote for interest. 5. Close with a strong statement. 6. Recommend any next steps that you or the listeners need to take.	1. State the objective. 2. State the present situation. 3. State the desired outcome. 4. State the potential strategies. 5. List the advantages and disadvantages of each. 6. Recommend one or more of the strategies and what to do next in order to carry them out.	1. List information using three or four major headings. 2. Explain the information. 3. Define buzz or jargon words. 4. Link the information to the listeners' interests. 5. If appropriate, explain its significance to the organization's goals.
Identify Potential Problems	**Sell a Product, Service, or Idea**	**Teach Skills**
1. State the goal. 2. List anticipated issues that may block achieving the goal. 3. Rate the seriousness of the issues. 4. State preventative and/or contingent actions. 5. Establish a framework identifying prime mover and deadlines.	1. State the objective. 2. State the needs of the listeners. If you are not sure, ask them about their needs. 3. List the features. 4. List the appropriate benefits relevant to the listeners. 5. Specify the next steps.	1. State the benefits of learning the skill to the participants. 2. State skill areas to be learned. 3. Cover areas using examples, handouts, questions, and exercises. 4. Conclude with a summary of major lessons of the day. 5. Suggest next steps in order to apply the information.
Report Progress	**Identify the Problem**	
1. Define the subject. 2. List three or four areas of discussion. 3. List issues under each area. 4. Prioritize the issues. 5. Delineate the action steps that have been taken and need to be taken for each issue.	1. State what you want to have happening versus what is actually happening. 2. Specify what things are happening that are the same. 3. Specify what things changed about the time the problem started. 4. Suggest the underlying problem(s). 5. Present the potential solution(s). 6. Suggest the next steps.	
Communicate Bad News	**Recommend a Decision Alternative**	
1. Discuss the background (such as facts, history, and other strategies considered). 2. State the bad news. 3. Present options among which to choose. 4. Conclude by reaffirming options. 5. Guide the person into choosing the most preferable option.	1. State the decision to be made. 2. List all the musts and wants. 3. Rate the importance of wants. 4. List the alternatives. 5. Eliminate alternatives not meeting "must" criteria. 6. Compare alternatives to see how much they satisfy the wants. 7. List any strong positive or negative consequences of each alternative. 8. Recommend one alternative and suggest steps for carrying it out.	

Figure 6.1. Ten presentation formats. [*Adapted from Claudyne Wilder,* The Presentations Kit *(New York: John Wiley & Sons, 1990), p.43 and pp. 47-48. Copyright © 1990 by Claudyne Wilder. Reprinted by permission of John Wiley & Sons, Inc.*]

Creating a Logic Tree[5]

Whatever format you choose, make sure that it flows logically and is easy for your audience to follow. "When a presentation fails, it's usually because it was not well-structured, not because the presenter spilled coffee on the visuals," says communications consultant Marya Holcombe.

If you are making a presentation to decision makers, Holcombe and her partner, Judy Stein, suggest drawing your ideas in the form of a logic tree (Fig. 6.2). The first step is to determine your objective—the one thing that you want the decision maker(s) in the audience to remember or do.

After choosing the main idea, write the major points that support the idea on the branches of the logic tree. Each branch or supporting point may have further supporting statements that appear as twigs (Fig. 6.3).

The supporting points should answer the questions that the decision makers in the audience will ask when they hear the main idea. Suppose the main idea is "We should buy the Kumquat spreadsheet program." The decision makers will naturally want to know why, and will likely be asking themselves questions such as *How much will this cost? How do we know it will improve productivity? What other options are available?* The branches of the logic tree should contain the answers to those questions (i.e., the reasons for recommending the Kumquat program).

During the presentation, the logic tree gives the presenter a clear picture of how ideas relate to each other. If, at any time during the presentation, the decision makers indicate verbally or through body language that they agree with a point, the presenter can cut the supporting details and move on.

One caution: When constructing your logic tree, be careful not to develop a topical outline instead. A topical outline lists ideas by category or sequence, typically with an introduction and conclusion. This approach, which most of us learned in eighth-grade English class, often results in talking about a topic rather than telling the decision makers what they need to know.

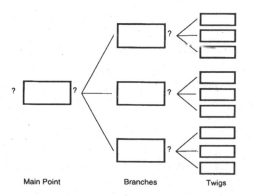

Main Point   Branches   Twigs   **Figure 6.2.** The logic tree.

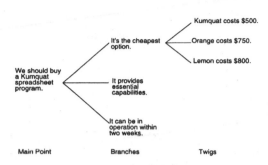

Figure 6.3. Example of a useful logic tree.

Crafting a Beginning and Ending

The next step is to develop a beginning and ending—the two parts of your presentation the audience will remember most. David Peoples writes: "You are an unknown quantity for only 120 seconds. After that, everything you say will be heard in the context of the impression from your first two minutes." In those two minutes, you have to answer the one question that will be on the minds of every person in the audience: "What's in it for me?"[6]

Your answer need not be as compelling as that of the flight instructor in the opening anecdote, but you must appeal to the self-interest of your audience right from the start. You might open your presentation with a provocative question or startling statistic about an issue that concerns the audience. You could display a relevant prop, as the flight instructor did. Or, you could relate a powerful story that strikes at the heart of your message.

However you begin, make sure to focus on what the audience needs to know, not on what you want to say. Don't boast about your background or expound on your experience unless the audience has a compelling need to know this information.

In crafting your opening, imagine that each person in your audience is wearing a sign on his or her forehead that reads: "So what?" If your opening effectively addresses that question, your presentation will be headed in the right direction. Resist the temptation to open with a joke, unless you are a professional comedian; the risk of bombing far exceeds the chance of succeeding. Avoid opening with dictionary definitions or quotations, as these are cliches and will more likely bore than inspire your listeners. And never begin with an apology, such as "I wish I'd had more time to prepare for this presentation." If you haven't taken the time to prepare, why should your audience take the time to listen?

A strong ending is as crucial as a solid beginning. The ending is your last chance to appeal to the audience and motivate them to make a decision or agree on a course of action.

Many of the techniques that are used to open a presentation also can be used to end it. For example, you might end with a powerful anecdote that reinforces the main idea of your presentation. If possible, tie the ending to the beginning; this will make both more memorable. (For other ideas on how to end your presentation, see Fig. 6.1.)

Creating Visuals

To maximize the impact of your presentation, incorporate visual aids. There is truth in the adage that "a picture is worth a thousand words." People absorb information more quickly and retain more information when it is communicated visually rather than in verbal or written form (see Fig. 6.4).

"When we see a picture or symbol, we grasp the totality of an idea," says Bill Korbus, who teaches visual design at the University of Texas at Austin. For example, it's more effective to see a picture of a proposed office building than to read about it or hear it being described. That's because words convey

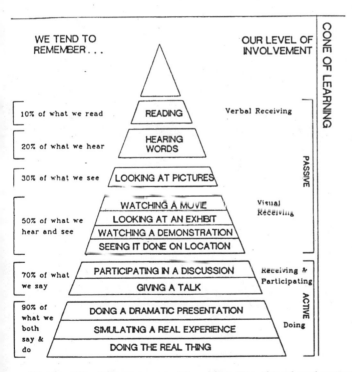

Figure 6.4. Experience and learning. (*Developed and revised by Bruce Nyland from material by Edgar Dale.*)

the message in pieces—such as the height, width, color, and shape of the building—while visuals provide a more complete picture.[7]

Research sponsored by the 3M Meeting Management Institute confirms the power of visual aids. A 3M-sponsored study by the Wharton Applied Research Center found that when presenters use overhead transparencies, the audience remembers up to 10 percent more of the information presented.[8] Subsequent research at the University of Minnesota showed that presenters who used computer-generated visual aids were 43 percent more persuasive.[9] Both studies found that presenters who use visual aids are perceived as better prepared, more professional, more highly credible, and more interesting than those who do not.

A follow-up study at the University of Arizona found that the use of computer technology in presentations further enhances effectiveness. Specifically, the researchers found that the selective use of animation and transition effects increases audience attention; aids comprehension; fosters agreement with the presenter; increases retention of the message; and positively affects the audience's perception of the speaker.[10]

When to Use Visuals

Visuals can be used for the following purposes:[11]

- *To hook the audience.* A cartoon, provocative quote, gripping statistic, or other compelling visual can instantly capture the attention of the audience.

- *To emphasize key ideas.* Visuals can be used to reinforce the most important points of the presentation.

- *To present complex or statistical data.* Presenters can avoid the tendency to "data dump" by transforming complex concepts or masses of data into visual information that is easy to grasp.

- *To show comparisons.* Visuals can be used to compare data at one point in time, such as the sales revenues for two divisions, or to show trends.

- *To show items too big or small to display.* Visuals such as a jet aircraft or a computer memory chip can be easily presented to the audience.

Visual Design Principles[12]

Visuals enhance a presentation only if they are properly designed. If not, they detract from the presentation and reflect poorly on the speaker. In developing your visuals, keep the following guidelines in mind:

- *Don't tell the whole story.* A visual aid is just that—an aid, not a substitute for the presentation. Don't spell out your entire presentation on visuals. The audience will read the visuals and not listen to you. Instead, use key words, charts, or pictures to illustrate what you're saying.

- *Keep it simple.* The most common mistake presenters make with visuals is "overloading them," according to Judy Stein. When using visuals, "you want the audience to look at the screen, quickly get the message, and then focus on you," says Stein. When viewers have to spend time reading, "you become the voice-over to a video and lose your effectiveness as a presenter."

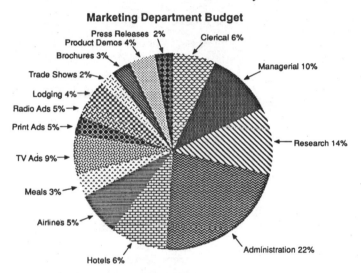

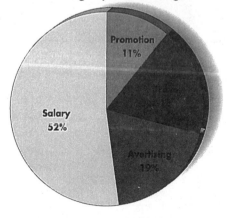

Figure 6.5. Keep it simple. *Top:* The message of this pie chart is lost in the clutter. *Bottom:* Reducing the number of slices and replacing black-and-white patterns with solid colors enhances the impact of the chart. (See Fig. C.1, Chap. 6 color insert.)

To prevent your visuals from stealing center stage, keep them simple. Present only one key idea per visual. In the text chart, use no more than six words per line and six lines per visual. If you want to provide more detail, include it in a handout to be distributed after the presentation. When creating pie charts, bar charts, or other commonly used visuals, minimize the number of elements so that your message will not be lost.

Resist the temptation to add boxes, grid lines or other devices that will clutter up the visual. "The more elements in an image, the less attention each one commands" says Margaret Rabb, editor of *The Presentation Design Book*.[13] She advises: "A clean, uncomplicated presentation is more professional than one cluttered with a lot of clip art and foreign matter."[14]

- *Make the message the heading.* Judy Stein says that presenters often make the mistake of putting a heading such as "Sales 1990-1995" at the top of a chart. This is a variation on the topical outline trap; the heading talks about a topic instead of conveying a message.

  "Your heading should always tell people what you want them to look for on a chart," says Stein. "An action statement or message will do that for you." An action statement has a verb and is a complete sentence, such as "Profits Rise for All Products but Widgets."

- *Make it readable.* One of the most common mistakes presenters make is creating visuals that are unreadable because the text is too small. Make sure the words and numerals on your visuals are at least four inches tall when projected. (Labels on charts, graphs, etc., can be slightly smaller but should also be readable.) Another good rule of thumb: If you can read your unprojected visuals from ten feet away, your audience should be able to read them projected in almost any meeting room arrangement.

Other ways to increase readability:

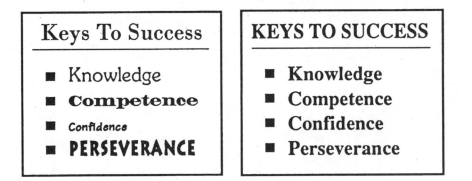

Figure 6.6. Make it readable: Because it combines several typefaces and sizes, the chart on the left is more difficult to read than the one on the right.

- *Make sure all letters and numerals read horizontally.* Don't permit them to run vertically up the side of the chart so viewers must tilt their heads to read them.

- *Fancy typefaces or multiple typefaces can also make your visual hard to read.* Restrict yourself to simple type styles and to a maximum of two type styles per visual.

- *Avoid using all capital letters, since these are hard to read.* Margaret Rabb notes two exceptions to this rule: (1) when type becomes too small to read, as in labels and legends, use uppercase; and (2) when there are words and numerals on the same line; uppercase letters make a better blend.[15]

- *Be consistent.* Your visuals will be easier to read if they are consistent. Consistency applies to format, word choice, type style, colors, alignment, background, and other design elements. By making visuals consistent, you are more likely to keep viewers from getting distracted from your message.

- *Use a variety of types.* While consistency of design is important, it's a good idea to vary the type of visuals you present, to keep your audience interested. A visual mix of bar graphs, pie charts, a prop and a video clip is more compelling than a sequence of line graphs in an identical format.

- *Avoid distortions.* Make sure that your visuals accurately communicate your message. All numerical axes should begin at zero, and only like variables should be compared.

Also, beware of design elements that can distort your message even if the information presented is technically accurate (see Fig. 6.7). That advice comes from Dona Meilach, a leading expert on computer-generated graphics. As an example, Meilach notes that "certain colors, like red and black, when assigned to some bars or lines, make them appear more important than those in yellow or light blue" and that solid bars "appear weightier and more important than those that are outlined."[16]

Adding Color

The Impact of Color

Color may soon become a requirement in meetings and presentations, according to Larry Brown, Process Manager for the Deskjet Printer Group of Hewlett-Packard. "Color is a powerful communication tool," says Brown. "It helps people stay interested, retain information better, make better decisions, even dream a little."[17]

Color affects us strongly because we react to it emotionally, says Brown. "It starts with the rods and cones in our eyes. We sense blues and greens as

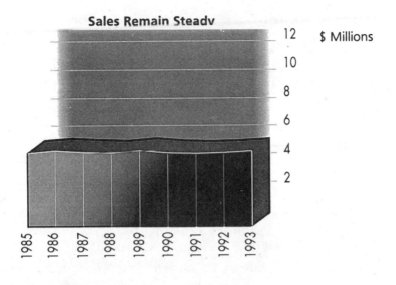

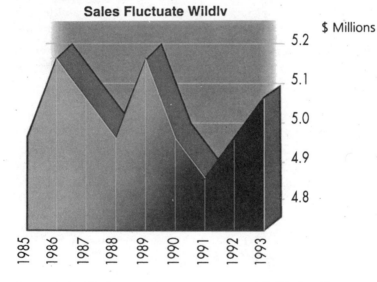

Figure 6.7. Which message is more accurate? Altering the range of the *y*-axis (*bottom*) results in a distortion of the profit picture. (*Charts produced using Adobe Illustrator 5.0. Reprinted courtesy of Adobe Systems, Incorporated, copyright © 1987-1993, Adobe Systems Incorporated. All rights reserved.*)

cool and calm, and reds as warmth or danger. We don't have to be told what these mean; we respond naturally."[18]

The power of color has been demonstrated in a variety of research studies. A 3M-sponsored study found that color visuals are significantly more persuasive than black and white.[19] Research by the Bureau of Advertising shows that color increases comprehension by as much as 73 percent, sells products and ideas more effectively by 50 to 85 percent, and enhances the clarity of visuals, to name just a few of its many proven benefits (see Fig. 6.8). Other business and academic studies have reported similar findings.

Uses of Color

There are many ways that color can be used to enhance the appeal and effectiveness of your visuals. Following are the more common uses of color:[20]

- *To differentiate.* Choose primary (red, yellow, and blue) or contrasting colors to help viewers distinguish between items, such as sales of product

---

The Impact of Color

According to research by the Bureau of Advertising, color visuals ...

- Attract attention and hold interest.
- Highlight vital information.
- Accelerate learning, retention, and recall by 55 to 78 percent.
- Increase comprehension by up to 73 percent.
- Increase willingness to read by up to 80 percent.
- Increase recognition up to 78 percent.
- Increase motivation and participation up to 80 percent.
- Reduce error count by 55 to 35 percent.
- Sell (products and ideas) more effectively by 50 to 85 percent.
- Increase clarity, providing more distinct differentiation between graphic elements.
- Add an extra dimension, creating more interest in the topic.
- Relate elements, making comparisons easier.
- Condense information, allowing more elements to be related without confusion.
- Add prestige, which reflects on the speaker.

Figure 6.8.

X (blue bar) compared to product Y (red bar) over five years. One exception: Avoid using red and green together. Color-blind viewers, 10 percent of the male population, perceive these as muddy brown.

To separate several items, choose colors close to each other on the color wheel, such as red, red-orange, and yellow. In a bar chart, place the darkest color (red) near the axis; otherwise the chart will appear to tip to one side. In a pie chart, stagger the darker colors for an even appearance.

- *To emphasize.* In a simple text chart, use one color for the text and a second color for the word or phrase that needs to stand out. In a graphics chart such as a U.S. map, use cool colors for all the states and a warm color for Wyoming, the state you wish to highlight. In a "build" chart that develops your argument point by point, use a bright color for the point you are discussing and subdued colors for the points you've already made.

    Choose bright colors for small objects that you want to emphasize and subtle colors for large objects and backgrounds. Blue works well as a background color because the retina contains fewer blue-sensitive cones than other color receptors.

- *To identify or group related items.* In a diagram illustrating the petroleum refining process, for example, choose one color (or color group) for the diesel-grade fuels and another color for the gasolines.

- *To order items.* Choose colors next to each other on the color wheel and assign them to items in sequence from most important to least important or vice versa.

- *To suggest a mood or trigger emotions.* Different colors produce different emotional effects. Use red to connote error, danger, or anger; green for growth or money; blue for trust or serenity; and yellow for cheerfulness. Pastels are associated with romance. Greens, yellows, and browns are associated with the outdoors. There are many other color connotations. One caution: Color connotations vary among cultures, so know your audience.

When adding color to your visuals, keep the following guidelines in mind:

- *Use color consistently.* When presenting information in a series of charts, be consistent. If you use orange to indicate energy costs in one pie chart, use orange for the same segment in the other pie charts in the series. If you're color coding by department, make sure departments keep the same color on every visual.

- *Don't overdo it.* The most common mistake novices make is using too many colors, and colors that are too bright. "Typically, we think more is better or brighter is better, but that's not true," says Larry Brown. Graph-

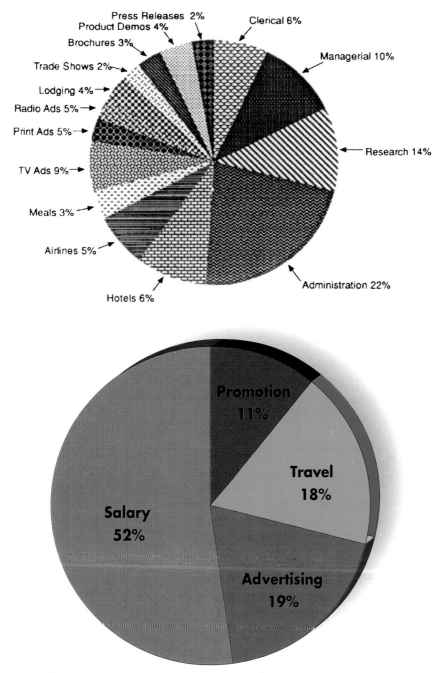

Figure C.1. Keep it simple. *Top:* The message of this pie chart is lost in the clutter. *Bottom:* Reducing the number of slices and replacing black-and-white patterns with solid colors enhances the impact of the chart. (*The top chart was produced using Aldus Freehand 3.0 software; the lower chart, Adobe Illustrator 5.0 software. Reprinted courtesy of Adobe Systems, Incorporated, copyright © 1987–1993, Adobe Systems Incorporated. All rights reserved.*)

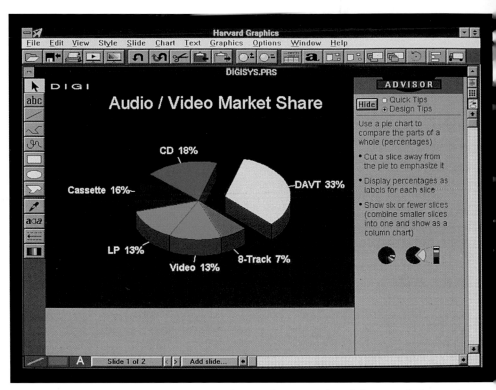

Figure C.2. Harvard Graphics® 3.0 software offers an "Advisor" feature, which provides users with tips on creating effective visuals, like this colorful pie chart. (*Courtesy Software Publishing Corporation, Santa Clara, California.*)

Percentage of Total Sales

Figure C.3. Bar charts are used to compare individual items or groups of related items: *Top:* horizontal bars; *bottom:* vertical bars. Note the addition of graphic art to reinforce the message of each chart. (*Charts produced using Adobe Illustrator 5.0. Reprinted courtesy of Adobe Systems, Incorporated, copyright © 1987–1993, Adobe Systems Incorporated. All rights reserved.*)

Minivan Sales Remain Strong

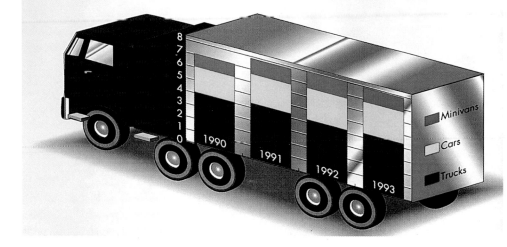

Computer Games Take the Lead

Figure C.3. (*Continued*) *Top:* stacked bars; *bottom:* series of stacked bars. (*Charts produced using Adobe Illustrator 5.0. Reprinted courtesy of Adobe Systems, Incorporated, copyright © 1987–1993, Adobe Systems Incorporated. All rights reserved.*)

Retail Sales Overtake Catalog Orders

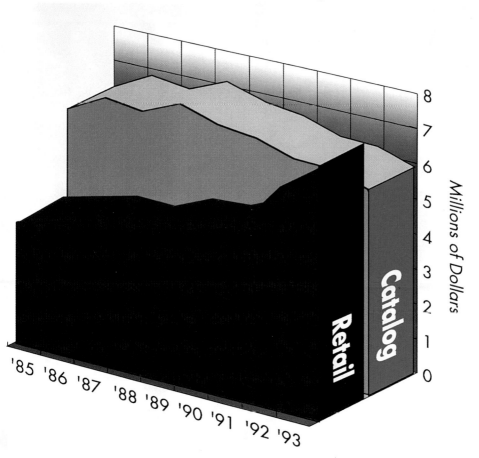

Figure C.4. The purpose of a line chart is to convey a trend, not to provide detailed data. (*Produced using Adobe Illustrator 5.0. Reprinted courtesy of Adobe Systems, Incorporated, copyright © 1987–1993, Adobe Systems Incorporated. All rights reserved.*)

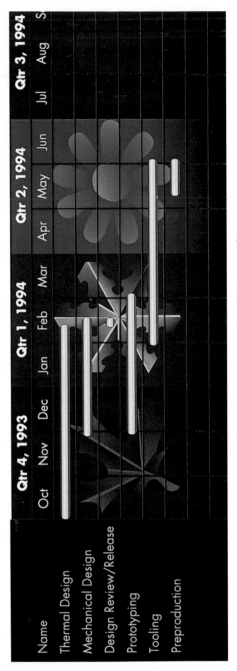

Figure C.5. The Gantt chart, showing the stages of a project, is a commonly used diagram. (Chart produced using Adobe Illustrator 5.0. Reprinted courtesy of Adobe Systems, Incorporated, copyright © 1987–1993, Adobe Systems Incorporated. All rights reserved.)

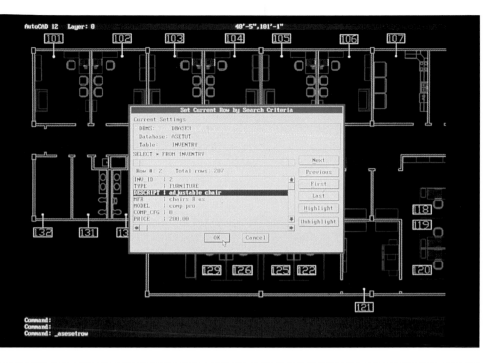

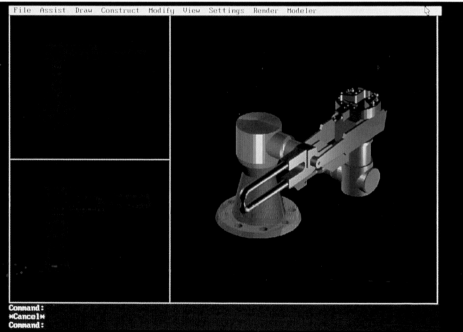

Figure C.6. Standard drawings. *Top:* This office facility floor plan illustrates how AutoCAD SQL Extension™ (ASE) is used to link AutoCAD Release 12 drawings to nongraphical data existing within database files. *Bottom:* This three-dimensional model of a welding machine was rendered in AutoCAD Release 12 using the completely integrated AVE Render feature. (*Courtesy Autodesk, Inc., Sausalito, California.*)

ics experts recommend working with as few colors as possible—no more than four in a single visual.

- *Study the pros.* Dona Meilach advises presenters to study the graphics used on television news broadcasts and the lead-ins to movies and TV shows. "Emulate those colors in your visuals and you'll be on target," says Meilach.[21]

Common Types of Visual Aids

With these general design and color guidelines in mind, let's explore the most common types of visuals used in business presentations.

Pie Charts

Pie charts are used to show relationships among items or between one item and a whole. (See Figs. C.1 and C.2, Chap. 6 color insert.) For example, a pie chart provides a quick visual image of market share, with the pie representing the entire market and each slice representing an individual competitor.

In constructing pie charts, observe the following rules:

- Limit the number of slices to six.
- Limit the number of pies on a single chart to three (preferably two) or the chart will be too cluttered and difficult to grasp.
- Make legends brief and large enough to read. They can be placed within or outside of the pie, next to the appropriate slice.
- Make sure there's enough contrast between colors or shading so that the pieces of the pie are clearly differentiated.
- Highlight a slice of the pie by giving it a bright color or by exploding it.
- Arrange segments in clockwise order, either from largest to smallest or vice versa, starting at the 12 o'clock position. One exception: If you wish to explode a segment, put that slice in the 12 o'clock position, regardless of its relative size.

Bar Charts

Bar charts show comparisons among individual items or sets of related items. They can also be used to illustrate trends. (See Fig. 6.9.) Bar charts can be horizontal or vertical. Use horizontal bars for comparing individual

Percentage of Total Sales

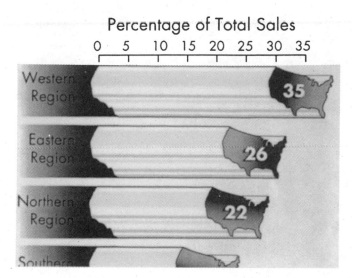

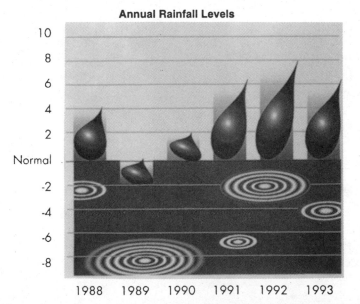

Figure 6.9. Bar charts are used to compare individual items or groups of related items: *Top:* horizontal bars; *bottom:* vertical bars. Note the addition of graphic art to reinforce the message of each chart. See Fig. C.3, Chap. 6 color insert. (*Charts produced using Adobe Illustrator 5.0. Reprinted courtesy of Adobe Systems, Incorporated, copyright © 1987-1993, Adobe Systems Incorporated. All rights reserved.*)

Minivan Sales Remain Strong

Computer Games Take The Lead

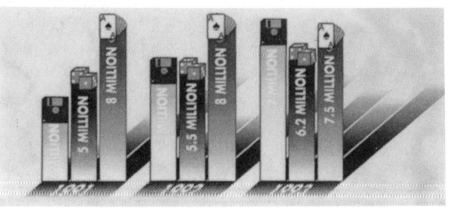

Computer Games

Board Games

Other Games

Figure 6.9. (*Continued*) *Top:* stacked bars; *bottom:* series of stacked bars. (See Fig. C.3, Chap. 6 color insert.) (*Charts produced using Adobe Illustrator 5.0. Reprinted courtesy of Adobe Systems, Incorporated, copyright © 1987-1993, Adobe Systems Incorporated. All rights reserved.*)

variables or sets of variables at a single point in time. For example, if you want to show the highest profit, the lowest interest rate, or the most products sold or you want to rank variables from largest to smallest (or vice versa), use a horizontal bar chart.

Use a vertical bar chart (also known as a column chart) if you want to compare variables at various points in time. Since we naturally associate left-to-right with the movement of time, vertical bars work better than horizontal bars for time series data. For example, a vertical bar chart can be used to show that administrative costs have risen faster than manufacturing costs over three years. (However, if you have more than five data points, use a line chart, described in the following section.)

Horizontal or vertical bars can be used to display positive and negative data. Segmented or stacked bar charts show relative proportions of two, three, or four wholes, with each bar representing the whole, and each segment representing a percentage. A series of stacked bars can be used to show how percentages change over time.

To enhance readability, limit charts to five bars, and make sure the bars are wider than the spaces that separate them.

In some cases, art graphics can be used in place of lines or bars. For example, a chart showing the increase in plant employees over a 10-year period might show three figures of workers: a small one representing the number of plant employees 10 years ago; a larger one showing plant employees five years ago; and the largest figure showing today's plant employment.

Use art graphics only if they enhance the message. If you want to show that employment doubled, a bar chart may convey the message more effectively than showing two workers of different sizes. Art graphics are more effective at communicating general trends than showing precise relationships.

Line Charts

Line charts are used to show changes in one or more variables over time. The details are generally less important than the trends indicated (see Fig. 6.10).

Use a line chart when a variable has more than five data points and you want to emphasize continuity over several months or years. If, for example, you want to show how college entrance test scores have changed over 30 years, use a line chart. The slope of the line tells viewers at a glance the direction of the trend.

When creating a line chart, use no more than three lines to compare changes or your visual may become confusing. Give each line a different color, so it will be easy for viewers to differentiate one line from another. If

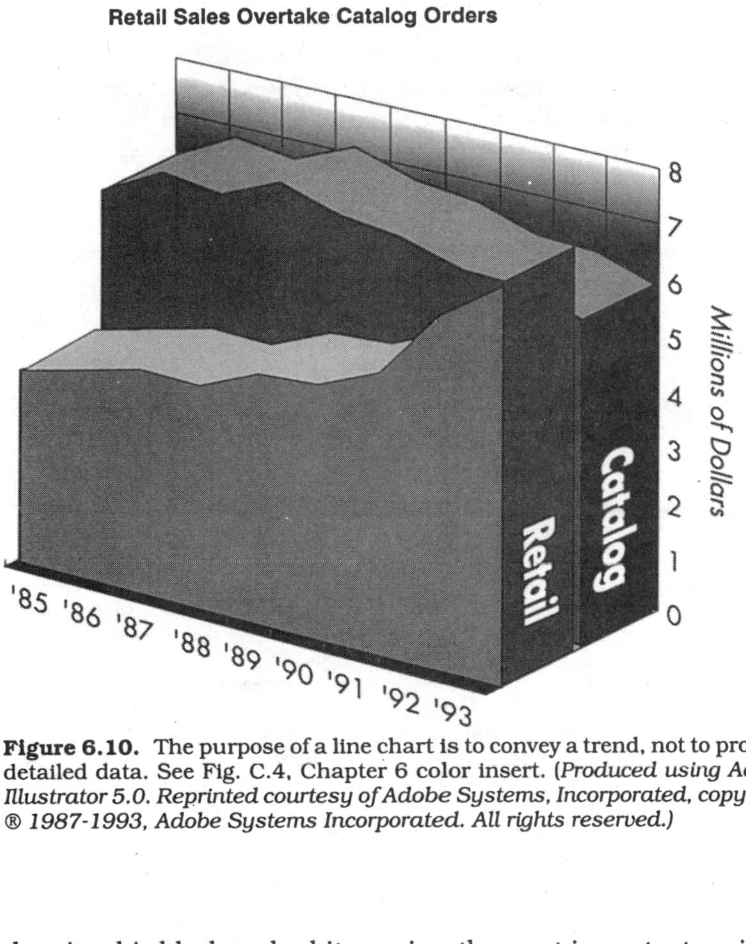

Retail Sales Overtake Catalog Orders

Figure 6.10. The purpose of a line chart is to convey a trend, not to provide detailed data. See Fig. C.4, Chapter 6 color insert. (*Produced using Adobe Illustrator 5.0. Reprinted courtesy of Adobe Systems, Incorporated, copyright ® 1987-1993, Adobe Systems Incorporated. All rights reserved.*)

the visual is black and white, assign the most important variable a solid, bold line and give the others broken lines of various types.

Title and Text Charts

Title charts are like billboards. Use them to focus attention on a single idea.

Text charts are more detailed; they usually include a title at the top followed by a number of related points. Use text charts to outline a topic for your audience.

To make your text charts more interesting, add images, but use discretion: Research shows that adding images creates interest, but it can also make a text visual slightly less clear. When in doubt, use text only.[22]

Tables

Tables, as shown in Fig. 6.11, are used to summarize and compare precise data. In creating a table, keep the number of rows and columns to a minimum—no more than needed to achieve your goal. Don't show sales figures for 10 consecutive years; the same point can be made by showing figures for 10 and 5 years ago along with this year's figures.

Keep the labels on columns and rows simple—one word per column or row, if possible. Long, narrow, and crowded columns are difficult to read at a distance.

To enhance readability, show figures in simple form—such as $420K rather than $419,826.32. Highlight key figures by giving them a bright color.

	1991	1992	1993
Total Sales ($ Millions)	$250.21	$283.76	$301.12
Western Region	72.68	82.22	87.79
Northern Region	68.35	76.34	79.88
Southern Region	56.47	62.13	68.21
Eastern Region	52.71	63.07	65.24
Total Expenses	231.43	260.70	276.74
Salary + Commission	157.08	177.28	188.18
Advertising & Promotion	34.71	39.10	41.51
Administration	24.30	27.37	29.06
Miscellaneous	15.34	32.29	17.99
Net Profit	18.78	23.06	24.38

	1991	1992	1993
Total Sales ($ Millions)	$250	$284	$301
Total Expenses ($ Millions)	$231	$261	$277
Net Profit	$19	$23	$24

Figure 6.11. The table on top contains too much information for the audience to grasp. The table on the bottom summarizes the data and communicates a clear message to the audience.

Make sure you verbalize the conclusion to be drawn from the table. Unlike other visuals, tables do not tell a story. For this reason, they should be used only when more graphic visuals, such as pie or bar charts, cannot be used.

Diagrams

Diagrams are useful devices for explaining relationships, processes, or logical connections that are difficult to explain in words. Use an *organizational chart* to depict the flow and functional relationship of a business or group; a *flow chart* to diagram a process (e.g., the manufacture of a product or the flow of paperwork between two offices); and a *Gantt chart* (Fig. C.5 of Chap. 6 color insert) to show the duration of different tasks across a calendar span.

Do not show too many details in a diagram or its effectiveness will be reduced. If you must show a complicated diagram, break it into parts and show them successively; then show the entire diagram so the audience is able to grasp the details and their relationship to the whole.

Maps

Maps provide easy identification of geographic distributions and comparisons. Use them to pinpoint key cities, regions, sales territories, and so on. Use color to highlight key areas of emphasis, travel routes, communication channels, or different products. When displaying a map with few distinguishable features, add city or street names to orient the reader.

Standard Drawings

There are three kinds of drawings that are commonly used in business presentations. The *scale drawing* is an accurate depiction of a physical object in exact proportions.

A *line drawing* is less concerned with portraying accurate measurements than with conveying the general appearance of the object. It is used to acquaint the audience with an object or place rather than to explore its details.

Schematic drawings use symbols to simplify complex material. Schematics are often used to illustrate electrical or mechanical systems. They should be used only if the audience understands the symbols involved, or their purpose will be defeated. (See Fig. C.6, Chap. 6 color insert, for examples of standard drawings.)

Photographs[23]

Photographs can be used when you wish to portray a subject with a reasonable degree of accuracy. However, be aware that photos can distort the subject or the relationship of the subject to its surroundings if a wide-angle or telephoto lens is used.

In selecting color photographs to include in your presentation, choose images that are sharply defined (in focus), evenly lit (natural shadows and no glare), and correctly exposed (neither too dark nor too bright or washed out). The colors in the photograph should have pleasing contrast, and they should be true; a summer sky on a sunny day should look blue, not gray or white. Avoid images that consist primarily of neutral colors (grays, tans, whites); they lack interest. The colors should have a wide range of values—light, medium, and dark; otherwise, the photo will lack depth and will look flat.

To get a feel for the kinds of photographs that work well, study the samples that appear in advertisements for color film. You will find multicolored balloons, clowns, children's birthday parties, brightly colored sailboats, and other colorful subjects with strongly contrasting colors.

If you use photographs in your presentation, have them taken by a professional or an experienced amateur with a good camera. Finally, make sure the photograph conveys your message at a glance. If the audience has to struggle to decipher its message, the photo is not a visual aid but an obstacle.

Choosing the Right
Graphic Medium

In what form should you display your visuals? There are a variety of graphic media available, from flip charts or Post-It® easel pads to overhead transparencies to 35 millimeter slides to multimedia presentations that combine video, audio, text, and graphics. Your choice will depend on the objective of your presentation, the size of your budget, the amount of preparation time involved, the characteristics of your audience, the level of formality of the presentation, the equipment you have available, and whether or not you want to interact with your audience. In this section we'll review several graphic media and discuss how and when each is most effectively used.

Overhead Transparencies

Overhead transparencies (also called foils) are favored by a majority of executives because they are inexpensive, informal, flexible, and easy to create and use.[24] They are particularly effective in meetings of 10 to 20 people where interaction is important.

As noted earlier, research shows that when presenters use overheads, they are perceived as better prepared, more professional, more credible, and more interesting. Another benefit: overhead transparencies can be used in a fully lighted room, making it easier for the audience to take notes and for the presenter to maintain eye contact with the group. Overheads also are easy to revise, even during the presentation, by rearranging, adding, or deleting transparencies, or by writing on them with a transparency marking pen. (See Fig. 6.12 for some tips when using overheads.)

There are several ways to create overhead transparencies. The simplest is to write or draw directly on the film, using a transparency marking pen.

To create transparencies on a plain paper copier, substitute clear or colored transparency film for paper in the paper tray. Check your copier first; some have optical sensors that require the transparency to be opaque on one side. Transparency film for plain paper copiers comes in three types: with a permanent sensing strip, with a removable one, or with no strip.

Another option is to make transparencies on an infrared copier (also called a thermofax). This method has three advantages over using a plain paper copier: (1) It is roughly three times as fast; (2) the infrared copier is electric; there are no chemicals or toner to change, and no pollution concerns; (3) infrared film varies in weight; a heavier film will produce a more durable transparency than you could create with a plain paper copier.

To produce color transparencies, you can buy tinted infrared film or clear film that reproduces an image in a single color.

Black-and-white or color transparencies also can be made from computer images, using a laser jet, ink jet, thermal transfer, pen plotter, or impact printer.

Other tips for creating effective overhead transparencies:

- Create horizontal, not vertical transparencies, or the audience's view of the lower edge of your image may be obstructed.
- Frame your transparencies, or buy them preframed. Frames block the light around the edge of the visual, add rigidity, and provide a border for notes. Preframed transparencies are easier to handle during presentations and to catalogue for reuse. They also make it easier to add color overlays.

  Another option is to use a Flip-Frame® reusable transparent envelope to hold each transparency. Opaque panels fold open to frame the transparency and provide space for notes. Flip-Frames are prepunched for insertion into a standard three-ring binder, so your transparencies can be easily organized. And you can jot notes on the frame.

Guidelines for Using Overhead Transparencies

- Start by projecting the title or outline of your presentation.

- Do not use a prepared script. Make notes on the frames of your transparencies.

- Use a pen or pointer by placing it on the stage of the overhead projector rather than on the screen.

- Use the "revelation technique" by placing a sheet of paper under the transparency and revealing information one line at a time to control pace and audience attention. Or use the overlay technique, in which a graphic is built up by placing one transparency over another (four is the limit).

- Turn the projector off to position the next transparency and to bring audience attention back to you when making a strong verbal point. (However, don't turn the projector on and off too frequently or you will distract and annoy the audience.)

- Address your remarks to the audience, not the screen.

- Use dual overhead projectors, one to focus on summary information, the other to focus on details.

- Do not turn on an overhead projector without showing an image.

- Do not leave an old visual on the screen when you move to a new subject.

- Don't walk between the overhead projector and the projection screen, to avoid casting a shadow.

Figure 6.12.

35 Millimeter Slides

For a formal presentation that does not require audience interaction, 35 millimeter slides may be a good choice. They also are appropriate for presentations to large audiences (more than 300 people). They are not appropriate for relaxed, informal gatherings.

Slides communicate professionalism, but there are some disadvantages to using them. For one thing, the room must be darkened to show them, so the potential for audience interaction is limited (and the potential for the audience to doze off is increased). Another drawback is the time required to process the film; however, with the proliferation of one-hour photo shops, this is no longer much of a concern.

Slides can be made from computer graphics as well as from photographs. The most common method of making a slide from a computer graphic is to photograph the computer screen. However, the quality of the end product is marginal, because the glass on the monitor can create glare and produce other distortions of the image on the screen. Also, the format of 35 millimeter film is rectangular and the format of a computer monitor is closer to square, so a photo of a computer monitor often includes part of the frame around the picture tube.

Another option is to feed the output from the computer into a film recorder, a peripheral device that plugs into the computer. However, there are two drawbacks to this method. One is cost: Even the least expensive film recorders can run into the thousands of dollars, and the highest-priced professional models go for tens of thousands of dollars. The other is skill: It takes a fair amount of expertise to balance color and master the other technical intricacies of operating a film recorder. As a result, these devices are used primarily by media professionals or semiprofessionals.

Computer Graphics

Until recently, making charts, graphs, and other visuals often required careful lettering or typesetting, drawing, cutting, and laying adhesive strips. In some cases, visuals were expensive and took days or even weeks to produce. Now there is a broad range of affordable computer software that makes it easy for presenters (including computer novices) to produce professional-looking visuals—everything from simple pictures, tables, and charts to complex diagrams, maps, and 3-D objects.

How to Choose a Presentation Software Program

At the start of 1994 there were about a dozen presentation software programs for the IBM-PC and about five for the Macintosh. Prices don't necessarily reflect quality, according to Dona Meilach: "A $49 package may do as much, or more, or perform better in some areas than a $400 package."[25]

Deciding which program to buy requires some research, says Meilach: "Graphics is no different from other software research. It requires asking people how they like the packages they bought, reading reviews, purchasing programs until, by trial and error, you find what you want. One, two, or more packages may be needed to satisfy your requirements."[26]

The first step in the research process is to identify your graphic needs, then determine the capabilities of your computer system. Here's what you have to know, according to William Coggshall, editor and publisher of *The Desktop Presentations Report* in Mountain View, California:[27]

- *Processor speed.* Most graphics software will run better on 80286-based or faster computers.
- *Hard disk.* Most packages work better on a hard disk, although some will use high-density floppies.
- *Video graphics array* (VGA) card. A VGA is especially helpful, although most packages will run with a monochrome or color graphics adapter (CGA) monitor.
- *Operating system.* Your choice of software will depend on whether your computer is a Macintosh or a DOS-based system.
- *Pointing device (mouse).* This is a must if the software runs on an Apple computer or a DOS-based computer under a Windows™ environment, or if you plan to make illustrations that resemble free-hand drawing.
- *Output device (printer).* All packages can run on dot matrix printers or plotters, but most audiences expect laser quality. Access to an ink jet or thermal transfer printer will widen your options in selecting software to produce color visuals.
- *Connectivity.* If the data for a visual will come from another database or computer, your package must have the ability to import or export files.

If you're not sure of your needs, Dona Meilach recommends that you start with a low-cost program, become familiar with how it works, and use it as a standard of comparison. There are many similarities among programs, in terms of the commands, symbols used, and so on. Once you've mastered the basics of one or two packages, subsequent programs will be easier to learn.[28]

No matter how much research you've done, you won't know how well a software package will meet your needs until you use it for a while. According to Meilach:

> You can read reviews and watch a demonstration. Sometimes you can test a program at a conference or in a dealer's showroom. Still, until you apply a program to your specific needs, it's like breaking in a new pair of shoes. It's hard to evaluate where it feels good and where it pinches until you break them in. Even if they pinch a little, you get used to them and wear them anyway.[29]

Graphic Mistakes

Most presentation software comes with default templates that have preset type fonts, colors, symbol placement, and other design elements.

This makes it easy for the novice to produce slick graphics quickly and easily. Unfortunately, these visuals may do a bad job of communicating your message.

The problem is that the people who create the software are engineers, not graphic artists. As a result, they often don't incorporate in the software the design principles discussed earlier in this chapter. As one reviewer warns: "Title and text sizes are too small to be read from the back of a large lecture hall. There may be inflexible positioning for legends and labels. The picture library is static and dull. In some programs, the chart you see on-screen is not what you get when it is printed."[30] Changing the default settings can help, but in some cases built-in deficiencies cannot be overcome.

Software manufacturers are becoming more aware of this problem and have developed a number of resources, including free seminars, videotapes, and booklets to help novices learn how to use their products effectively. Training is available from independent companies as well and may be a good investment for the novice.

Video and Laser Disk

Video and laser disk technology are increasingly being integrated into presentations. Images on videotapes or laser disks can be displayed through video monitors placed within viewing distance of the audience or through an overhead projector using a liquid crystal display (LCD) projection panel.

LCD Projection Panels and Projectors

An LCD projection panel (Fig. 6.13) is a variation on the screen of a laptop computer. When connected to a computer or video source (such as a laser disk or videotape) and placed on the stage of a transmissive overhead projector, the LCD panel projects the images produced by the computer or video source.

Most projection panels offer remote controls, giving you the ability to move about the room as you control the presentation sequence. Options such as magnification features and on-screen pointers are also available, giving you more flexibility and control over your images.

LCD panels are typically small and lightweight. Used with notebook computers, they create a powerful portable presentation system.

The prices of LCD panels vary, depending on the features they offer (including color and the capability to accept audio and video input), but there's a broad range of models to fit even limited budgets. Prices are expected to decline and color and resolution to improve over the next few years.

LCD *projectors* are another option. These are devices that integrate a light source and the LCD screen into a single self-contained unit.

LCD projectors come in two sizes. The combination projector is the same size as a standard overhead projector. There is also a compact unit, which is slightly smaller than a briefcase. The compact LCD projector is more portable, but the screen is smaller, which limits the size of the images it can project.

Multimedia

With the increasing sophistication of personal computers and software, as well as the advent of LCD technology, multimedia is quickly becoming a viable presentation option. True multimedia presentations incorporate text, graphics, video, animation, and sound that can be presented live or compiled on computer disk or CD-ROMs for presentation as needed.

Audio and video input for a multimedia presentation can be generated by your computer and/or it can come from any external digital audio or video device, such as a compact disk player, VCR, or laser disk machine. Most multimedia systems also are able to convert input from analog devices such as audiocassette tape decks to the digital format required.

With this technology, you could, for example, extract film clips from *Gone with the Wind* along with essays about film production from an encyclopedia stored on a CD-ROM inside your computer, add background music from a

Figure 6.13. LCD projection panels can be linked to notebook computers to create powerful, portable presentation systems.

CD player plugged into your PC and synthesized voices generated by a software program, and intersperse computer graphics you created for the presentation. The entire production would be coordinated by your PC and controlled by you through your computer keyboard or mouse.

If the group is small, your multimedia presentation can be given right at your desk, using a PC, laptop, or notebook computer. For a larger group, the presentation can be delivered with video monitors or a LCD projector device. For a multimedia videoconference presentation, you can transmit through a cable television channel.

Delivering Your Presentation

Once you've developed your presentation and created visual aids, it's time to rehearse, preferably in front of one or more colleagues who can give you constructive feedback.

During rehearsals, practice your timing and pacing. Marya Holcombe and Judy Stein recommend that you talk through the entire presentation, then subtract 15 to 20 percent from the total time to allow for handling visuals and discussion. Once you know how long it takes to deliver the presentation, divide it into sections and rehearse again, so you know where you should be one quarter of the way through the presentation, at the halfway point, and so forth. This will enable you to maintain an even pacing and will prevent a "last-minute flurry to finish."[31]

Controlling Your Nerves

No matter how thoroughly you know your subject matter, no matter how much you've rehearsed, you're bound to be nervous on the day of the presentation. Don't worry; a slight case of nerves is normal, even for experienced presenters. Usually the butterflies land a few minutes after you begin to speak.

To combat nervousness, try these proven techniques:

- *Slow down*. Presenters who are nervous tend to speak more rapidly, and this exacerbates the problem. The physical act of slowing your speech will help to calm your nerves.

- *Focus on your presentation, not your nerves*. Concentrate on what you want to achieve, and your nervousness will subside.

- *Make sure you are thoroughly prepared for the presentation.* Fear of blanking out or being unable to respond to the audience because you haven't done your homework will ensure a bad case of nerves.

- *Get plenty of exercise and a good night's sleep.* If you arrive at the presentation site relaxed and refreshed, you will be better able to cope with a slight case of nervousness.

- *Memorize the first two to three minutes of the presentation.* That's when your nervousness will be at its peak, and when people will be forming their impressions of you.

Monitoring and Involving the Audience

As you speak, monitor the audience for nonverbal cues that reveal their reaction to what you are saying, and adjust your presentation accordingly (see Fig. 6.14). If you notice that several people in the back of the auditorium are nodding off, it may be time to pick up the pace. If you find yourself staring at a sea of puzzled faces, you may need to stop and ask questions to find out what has confused the audience. On the other hand, if most members of the audience are nodding in agreement, keep going; don't tinker with a winning formula.

To keep interest high, involve the audience in the presentation as much as possible. Ask questions. Call people by name. Solicit volunteers to participate in an exercise or demonstration.

Don't remain stuck behind the podium. If possible, move out into the audience every now and then. If this is not practical, at least move toward the front of the stage.

Anticipate questions and objections from the audience, and be prepared to address them. To handle a hostile audience, try some of the techniques outlined in Chap. 2, under "Managing Conflict."*

Take care to avoid annoying habits (see Fig. 6.15). David Peoples recalls a woman who was an excellent presenter but had the irritating habit of popping the top of a Magic Marker every ten seconds or so: "Well, the popping of the top of a Magic Marker doesn't make a very loud noise, but if you're doing it every ten seconds that's six times a minute, or 360 times an hour. By the time you get up to pop number 125, they start to sound like rifle shots."[38]

---

*Also see Marya Holcombe and Judith Stein, *Presentations for Decision Makers*, pp.140-143, and Claudyne Wilder, *The Presentations Kit*, Step 8, "Managing Questions and Objections," pp. 213-235.

How to Read Your Audience

Here are some of the most common body language signals you may encounter as a presenter:

Someone who is receptive or agreeable:
- Readily makes eye contact.
- Sits in a relaxed, open manner, sometimes leaning forward.
- Has unclenched hands.
- Participates in discussions.
- Nods and shows agreement through facial expressions.

Someone who is bored or frustrated:
- Has a vacant, far-away gaze.
- Fidgets.
- Sits with her head in her hands.
- Runs her hands through her hair or rubs the back of her neck.

Someone who is hostile or unaccepting:
- Sits back and crosses his arms in a "show me" position.
- Refuses to look at the presenters.
- Scowls and frowns.

Someone who wants to interrupt or join in the discussion:
- Leans forward.
- Raises a hand.
- Puts a finger to his lips.
- Tugs once at his ear (repeated tugging is a sign of nervousness).

Figure 6.14. [*Source: Marya W. Holcombe and Judith K. Stein, Presentations for Decision Makers (Van Nostrand Reinhold, 1990), pp. 138-139.*]

Evaluating and Improving Your Performance

To enhance your presentation skills, have someone critique your performance—preferably someone who is an experienced presenter. And conduct your own evaluation after the presentation (use the criteria found in Fig. 6.16).

Guaranteed Distractions

Here are some bad habits that are guaranteed to take the mind of the audience off the subject:

- Rattling keys or coins in your pocket
- The habitual and continuing use of "uhs" or "ahs." Some people double-clutch it and say "uh-uh" or "ah-ah"
- Sucking the teeth
- Ring twisting
- Stroking a beard
- Lip licking
- Tugging your ear
- Lip biting
- Cracking knuckles
- Pushing the bridge of your glasses
- Playing with a watch
- Drumming your finger
- Bouncing a pencil on its eraser
- Blowing hair out of your eyes
- Popping the top of a Magic Marker

Figure 6.15. [*Adapted from David A. Peoples,* Presentations Plus *(John Wiley & Sons, Second Ed., 1992), p. 188. Copyright © 1992 by David A. Peoples. Reprinted by permission of John Wiley and Sons, Inc.*]

To make a dramatic improvement in your performance in a short period of time, have the presentation videotaped. If you are not already convinced of the power of visual communication, we guarantee this technique will make a believer out of you.

Your friends and colleagues may minimize your shortcomings, but the camera won't lie. If you adjust your glasses, scratch your nose, drum your fingers, twiddle your thumbs, or cling to the podium for dear life, it will be dutifully recorded. There is no surer way to cure a bad habit than to watch yourself perform it in living color—over and over again.

If you don't have access to video equipment, consider enrolling in a presentation training program in which your performance is videotaped

---

Checklist for Evaluating the Presentation

- Did I effectively communicate my main point? Did I leave the audience knowing what the next steps are?
- Was the structure appropriate for the audience?
- Was I comfortable with myself? If not, why not?
- Did I help the audience feel comfortable?
- Did I respond to the concerns of the audience?
- Have I taken steps to follow up on any new issues that came up in the meeting?
- Did I use visual aids effectively to enhance the presentation?
- Did I achieve my goal? Did the audience say "yes" to what I wanted?
- What would I change next time?

Figure 6.16. [*Source: Marya Holcombe and Judith K. Stein,* Presentations for Decision Makers *(New York: Van Nostrand Reinhold, 1990), p.135. Reprinted with permission.*]

and analyzed. There are many such programs available through communications consultants and training and development firms.

However, keep in mind that training has its limitations. It may help you to become a polished presenter but it won't necessarily make you an effective one. To be a truly effective presenter, you must believe in yourself and in your message. No amount of technique or technology can make up for a lack of confidence or conviction.

7
Emerging Issues in Meeting Management

"My grandmother instilled in me the notion of hate thy neighbor, if they are different than you. Especially ... Italians. She once hit me upside the head for wearing a red shirt because, she said, it made me look Italian. She used a different word than 'Italian.'"[1]

The speaker is Al Wann, Washington, D.C. public relations director for AT&T. Later in his speech, before a meeting of the International Association of Business Communicators, he reflected:

> My relatives were ignorant. But time has passed. Attitudes have shifted. If my grandmother were alive today, she'd roll over in her grave. She'd see her beautiful blonde, blue-eyed great-granddaughter is married to a successful dentist in Long Island. His name is Mongiello. She'd see these wonderful blonde, brown-eyed great-great grandchildren—with straight teeth, I might add. They've inherited the best qualities of both sides of their family tree. What a strong gene pool they sprang from.

What holds true for families holds true for businesses. "In business, as in human beings, it is the differences that result in progressive, evolutionary change," says Wann. "Inbreeding, in business and people, ultimately produces idiots.

"In business, if everybody thought the same and acted the same, and believed the same things, the business would die a certain, boring death. Many did and many will."

In this chapter we'll discuss how growing diversity is making its impact felt in the meeting room, and how organizations can learn to seize the opportunities it affords. And we'll explore three other issues that will have a significant impact on meeting management in the coming years: the growth of international meetings; the emergence of teams as a fundamental work unit; and the impact of two-person meetings on the productivity of the organization.

Diversity in the Meeting Room[2]

"Dealer incentives—that's the key," says Harriet Nixon in the brainstorming session. "I saw some sales figures...."

"Better packaging," interrupts Chris Cox. "Let's simplify the graphic design and change the colors."

Others join in, voicing their ideas and challenging others' statements. After a few minutes of spirited discussion, the meeting leader turns to Mike Nakimoto and says, "You've been awfully quiet. What do you think?"

"I plan to study the sales figures," he says, looking up from the tabletop. "I'll send you a full report tomorrow."

As a meeting manager, how would you react to Mike's statement? Would you question his competence? Would you assume he's too shy to voice his opinions, and conclude that he's "not management material"? Would you wonder whether he is withholding ideas he plans to use elsewhere? Or would you recognize the real reason for Mike's reticence: He is simply behaving true to his Asian culture. He has been taught that ideas should be contemplated carefully before they are shared, and that meetings are vehicles for communicating decisions made beforehand.

An Equal Right to Be Different

Culturally influenced behavior will appear increasingly in America's conference rooms in the years ahead, the result of growing diversity in the workforce and a steady increase in international business. Meeting managers will have to learn how to manage this diversity, creating environments in which all participants can be productive.

A return to the Affirmative Action and Equal Employment Opportunity policies of the 1960s and 1970s isn't the answer. Those policies "tried to treat everyone the same," says Lewis Griggs, whose San Francisco firm, Griggs

Productions, produces the seven-part "Valuing Diversity®" film series. But we're not all the same, Griggs asserts, and we have "an equal right to be different."

Minority groups within the United States traditionally have been viewed as blending into a melting pot. This viewpoint doesn't allow for the acknowledgment of genuine differences among people of different ethnic and cultural backgrounds. "When we perceive a difference, we're supposed to either deny it or consider it irrelevant," says Griggs.

Griggs believes it's time to discard the melting pot and adopt a "stew pot" approach in which we acknowledge that "some differences are real and relevant"—and positive: "There are more similarities than differences between us. All else being so similar, isn't it our differences that are precisely our greatest gifts to one another? Instead of tolerating and toning them down, why not exaggerate and value them?"

The first step in learning to value differences is to become aware of the unconscious assumptions we hold about others who are different from us. For example, says Tom Peters, "it's a Caucasian male American bias that if you don't speak up, you have nothing to say," and that "if you don't interrupt, something's wrong with your mental process."

It's often easier to spot the biases of others than to identify our own. For example, ask yourself: If there are nonnative English speakers in a meeting (and you are not one of them), do you automatically equate poor grammar with a lack of intelligence? When two Hispanic participants speak Spanish to each other, do you assume they are conspiring about something? As a meeting leader or participant, do you unintentionally ignore or discount the contributions of others?

The Gender Gap

Some men treat women as though they are "invisible," says Griggs. "They do not fully see them for who they are," or they unconsciously withhold important information and thus engage in subtle sabotage.

Because gender cuts across culture and ethnicity, it is a primary diversity issue, and its impact is felt in the meeting room, where women are not always equal participants. In some cases, their own behavior contributes to the inequity. Says Karen Anderson, a trainer for National Seminars Group in Shawnee Mission, Kansas: "As women, we are socialized to please everybody, so we tend to smile too fast and too often." Many women also speak softly, avert their eyes, qualify their remarks, start sentences with a disclaimer ("this may not be a good idea, but ..."), use tag questions ("I think those figures are misleading, don't you?") and practice other habits that reduce their credibility.[3]

Anderson says women can bolster their impact at meetings by replacing these habits with more assertive behavior. But such surface alterations may not always work, according to Robin Lakoff, a linguist at the University of California at Berkeley. "Until recently, women were almost totally absent from the corporate conference room," says Lakoff. "Since men were the only ones participating, they made all the rules. Consequently, their rules became the norm and the standards that everyone is expected to follow."[4]

Thus, to be effective in meetings, women have learned they must "speak like a man"—that is, directly and forcefully. Unfortunately, this speaking style sometimes leads to a perception of women as "aggressive" and "bitchy," Lakoff notes.[5]

Deborah Tannen, a linguist at Georgetown University and a former student of Lakoff, cites research to support the contention that men and women are often viewed differently regardless of what they say in a meeting. For example, she notes that most studies show women use more tag questions. But even when they don't, people think they do.[6]

Furthermore, research shows that men and women who use the same approaches may not have the same credibility:

> One study found that when women used tag questions and disclaimers, subjects judged them as less intelligent and knowledgeable *than men who also used them*. When women did not give support for their arguments, they were judged less intelligent and knowledgeable, *but men who advanced arguments without support were not* ... So it is not the ways of talking that are having the effect so much as people's attitudes toward women and men.[7]

Tannen believes these attitudes stem from the fact that boys and girls "grow up in what are essentially different cultures."[8] For example, boys are expected to be competitive. But although "some girls are certainly more skilled than others, girls are expected not to boast about it, or show that they think they are better than the others."[9]

Such cultural differences show up in conversational styles. For example, men's conversations tend to focus more on gaining status, while women's tend to focus primarily on making connections and gaining consensus. These style differences can lead to misunderstanding even when both genders respect and sincerely want to communicate with one another.[10]

The answer, according to Tannen, is not to pretend that "women and men are the same."[11] Instead, she believes the solution is for each gender to recognize and accept the other's style of communication: "Understanding style differences ... allows for 'no-fault negotiation' between men and women: You can ask for or make adjustments without casting or taking blame."[12]

"The biggest mistake is believing there is one right way to listen, to talk, to have a conversation," Tannen suggests. "Nothing hurts more than being told your intentions are bad when you know they are good, or being told you are doing something wrong when you know you're just doing it your way."[13]

However, Robin Lakoff cautions that understanding language differences may not be enough to bridge the gender gap: "If you don't change inside, your communication will be hollow. Real understanding will only come with changes in attitudes."[14]

"A Marriage Without Courtship"

Communication styles and other differences may be even more pronounced when people from different cultural and ethnic backgrounds meet. In making meetings more sensitive to these differences, managers have two options, according to Lewis Griggs: Change the meeting to fit the different cultural groups represented or inform the groups about the organization's meeting traditions and invite their participation. In either case, you've acknowledged rather than ignored the differences.

Meeting managers also should allow extra time for participants to get to know one another, says Tom Peters: "When you bring diverse groups together, you must give them the time to adjust to one another before you try to work productively together. Trying to rush the relationship is like having a marriage without any courtship, and you won't pull it off." The meeting leader can facilitate the courtship process by paying attention to what Peters calls "social atmospherics," such as planning a 30-minute coffee break rather than the usual 10 or 15 minutes, and scheduling a long lunch hour.[15]

Diversity training is another important part of the process. "People need a safe place to talk about differences," says Lewis Griggs. The training room provides a safe haven for employees to air their feelings openly and honestly, and to learn to appreciate those with different backgrounds and beliefs.

"I believe 100% in training," says Tom Peters. "There's no question that top diversity programs can really help, at least at the margin, to raise everyone's awareness as to why radical differences in style lead to a total lack of communication."[16] Hewlett-Packard, Procter & Gamble, Corning, Honeywell, 3M, Xerox, and scores of other corporations have implemented successful diversity training programs.

For these programs to be effective, senior management must demonstrate a clear commitment to valuing diversity (see Fig. 7.1), with the understanding that "sometimes we will make mistakes." The only serious mistake, in a time of growing diversity, is to avoid the issue.

Self-Assessment Checklist for Managers

To assess how hard you will have to work to effectively manage diversity, rate yourself on your responses to the statements below. Use a scale of 1 to 5 to rate how strongly you agree with the statements, 1 being low agreement and 5 being high.

1. I regularly assess my strengths and weaknesses, and consciously try to improve myself.

2. I am interested in the ideas of people who do not think as I think, and I respect their opinions even when I disagree with them.

3. Some of my friends or associates are different from me in age, race, gender, physical abilities, economic status, and education.

4. If I were at a party with people outside of my own group, I would go out of my way to meet them.

5. I do not need to understand everything going on around me. I tolerate ambiguity.

6. I am able to change course quickly. I readily change my plans or expectations to adapt to a new situation.

7. I recognize that I am a product of my upbringing and my way is not the only way.

8. I am patient and flexible. I can accept different ways of getting a job done as long as the results are good.

9. I am always asking questions, reading, exploring. I am curious about new things, people, and places.

10. I am interested in human dynamics and often find myself thinking, "what's really going on here?"

11. I can see two sides on most issues.

12. I have made mistakes and I have learned from them.

13. In an unfamiliar situation, I watch and listen before acting.

14. I listen carefully.

15. When I am lost, I ask for directions.

16. When I don't understand what someone is saying, I ask for clarification.

17. I sincerely do not want to offend others.

18. I like people and accept them as they are.

19. I am sensitive to the feelings of others and observe their reactions when I am talking.

20. I am aware of my prejudices and consciously try to control my assumptions about people.

How to score:

Total your answers. If your score is 80 or above, you probably value diversity and are able to manage people who are different from yourself—but you certainly have room for improvement. If your score is below 50 you probably experience much difficulty managing diversity and could benefit from further training.

Figure 7.1. (*Copyright © Griggs Productions, San Francisco, California. Cannot be reproduced without written permission from Griggs Productions.*)

International Meetings

The rise of global business has brought the issue of diversity, and the need for effective meeting management, to the forefront. "We're not just shipping products between countries," says Mike Wadino, former international marketing manager and now sales manager for the 3M Visual Systems Division. "We're also meeting to discuss how to do that. How can you communicate if you don't have meetings?"[17] And how can you communicate effectively if participants speak different languages?

Bridging the Language Gap

International business travelers may quickly discover that the same word can have a different meaning in another language. "Call something 'fantastic' or 'fabulous' and an unsuspecting foreigner may think you mean unreal or imaginary," Roger Axtell warns. Axtell is the author of several popular books on the subject of international travel and cross-cultural communications. "To us a disaster can be anything slightly less than perfect ('Lunch was a disaster—they ran out of fresh chives'). People on other continents think of disaster as pestilence, war, famine and death."[18] (Figure 7.2 provides some tips for avoiding misunderstanding in international communications.)

Even commonly used business terms may vary from one country to the next. For example, when Americans table a matter, they put it aside for later review. When Europeans table a matter, they bring it up for immediate discussion. Such differences in meaning can obviously lead to confusion.

Bob Green learned this lesson when he was director of meeting planning and corporate travel for Ralston Purina. He asked the staff of a Madrid hotel for a blackboard to use in a meeting. "What I got was a square piece of plywood painted black," says Green. "I've learned since to ask for a chalkboard—and to make sure that words mean what I think they mean."[19]

Watch Your Pronunciation

Pronouncing words correctly is as vital as choosing the correct words. Roger Axtell relates a story that makes the reason clear:

> As the honored guests at one of China's famous twelve-course governmental dinners, a delegation of heavy-duty equipment manufacturers from the Midwest had just laid down their chopsticks. It was time for a word, in quickly memorized phonetic Chinese, from our side. "Thank you very much for the dinner. I am so full I must loosen my belt" is the toast the Americans had prepared. But through the vagaries of the language what was actually delivered was, "The girth of thy donkey's saddle is loose."[20]

Do's and Taboos Around the World

- Keep a constant lookout for the glazed expression and the wandering or sleepy eye that tell you that you have lost your audience.
- "Is that perfectly clear?" Don't guess, ask. Nods and smiles do not necessarily signify understanding.
- Don't wait until the end of a speech or even a sentence before checking for comprehension. Never go on to B until A is thoroughly grasped.
- Don't take yes for an answer. Ask probing questions that prove how much your listener is really absorbing.
- If possible, meet with your opposite number for a quiet one-on-one double check of understanding on both sides.
- Enunciate distinctly and slowly.
- Overpunctuate with pauses and full stops.
- Make one point at a time, one sentence at a time.
- Paraphrase and ask others to do the same.
- Avoid questions that can be answered yes or no.
- If there is a misunderstanding, take the blame.
- Use visual aids (photos, sketches, diagrams, graphs).
- Use both languages in visual presentations like flip charts, video-tapes, and slide shows.
- Put what you are going to say in writing *before* you say it.
- Write and distribute a report on what was said as soon as possible after the meeting.
- Never use numbers without writing them out for all to see.
- If possible, say numbers in both languages.
- Send a follow-up telex, fax, or letter to confirm what was said by telephone.
- Let your host set the pace of negotiations.
- Greet foreigners in their language, especially if it is an uncommon one like Arabic, Urdu, or Hindi.
- In Japan learn terms of greeting and departure phonetically so you will be understood.
- Take a foreign language cassette with you to practice pronunciation as you go along.
- Do not speak whole sentences in a language you have not thoroughly mastered.
- Never interrupt.
- Adjust the level of your English to your counterpart's.

Figure 7.2. (*Adapted from* Do's and Taboos Around the World, *edited by Roger E. Axtell. John Wiley & Sons, 1993, pp. 170-171. Copyright © 1993 by The Parker Pen Company. Reprinted by permission of John Wiley & Sons, Inc.*)

Pronunciation is particularly important when calling a person by name. A person's name is central to his or her identity, and most people are sensitive about having their names pronounced or spelled incorrectly. One solution is to ask international meeting participants to pronounce their names. Another is to include a phonetic pronunciation guide with the roster of participants, or as a subline on name badges.[21]

Make Yourself Understandable

To ensure that your words will be heard and understood by a multicultural audience, use simple words and short sentences, speak slowly, and frequently "check in" with the audience. Don't assume that, just because someone doesn't respond to a question, he or she doesn't know the answer. Silence may mean that the person doesn't understand the question or is afraid to make a mistake in another language.

Never assume that because a person has a good command of spoken English, he or she understands everything that is said. Verbal language skills develop more rapidly than do listening skills.

Avoid Idioms, Acronyms, Jargon, and Slang

Avoid using idioms, such as "in a nutshell," or "off the top of my head," which will only confuse a multicultural audience. Avoid acronyms, even common business acronyms such as *P&L, ASAP,* and *CEO.* If you must use acronyms to get your message across, define them clearly at the start of the meeting.

Also beware of business jargon such as "interface," "bottom line," "fast track," "input," and "feedback." Such terms may be meaningless to many people outside of corporate America. Or they may be taken literally. (You don't want to find out too late what the "shotgun approach" may mean in a distant culture.)

Never use slang. Take a cue from the American who ordered dinner in a Japanese restaurant, then changed his mind and told the waiter to "scratch the sushi." The sushi was promptly served, "presumably properly scratched, as ordered."[22]

Hear the One About the German and the Scot? Keep It to Yourself

If it is dangerous to make jokes in meetings among colleagues who share the same language and culture, the danger is multiplied when a second language and culture are added. Says one well-traveled executive: "If there is one thing that isn't funny in a foreign country, it's humor."[23]

Even if your audience laughs, it's no guarantee that your joke was understood or appreciated. Perhaps the translator told the audience to laugh, or they laughed out of politeness.

Other Ways to Bridge the Language Gap

Visual Aids

Visual aids also can be helpful in bridging the language gap. One strategy for an international meeting involving only two languages is for the speaker to show major points of a presentation in outline form on an overhead projector. Or, the speaker can use two or more overhead projectors—one to show visuals in the speaker's native language and the others to show the same information in other languages.

While we do not generally recommend distributing visuals before most meetings, international meetings are an exception, as noted in Chap. 2. If you plan to use overhead transparencies, mail hard copies to participants ahead of time or distribute them before the meeting begins, to give them extra time to review the material and formulate questions.

Technology

Computer technology can help to enhance international communications. Gary Tritle, manager of technical planning for the Information, Imaging and Electronics Sector of 3M, recalls how computers were used to produce instant minutes of two global strategic planning meetings during the late 1980s. These week-long planning sessions involved 3M employees in approximately 20 countries.

Several of the people attending the meetings had difficulty understanding spoken English or the languages of other participants, but everyone could read English. So the meeting planners, including Tritle, decided to create simple computer-generated documentation throughout the week, to make sure that the group stayed on track.

Instant minutes were distributed at the end of each presentation, in a simple outline form. At the end of the week, participants were given a notebook containing copies of the discussion outlines, the global plan for 3M, and their country's plan.

The individual country plans were generated by teams of two people: the country representative and a U.S. representative. The U.S. team members developed an in-depth understanding of the business conditions in other countries, and were available to help with any problems with the English language.

"I think the computer capability was a major contributor to the success of those meetings," Tritle says. "Giving everyone a notebook at the end of the meeting really impressed them," he adds. And it impressed their managers, says Tritle. "It was much better than coming back and telling the boss, 'I'll get minutes in a week or two'; by then the boss has concluded that the money [to travel to the meeting] wasn't well spent."

Software Translation

If international meeting participants cannot read English, you might consider using a new category of software known as cross-cultural groupware, which enables participants to view translated versions of what is being discussed in the meeting.[24]

You can also purchase software that will enable you to translate materials ahead of time, for distribution during or after the meeting.

However, be careful in purchasing translation software. "You still have to correct it," warns Sheila Fanning, conference and meeting services director for the New York-based Society of Incentive Travel Executives (SITE), whose membership roster includes 69 countries. "A lot of computer programs translate, but give you a prompt when they're stuck on a word," Fanning explains. "If you can't understand the language, you can't translate it."[25]

Interpreters

When more than two languages are represented in a meeting, it may be necessary to hire interpreters and even provide instantaneous translations in individual soundproof booths. Maria Elena Perez de Pardi, manager of the International Association of Conference Interpreters, offers the following ten rules for hiring an interpreter:[26]

1. Book well ahead. Do not expect an interpreter to be available at a day's notice. Good interpreters are much in demand.

2. Brief your interpreter in advance on the subject of the meeting.

3. If your work is of a highly technical nature, brief your interpreter on any specific terms, especially acronyms and abbreviations. A good interpreter can handle any type of meeting provided he or she is properly briefed.

4. Let your interpreter know in advance precisely what you expect of him or her. Dinner engagements and theater visits may be relaxing for you, but they are extra work for an interpreter.

5. Hire a professional. The interpreter might well be your client's chief point of contact.

6. Treat the interpreter as a business traveler. Be prepared to offer the same standards of travel, hotels, and restaurants as you would provide for yourself.

7. Expect the interpreter to feel exhausted at day's end. Interpreters have to concentrate continuously while you have breaks between asking questions and receiving answers.

8. Be honest about your own language abilities. If you keep interrupting the interpreter, he or she will feel undermined and confused.

9. If you are not prepared to trust an interpreter with confidential information, don't use one. Hiring a member of a professional association is your guarantee of strict confidentiality.

10. Don't skimp. Apply the same professional standards you would use in hiring an accountant or legal adviser. Hiring the best could mean the difference between clinching a deal and going home empty-handed.

Language Training

Don't overlook the possibility of learning another language, particularly if you are a frequent participant in international meetings. No interpreter or software package can generate the level of rapport that comes from demonstrating you have taken the time to learn a foreign colleague's language.

Another advantage of learning a new language is that it gives you a strong appreciation for the difficulties others face in adapting to English. As you struggle to master French, Portuguese, or Japanese, you soon realize how difficult it is to understand someone who speaks too rapidly, uses slang, or tries to joke in a language that's unfamiliar to you.

Body Language

Milton Neshek, a lawyer and officer of a Japanese-owned company located in the Midwest, once travelled to Japan with the governor of his state, as part of a trade mission. In Japan, the governor made a presentation to a "large and distinguished audience of Japanese officials."

Afterward the governor, who was "visibly upset," cornered Neshek and lamented,

"My speech was a disaster! I shouldn't have delivered it. Why didn't my staff warn me?" Confused, Neshek asked "What made you think it was so bad?" The governor complained he had seen many members of the audience asleep, even nodding their heads. Relieved, Neshek quickly explained that among the Japanese a common way to show concentration and attentiveness was to close the eyes in contemplation and nod the head slightly, up and down. What the governor read as boredom was actually a signal of respect and attention."[27]

As the anecdote above makes clear, body language is a vital component of cross-cultural communication. Like the language of words, body language can vary dramatically from one country to the next. For example:

- In most countries, nodding the head means "yes"; in Bulgaria and Greece, it means "no."

- In the United States, a thumbs-up signal acknowledges success. Thumbs-up in Australia, loosely translated, means "up yours."

- The correct form of waving hello and goodbye in Europe is palm out, hand and arm stationary, fingers wagging up and down. The common American wave with the whole hand in motion means "no"— except in Greece, where it is an insult that is likely to get you into big trouble."[28]

There are dozens of other gestures that are common to cultures around the world. Before you conduct an international meeting, educate yourself about the particular gestures of the countries that will be represented.

Roger Axtell notes that there is one, and only one, gesture that is universally understood, one that can help people get out of the most difficult situations: the smile. He advises those who conduct international business to use it freely and often.[29]

Customs

The Ghost of the Ugly American

Roger Axtell writes: "The Ugly American about whom we used to read so much may be dead, but here and there the ghost still wobbles out of the closet."[30] He cites this scene in a Chinese cemetery: "Watching a Chinese reverently placing fresh fruit on a grave, an American visitor asked, 'When do you expect your ancestors to get up and eat the fruit?' The Chinese replied, 'As soon as your ancestors get up and smell the flowers.'"[31]

If it is important to appreciate the language and gestures of other cultures, it is equally important to honor their customs. Customs vary significantly from one country or region to the next, so it's important to do your homework. Almost every country has certain customs regarding food and drink. For example, alcoholic beverages may be welcomed or forbidden, and certain types of food, such as pork, may be taboo.

Other customs may cover everything from style of dress to relationships between men and women. For example, there is still a ban on mixing the sexes in Muslim and Buddhist countries. And in Islamic countries, men are forbidden to touch women to whom they are not related, so shaking hands is taboo. To avoid offending another culture or unwittingly breaking the law, learn about customs in advance.

It's also important to be aware of differences in protocol among cultures. For example, in certain countries it may make a great deal of difference who is the first to walk in a room, or the first to speak. "Even in small meetings, the Japanese will always defer to the lead man in the company to ask the first question," says Ed Crego, managing director with The TQS Group, a Chicago-based quality and customer focus consultant.[32] Learn about protocol ahead of time to avoid making a blunder during the meeting.

International Meeting Styles

Meeting styles also vary around the world. For example, in Europe people often make presentations while sitting rather than standing. The idea is to create a more collegial atmosphere and avoid the appearance of talking down to the audience. Sit-down presentations also foster more interaction and are easier on the presenter.

In Japan and other parts of Asia, many presentations also are sit-down, but the structure is different. In the West, meetings may be used to brainstorm ideas or solve problems. In Japan, decisions are made beforehand, in a series of one-to-one exchanges.

Kieko Saito, president of ILCC (Integrating Language and Culture in Communications) in Tokyo, compares these premeetings to the concept of *namawashi*—preparing a tree for transplanting. An individual must do the groundwork—that is, propose an idea to one person and get feedback, propose the idea to others, perhaps revise the idea, and go back and get tacit agreement. When finished, the individuals hold a group meeting to ensure confirmation and consensus.[33]

Meeting behavior also varies from East to West. In the United States, it's "not unusual for us to interrupt each other," Mike Wadino notes. By contrast, in Japan, participants often "look at the presenter as a teacher," he says. They are "very polite" and wouldn't think of challenging the speaker.[34]

Saito explains that Japanese culture permits two individuals to speak candidly and directly to each other. When a third person enters the scene, they become a group and must speak indirectly to avoid conflict.

Avoiding conflict is consistent with *wa*, the concept of harmony, the notion that "it's better to keep the water smooth instead of making waves," says Saito.[35] For American managers accustomed to making plenty of waves, the adjustment can be difficult.

There are many other cultural and national differences in meeting style. As business becomes a more global affair, we can expect to see a gradual overlapping of meeting traditions. This is already happening to some extent. For example, Japanese multinationals are developing Western-style presentations for their Western customers, and many American managers are adopting the European style of sit-down presentations.

However, it's unlikely that local customs ever will be completely abandoned in favor of a universal meeting style. When in Rome, it's still wise to prepare to do as the Romans.

Planning an International Meeting[36]

From this discussion it should be clear that careful planning is vital to the success of any international meeting. Because of all the peculiarities involved, it's important to begin the planning process well in advance of the meeting.

The first step is to list potential participants and their languages, nationalities, and cultural characteristics so that all arrangements will be sensitive to special needs.

The next step is to plan and distribute the agenda, just as you would for any other meeting, with one exception: include fewer items and allow more time for each, to accommodate language differences.

For international meetings, it's particularly important to let participants know in advance exactly what you expect from them. Some cultural groups feel uncomfortable, for example, if they are asked to speak spontaneously about their company or background. Make sure you give everyone time to prepare their remarks.

Don't schedule a long day of international meetings. It takes an enormous amount of energy to communicate across languages, and participants can quickly become exhausted. Allow enough time for travellers to recover from jet lag. And allocate extra hours for logistical problems, which are inevitable.

Logistics planning for international meetings can be fraught with challenges. Foreign hotels are usually smaller than those in the United States, and hotel personnel sometimes do not understand the importance of seating arrangements. Mike Wadino recalls: "The night before a meeting in the Philippines, I was up late rearranging the room, even though I had sent them a diagram in advance."

Furthermore, hotels abroad cannot always provide suitable audiovisual equipment, and equipment brought from the United States is often incompatible with the electrical current in foreign countries.

Meeting rooms must be inspected in advance of the meeting. If food is to be served at the meeting, it should be sampled in advance.

In planning logistics, it helps to work through a colleague in a company subsidiary overseas, but even then "everything has to be spelled out," Wadino says. Even when it is, problems can arise, so it's best to factor this into the planning equation.

Where to Go for Help

If planning an international meeting seems like an overwhelming undertaking, do not despair: There are a growing number of support services available, from private consultants to foreign consulates in major U.S. cities to the international sections of business schools, which offer everything from library materials to full-scale outreach programs.

Once you've done your planning, relax. You're likely to encounter a few glitches no matter how carefully you've considered cultural nuances. For example, Robert Hayles, diversity vice president of Grand Metropolitan, a Minneapolis-based food company, led a meeting of Europeans and told the group that, for the sake of clarity, they would use Roberts' Rules of Order. "But why," a German participant asked during a break, "must we use your rules?"[37]

Team Meetings

A growing number of meetings, whether domestic or international, are being held for the purpose of coordinating team efforts. As noted in Chap. 5, more and more companies are turning to teamwork in order to improve quality, cut costs, compress the product development cycle and thereby become more competitive. Work teams in major corporations around the globe are now doing everything from assembly work on the factory floor to marketing, planning, and managing departments. For example:

- At Corning, Incorporated, factory workers meet periodically in quality circles to solve problems and find ways to enhance productivity. In addition, every unit within the corporation—including the legal department and accounting—has a Quality Improvement Team (QIT), which meets routinely to manage the quality of that unit's work. More than 60 percent of the company's 20,000 employees worldwide serve on teams, and the goal is 100 percent.

- In 1991, Hewlett-Packard began experimenting with self-managed, cross-functional work teams. Larry Brown, Process Manager for the Deskjet Printer Group, says that so far the effects have been positive, with production times consistently ahead of schedule.

- At 3M, cross-functional, cross-divisional, cross-national, and cross-company teams are responsible for everything from product development to improving morale to planning Christmas parties. Team performance is gradually being adopted throughout the company as a factor in individual performance appraisals.

The Team Performance Model[38]

Teams have special meeting needs. In order to understand those needs, meeting managers and team leaders must understand the process by which a team evolves.

Bob Johansen, who has been studying teams for more than two decades, favors the seven-stage Drexler/Sibbet Team Performance® Model, developed by psychologist Allan Drexler and organizational change consultant David Sibbet. The model describes the "generic, recurring stages that teams encounter":

Stage 1: Orientation. As people come together, they ask, "Why am I here?" They want to know why a team should be formed, what its mandate is, and how seriously top management will view its work.

Stage 2: Trust building. At this stage team members want to know: "Who are you?" and "What will you expect of me?" They need to feel safe in expressing ideas, especially when the work demands creativity. During this stage, team members will begin to evaluate each other's expertise. This evaluation will not happen all at once, Johansen says, but rather occur as a gradual "sniffing" in which members learn about each other and what they bring to the team. Trust building may take longer if the team is composed of members from different divisions, companies, or countries.

Stage 3: Goal/role clarification. During the early stages, team members evaluate each other's expertise and gradually get to know one another and learn what each can contribute to the team. At Stage 3, they turn their attention to what the team must do and begin to clarify goals and roles. There is bound to be some misunderstanding among team members as a result of differences in language, work styles, culture (including corporate culture, in the case of cross-company teams), and values. But agreeing on goals and roles is essential if the team is to function effectively.

However, there is always room for renegotiation: "Goal clarification is an ongoing process," says Johansen. "You cannot just do it and forget it."

Stage 4: Commitment. At some point the discussion must end and the team must make commitments about its structure, resources, and budget. The team faces a major turning point as it works to agree on how to proceed.

"Most teams do not consciously think about how things will work within their teams," Johansen says. They assume they will use operating procedures from their individual departments or past teams. The team leader, or the senior manager who created the team, should lead the way in setting ground rules.

Stage 5: Implementation. Once a collective commitment has been made, team members decide who does what, when, and where. Since team members may be drawn from different parts of the organization, or even from different companies, each member has regular job duties and another boss to worry about. How supportive those other bosses are can greatly affect the team's work.

Stage 6: High performance. This is the peak performance stage during which team members "work in synch, sensing each other's moves and needs and responding accordingly," Johansen says. During this stage (which not all teams achieve), the team performs almost as if it were unconscious, responding intuitively and flexibly to "fast-breaking conditions."[39] Johansen likens this stage to the fast break in basketball: "You have a general sense of what you will do but the specifics are governed by instinct."

Stage 7: Renewal. Even if a team achieves peak performance, this is not a steady state. Tension can build to the breaking point, burnout can occur, or people can become tired or bored. They may wonder, "Why continue?" The team may abandon its project or it may move to a new level, and the seven-stage process begins again.

Teams move through the seven stages at different speeds and repeat stages in varying ways, with each stage building on the previous ones. Occasionally a team must backtrack and work through a previous stage before it can move on to a higher level.

Teams from different cultures progress through the stages differently. Japanese business teams, Johansen says, tend to emphasize activity that falls within the first two stages of the team performance model. These teams generally do not produce quick results, but because of their early investment in getting to know one another and building trust, they typically have

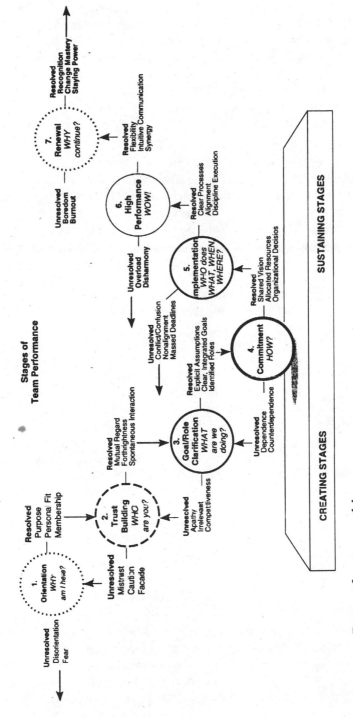

Figure 7.3. Team performance model.

little trouble making commitments and moving to the implementation stage. American teams, on the other hand, often move quickly to implementation and later, realizing that team members do not trust each other, take a remedial cycle through the first two stages.

Different Stages, Different Meeting Needs

Meeting requirements vary according to a team's stage of evolution. During the orientation and trust-building stages of a team, face-to-face meetings are essential so that team members can get to know one another and feel comfortable working with each other. These meetings derive their tone from the team leader, whose charisma and style can make people feel comfortable and significant. Some teams at this stage benefit from a professional facilitator who can draw out the best in people and smooth over organizational or cultural differences.

During the goal/role clarification and commitment stages, face-to-face meetings may not be needed if team members have developed a good measure of trust. If team members are located in different states or countries, face-to-face meetings may be difficult and prohibitively expensive. In either case, the team can meet at a distance to share ideas and keep in touch, using same-time/different-place tools such as audioconferencing, videoconferencing, and computer conferencing.

During the implementation and high-performance stages, a busy team will often have trouble meeting at any one time or place. To coordinate efforts during these stages, the team can use different-time/different-place tools such as voice mail, electronic mail, and computer conferencing. If they are in the same company and location, team members can use same-place/different-time groupware.

The renewal stage, whether the end of a phase or the end of a project, often finds people wanting same-time/same-place familiarity. A face-to-face meeting at this stage allows team members to deal with emotional needs, which may include celebrating (if the team has succeeded or scored a breakthrough) or saying goodbye.

Cross-Company Team Meetings

Cross-company team meetings pose special challenges for planners and participants, according to Mike Wadino, sales manager for 3M's Visual Systems Division. One key issue that must be addressed is how—and how much—information will be shared. "Perhaps one of the critical differences in a cross-company meeting is that people are concerned about disclosing proprietary information," says Wadino. Because cross-company teams are often formed for the purpose of joint product development, it's vital that some proprietary information be shared. To protect each company's technology and other interests, all team members should sign a nondisclure agreement to ensure that what is said in the meeting room is kept confidential.

Meeting preparation takes on greater importance when two companies are involved. Not only are scheduling difficulties multiplied, but it's tougher to monitor follow-up activities, and this must be factored into the planning equation. "We include detailed action items on each meeting agenda. They are reviewed at the next meeting to see if everyone completed their assignments, and if not, why not," says Wadino.

More thought goes into the preparation of visuals as well. "You really make an effort to ensure they're high-quality, color visuals and that the facts are doublechecked several times," says Wadino. "We want to put our best foot forward," he adds.

It's vital that cross-company meeting planners ensure that participants are given enough time to get acquainted. That might mean scheduling dinner meetings or extended lunch hours, or planning other activities so that team members can socialize with one another and begin to build trusting relationships.

Finally, cross-company meeting planners must anticipate differences in corporate culture and develop strategies to minimize or overcome them. For example, if one company's style is to manage from the top and the other's is to delegate, the team must decide which style it will use. Likewise, differences in values, use of technology, and other fundamental elements of corporate culture must be reconciled if the cross-company team is to function effectively.

Training and Rewards[40]

If teams are to succeed in meeting the difficult challenges previously outlined, companies must provide them with the proper training. To assist in the transition to work teams, Hewlett-Packard provides an assortment of training opportunities in such areas as group interaction, meeting management, and electronic communication for all employees. Corning requires that all salaried personnel receive training in group dynamics, and trains certain employees in problem solving techniques so they can serve effectively as facilitators. At 3M, employees throughout the company are encouraged to attend classes to learn how to function effectively as team members and leaders (see Fig. 7.4). Without such training, teams may not realize their full potential and in the worst cases may cause productivity to decline rather than increase.

Profile of Effective Team Leaders and Members

Effective team leaders:

- Are competent relative to the content of the team's work.
- Know how things get done and how to get things done in their host environment.
- Are practical. They make things obvious, not abstract.
- Are results-oriented, tough as needed and focused on key issues.
- Understand the importance of "process" (how well the team works together) for team success.
- Keep objectives clear and prioritized.
- Set well defined expectations that encourage team members to "stretch."
- Are timely and thorough communicators.
- Are reasoned and deliberate, not rash and emotional.
- Are flexible in their own personal style.
- Acknowledge their own weaknesses.
- Are comfortable with conflict and skilled in its resolution.
- Welcome diversity and encourage debate.
- Assure that appropriate information and people are brought into decision-making/problem-solving processes.
- Are inclined to help.
- Monitor team progress and communicate same to management.
- Celebrate team successes.
- Are ethical.

Effective team members:

- Are competent relative to the content of the team's work.
- Are committed to the team's purpose (goal or mission statement).
- Understand group dynamics and build positive relationships with other team members.
- Are flexible around people's style differences.
- Value diversity and treat others with respect.
- Seek and give effective feedback.
- Are comfortable with disagreement.
- Are adaptive to change.
- Demonstrate initiative and follow-through.
- Keep their managers informed of their team activities.
- Support the team agenda, not personal agendas.

Figure 7.4.

It's also crucial for the team to receive sufficient rewards throughout the seven-stage process. "If you want a desirable pattern of behavior, reward it—that's a basic lesson in psychology," says Judith Mower, an organizational psychologist and consultant in Syracuse, New York, who has studied team rewards. Furthermore, she says, research shows that when a group is rewarded as a unit rather than as individuals, the group turns in the best team *and* individual performances.

In rewarding teams, managers and team leaders must understand a few principles:

1. *A reward is different from an incentive.* "An incentive is something promised in advance if the team accomplishes an objective," she says. "It's often a ploy to get people to do something, and it can make them feel manipulated." A true reward, by contrast, is "something unexpected, given after the team has started or finished its work. It represents real appreciation, and it is often motivating."

2. *A reward need not be a cash bonus.* As long as team members earn adequate salaries, public recognition may be a more meaningful reward. Recognition might take the form of an article in the company newspaper, an acknowledgement at a company gathering, or letters of praise for team members' personnel files.

Mower suggests awarding small, tangible gifts such as mugs, T-shirts, or hats. Team members "may scoff at such items at first, but they really do work," she says.

Other team rewards can include a special dinner with the CEO for team members and spouses, a subscription to a new journal, a trip to a conference, a grant to a charity of the team's choosing, or a scholarship in the team's name.

3. *Some team members prefer intrinsic rewards.* Team members enjoy the inner satisfaction that comes with creating something new, working for the love of it. Mower remembers one scientist she interviewed who spoke of the "self-pride and respect" the team felt as a group for a job well done. For this man, a supervisor's praise would have felt uncomfortable, and money would have been an insult.

Team rewards that appeal to intrinsic motivation include an opportunity to learn and use new technology, rotation of team leadership responsibility, increased freedom and flexibility, an increasing variety of work, and a new and more difficult team challenge.

4. *Rewards should be given throughout a project's life, not just at its completion.* Some team projects can last two years or more, and team members may become discouraged if they receive little or no positive feedback until the bottom-line results come in.

"If you can afford only one party, have it when the project reaches the three-quarters point," says Mower. "That's when morale typically declines. That's when the team leader is likely to get the most criticism, and when people begin to grieve because they sense their project is coming to an end."

Other times to offer rewards:

- at the start of the project;
- at the beginning and end of every team meeting;
- when the team reaches a milestone;
- after the team solves a tough problem or weathers a crisis; and
- at the end of the project, to celebrate and say goodbye.

5. *The strongest reward is one the team invents for itself.* Once team members gain each other's trust and respect, they create their own rituals and generate their own rewards. In one insurance company, Mower recalls, team members began meeting for lunch every Friday. "No one planned it that way; it just happened."

Team leaders need to be sensitive to the rewards that evolve within teams and not interfere. "It's probably not a good idea to overplan ceremonies," Mower says. In the early stages of a project, however, a team leader can encourage self-generation of rewards by giving the team its own work room, a bulletin board, or wall space and "letting them decide what they want to do with it."

Should organizations eliminate rewards to individuals? By no means, says Mower. "It's appropriate to reward an individual when that person has clearly gone the extra mile, and everyone on the team knows it." Individual rewards also are appropriate when a team has ignored a person's contribution, when someone leaves a team, when a new person joins the team, or when a team gets stuck in groupthink.

Aside from these specific reasons for rewarding individuals, there is a broader rationale. Unfortunately, says Judith Mower, "this country is oriented to individual achievement." Schools single out students for academic honors, sports figures are honored more often than their teams, and businesses give bonuses based on individual performance, not teamwork.

Larry Brown of Hewlett-Packard agrees that individual rewards are necessary for work teams in the United States: "We have adopted an experimental pay policy called 'Pay for Contribution,' which augments work team pay with bonuses for individual contributions, based on skill levels that are demonstrated through testing and training. The more individuals can increase their skill level," says Brown, "the more they can make as an individual. This is in response to American culture.

Overseas, there's no need for individual programs; the team pay concept seems to be sufficient."

Two-Person Meetings[41]

So far in this book we have focused on meetings involving three or more people. However, some of the most important meetings that take place in organizations are informal, two-person interactions. So says Raymond Panko, a professor of decision sciences in the College of Business Administration of the University of Hawaii. Panko and his colleague, Susan Kinney, assistant professor in the Graduate School of Management of Wake Forest University, have done extensive research into the role of two-person relationships, or *dyads*, in the life of organizations.

Two-person communication is "pervasive in organizations," according to Panko and Kinney. Studies show that managers spend about 25 percent of their days communicating one-on-one, and these encounters (often informal and unscheduled) make up 40 to 45 percent of all face-to-face meeting time. When telephone conversations are included in the definition of meetings, the extent of dyadic communication is even greater.

"Organizations depend heavily on relatively voluntary dyads working together," says Panko. Research suggests that much of the organization's work is done by small teams, many of them dyadic. These teams can develop ideas inexpensively and quickly, then present them to larger groups for consideration.

Even large groups tend to subdivide into smaller units, researchers have found. One study showed that in groups of three or more, individuals "responded to the addition of more group members by voluntarily partitioning themselves into smaller units, typically the dyad."

Although no research has focused specifically on whether and how cross-functional and other types of work teams subdivide, Panko believes it's likely that the same dynamic occurs, and he has some evidence to back it up. He and Susan Kinney gathered data from executive MBA students regarding 35 project meetings they had attended. The vast majority (83%) said they worked on the projects with one other person outside the project meetings.[42]

Differences Between Dyads and Large Groups

"A dyad is not just a 'little meeting,'" Panko emphasizes. Scott Poole and Julie Billingsley have identified five differences in human dynamics:[43]

- A dyad has a longer attention span than does a group. It's easier for a dyad to focus on an issue than it is for a group, because only two points of view must be reconciled.

- A person in a dyad has greater influence on the decision than does the average member of a group. The larger the group, the greater the tendency for influence to be concentrated among a few members. As a result, people in a dyad may be more highly motivated than the average member of a group.

- People in a dyad have greater latitude and influence over each other than do people in a group. This is generally a positive feature of dyads, Panko believes, because it tends to lead to greater fairness. It's more difficult to wield negative power over another person with whom you must work closely than over someone in a large group to whom you are only loosely connected.

- Both parties feel pressure to be present; they can't let their attention wander or miss meetings. This enhanced pressure may also serve to boost productivity.

- The dyadic relationship is more critical than relationships in a group. If the two people in a dyad do not get along well, the dyad will have more trouble functioning effectively than if two people in a group of ten do not relate well.

Research suggests that dyads may be better than larger groups at solving problems. They also may be less susceptible to groupthink.

One drawback of the dyad is its fragile nature. While larger groups can survive even if some of their members leave, the dyad cannot.

This inherent fragility can cause problems. People in dyads may be hesitant to push too hard when differences arise, for fear of jeopardizing the relationship. This may cause them to avoid issues that need to be addressed. Dyads also may be less likely to ask for orientation or offer suggestions to one another, presumably because of increased sensitivity to the other person's point of view.

Understanding the dynamics of two-person interactions can help organizations to maximize their impact and minimize the problems they can generate. For example, managers might actively encourage dyadic communication when a difficult problem must be solved and discourage it when a sensitive issue needs to be addressed.

Work Tools for Dyads

Since two-person meetings are commonplace and vital to the functioning of the organization, Panko and his colleagues are studying ways to enhance them through small-group tools, such as electronic mail, networked laptop computers, and portable overhead projectors.

One idea is an electronic blackboard turned on its side, like a table. "It's not normal for two people to stand at a blackboard and work. Usually they will sit with a pad and pencil, writing or sketching at the same time," says Panko. If they could write, doodle, and erase on the tabletop and then photocopy their work instantly, they might work more efficiently, Panko notes.

Another idea is an intimate conference room, a small room with linked workstations where two or three people share ideas and work together. One arrangement calls for a single computer with two linked keyboards, while another setup uses two computers with locked screens that operate in unison.

Since computer screens are small, participants might view their work on a larger public screen on the wall. Farther into the future, they might wear virtual reality eyepieces that enable them to see an infinite blackboard.

Two people in distant locations might interact through desktop videoconferencing. Each person's screen would have a window for displaying a live video image of the other person as well as windows they would use for sharing information. The screen might also hold several private windows that only the user can see. The information in these windows could be pasted into public windows, and vice versa. Multimedia desktop computers with many of these capabilities are already on the market, and in a few years they are likely to be commonplace.

The Need for More Research

Panko and Kinney are continuing to conduct research into dyadic communications. More information is needed, for example, about the life cycle of dyads—how they are formed, how they grow, and how they disband. The two also want to learn more about how dyads use electronic media to communicate across long distances.

As organizations continue to move toward flatter hierarchies and flexible teams, informal two-person meetings will likely increase in importance and frequency. Meeting managers cannot afford to overlook this fundamental source of organizational productivity.

8

Improving Meeting Systems

In this book we've discussed tools and techniques you can use to improve the quality of your meetings, from preparing effective agendas to using meeting procedures to adopting group technology. Each of the topics we've covered is necessary but not sufficient to ensure that meeting quality will be consistently improved throughout the organization.

Piecemeal measures to improve meeting quality will have a limited impact because, as we noted in Chap. 1, meetings are interconnected events. Significant improvement will come about only when the problems of the organization's *meeting systems* are addressed.

The Meeting Audit

Meeting managers can start along the path of improvement by asking themselves the following questions: How effective are our meeting systems? How does our organization use meetings in series to plan and direct work, make decisions, and carry out its mission? How can we make our meeting systems more effective?

To help organizations answer those questions, management consultants Dick Byrd and John Johnson have developed a meeting systems audit. The audit is designed to help organizations assess their meeting patterns, practices, and problems, and develop a plan to improve their meeting systems. It consists of a battery of measurement instruments, including in-depth interviews with senior management about meeting patterns, surveys of meeting managers about the efficiency and effectiveness of their meetings, and structured observations of a sample of typical meetings.[1]

The Meeting Systems Profile

The objective is to produce a profile of current meeting practices and patterns, compare it to the organization's vision of what it wants to achieve through its meetings, and then develop a plan for realizing the vision.
   The profile answers critical questions such as:

- How much time and money are spent preparing for meetings, attending them, and following up?
- Do the organization's meetings reflect its values and vision?
- Which meetings are most critical to the organization?
- How well are the most critical meetings being managed?
- How effective are the organization's meeting managers?
- How satisfied are meeting participants?
- What processes and technologies are used in meetings?
- How do meeting practices vary throughout the organization?
- How well are meetings coordinated throughout the organization?
- Which areas of the organization have too many meetings or too few?
- Is the organization providing sufficient training in meeting management skills?
- Where can improvement efforts be focused so that they produce maximum benefits?

The Improvement Plan

With this profile in hand, the organization can begin to develop an effective plan for improving its meeting systems. That plan should include the following:

- Methods of monitoring meetings to determine whether they are achieving their objectives
- Policies to improve the productivity of the organization's meeting systems (e.g., stricter guidelines for meetings involving international travel)

- Process improvements (e.g., the adoption of decision-making and problem-solving procedures and the implementation of information systems across meetings)
- Budgeting changes (e.g., allocation of more funds for meeting technology and less money for travel)
- Structure and staffing changes (e.g., elimination of certain management positions as the meeting system assumes more of the control function)
- Formal training and ongoing coaching in meeting management techniques

Typical Audit Findings[2]

What kind of information does a meeting audit produce? Byrd and Johnson conducted their first full-scale audit—of the finance and information departments of a successful, high-growth Midwestern corporation—in 1991. They administered an extensive written survey to 51 meeting managers (leaders and facilitators) and a briefer version to 100 participants. They also interviewed 17 meeting leaders and observed a meeting led by each.

Although the audit showed that while the company was doing some things well (for example, setting agendas and starting meetings on time), there were still several problems. The six key findings demonstrate the need for even the most successful organizations to improve their meeting systems:

1. *High cost.* The "most astonishing" finding for managers was how much time and money were being spent on meetings: $2 million annually, including the cost of preparation, follow-up, and travel.

2. *Low productivity.* Despite the high price tag, productivity was low, partly because meetings were not being run efficiently. Many meetings included 10 to 12 people when only four or five should have attended. Some meetings were twice as long as they needed to be.

Another reason for low productivity was arbitrary scheduling. Meetings ran on a rigid schedule—weekly, monthly, or quarterly—with no consideration of whether or not a different or more flexible schedule would make the organization more responsive to market changes. Work handoffs from one meeting group to another waited until the regularly scheduled meeting time.

3. *Lost opportunity.* Management was dismayed to recognize the lost opportunities that resulted from ineffective meetings. They realized, for example, that taking six months rather than three to make a decision about investing in new hardware, changing data collection, or discontinuing a service could measurably affect the organization's profits far beyond the meetings' actual cost.

Meeting managers had trouble recognizing critical moments of choice—that is, times when the group was poised for a breakthrough, when thinking was about to converge, or when someone finally mustered up the courage to voice opposition to the matter being discussed. Instead, many leaders ignored those moments of choice, thus losing opportunities for productive discussion and resolution.

4. *Lack of procedures*. Formal procedures were not being used. Leaders arrived at their meetings with no specific decision-making or problem-solving procedures in mind, intending merely to talk about the issue or problem and decide what to do.

5. *Lack of technology*. The organization was not taking advantage of computer support or other meeting technology. (To determine how effectively your organization uses technology to improve meetings, take the "Meeting IQ Test" shown in Fig. 8.1.)

6. *Lack of commitment*. Few people took the organization's meetings seriously. Many participants experienced meetings as brief vacations during the work day—times to rest, turn off the thinking engine, and perhaps criticize those in charge.

Furthermore, no one was responsible for overseeing the organization's meeting systems. "With all their other tight controls, management had a loose cannon on the deck of the ship," Byrd and Johnson noted.

Recommendations

Based on the audit findings, Byrd and Johnson advised company leaders to appoint a high-level manager to oversee and improve the meeting system. They suggested that meeting managers adopt groupware and videoconferencing technology. They prescribed training for managers in problem-solving, decision-making, conflict resolution, and other meeting management techniques. Finally, they recommended that managers schedule timely (not just quarterly) cross-functional meetings and establish a mechanism for tracking variations in meeting processes and outcomes across the organization.

Raising Awareness

The audit "raised the level of consciousness about the impact meetings have" in this Midwestern company, according to Byrd and Johnson. Participants no longer view meetings as mini-vacations; they know they will be expected to come to the meeting room well prepared and ready to contrib-

MEETING SYSTEM IQ TEST

"Smart" meeting systems support productive communication before, during and after meetings. Evaluate the "intelligence" of your meeting system according to the 23 following measures of productive communication. For each measure, determine how closely your meeting system can be described (on a scale of 10 to 0) as NOT-SO-SMART (0) to SMART (10). A score of 230 is possible, a score greater than 100 is above average.

NOT-SO-SMART: No direct access between team and information technology, and even less Smart, no direct access between team and communication technology.

SMART: At least one computer is being used in the meeting room, connected to a printer, a screen large enough to share, and Smarter still, to computer networks.

BEFORE MEETINGS

TOTAL ▢

Continuity .... ▢

NOT-SO-SMART: Minutes filed somewhere. Project status reports filed somewhere else. In other words, start the meeting from scratch.

SMART: Minutes of previous meetings, action items, project status, etc., available on-line.

Logistics .... ▢

NOT-SO-SMART: Using phone and memo, maybe even fax, days are spent trying to get everyone to the same place at the same time.

SMART: Using computer network and calendaring software, less than an hour is needed to arrange meeting time and place.

Opportunity to prepare .... ▢

NOT-SO-SMART: Agenda is distributed late, if at all. Developed unilaterally, or maybe by a few. Presentation material not available until the day of the meeting, if at all.

SMART: Agenda developed collaboratively via network. Presentation material and references available before and during meeting.

Presentation Costs .... ▢

NOT-SO-SMART: Lots of money and time just to translate computer-produced presentations into color slides, hand-outs, posters, etc., that usually get thrown or stored away.

SMART: Information projected directly from computer. Materials remain instantly accessible, reusable, and brought-up-to-date-able.

Timeliness of meeting date .... ▢

NOT-SO-SMART: Meeting delayed for perhaps days because of absence of one or another key person.

SMART: Meeting arranged and conducted well ahead of decision deadlines. People who can't make it to the meeting room participate via phone and network.

Meeting System IQ

© 1993, Institute for Better Meetings, Palo Alto, CA

Figure 8.1. Meeting system IQ test.

Not-So-Smart	Smart
0←	→10

During Meetings   Total ☐

☐

Action Items .... ☐

Not-So-Smart: Action items are tracked by separate people, if tracked at all. People leave with different ideas of who is supposed to do what, when, and some things don't get done, ever.

Smart: Action items are evaluated, synthesized, organized, approved and posted continuously, as needed, during the entire meeting, assigned before the meeting is over, recorded and distributed via hard- and electronic copy.

☐

Agenda ....

Not-So-Smart: The "real agenda" is hidden. If there is an agenda, most items are new for most people. Need to define, challenge and reprioritize.

Smart: Up-to-date agreed-on agenda for review and last-minute prioritization. Can be collaboratively edited, reprioritized, used as a tool throughout meeting to help structure and re-assess priorities.

☐

Consensus ....

Not-So-Smart: Decisions are made by vote or by hollering at each other. Minority opinions forgotten.

Smart: Participants see their own and each other's contributions carefully and accurately noted. People work together to create on-screen summaries, define areas of consensus, describe their disagreements.

☐

Decision Support..

Not-So-Smart: Complex decisions lead to alternate solutions, each of which results in another meeting.

Smart: Participants model complex decisions on the computer via spread sheet, or planning tool. They generate alternate solutions using "what-if" capabilities.

☐

Leadership ....

Not-So-Smart: Unresponsive leadership using unresponsive media: pre-printed posters, packaged presentations, flipcharts and whiteboards that only the leader gets to use.

Smart: Leader uses information management software to support collaboration, participation, productivity. Team is self-facilitating, using the computer and other media to work together.

☐

Minutes, notes ....

Not-So-Smart: Everybody leaves with a different interpretation of what happened. "Official" minutes arrive too late to make a difference.

Smart: Minutes approved as they are being developed, becomes collaborative process, basis for producing memos, summaries, reports.

Figure 8.1. (*Continued*)

Not-So-Smart	Smart
0←	→10

Participation ....

NOT-SO-SMART: Participation is not invited. Meeting is formal and linear. People bored or anxious for it to be over.

SMART: Leader, presenter use computer to share information, leadership, responsibility for learning.

Productivity ....

NOT-SO-SMART: No tangible results. At best a set of out-dated, questionably thorough, poorly authorized meeting Minutes to file.

SMART: Electronic records of all major decisions. Distribution of approved results within a day. Co-owned, co-created, co-authored, co-produced: files, resources, reports, templates, tools, methods.

Questions and comments ....

NOT-SO-SMART: Questions and comments might eventually be found in the Minutes, maybe.

SMART: Questions and comments can be added to and stored with the presentation data, cross-indexed by project. Participants can edit questions and comments, creating co-authored and co-owned summaries and action items.

Timeliness of information ....

NOT-SO-SMART: Presentation is a mix of handouts, foils or slides, showing out-of-date material that most people haven't had time to think about.

SMART: Information is on-line. Presenter can check and update presentation data at the last minute. Presentation is displayed live, directly from the computer, providing interactive, responsive, random-accessible, updatable, full-colored, animated detail.

Verifiability ....

NOT-SO-SMART: Presenter is on the defensive: needs to document source, verbally defend position, information.

SMART: Presenter can retrieve on-demand, on-line background data to support conclusions and respond to questions. Presenter and group together use computer to research, combining expertise, search skills.

Figure 8.1. (*Continued*)

Not-So-Smart	Smart
0←	→10

AFTER MEETINGS   **TOTAL** ☐

☐

Accomplishment... ☐

NOT-SO-SMART: Not sure what was agreed to   **SMART**: Hard copy in hand.
or what you got noted for or as.

Accountability... ☐

NOT-SO-SMART: Not sure who's supposed to   **SMART**: In hard- and electronic copy for all to
do what, when. .   see: your name, what you agreed to do, when,
   with whom, who you're supposed to tell when
   it's finished.

☐

Alignment... ☐

NOT-SO-SMART: Everyone has a different   **SMART**: Everyone has the same set of notes.
interpretation of what was decided.

Follow-Up.. ☐

NOT-SO-SMART: Follow what up?   **SMART**: On-going, via network, phone, fax and
   collaborative software.

☐

Records.. ☐

NOT-SO-SMART: Minutes not taken, or not   **SMART**: Accurate, approved records of key
distributed until days or weeks after the   decisions available within the hour, on-line,
meeting, produced on paper and then filed   cross-indexed by project and meeting date, for
somewhere.   anyone whose business it is to know.

☐

Value to Organization... ☐

NOT-SO-SMART: People walk away clearer   **SMART**: Clear, collaborative, productive
about who's who, and less clear about what's   communication. Electronic production,
what.   distribution and storage of results and
   notification of accountability.

☐

TOTAL MEETING SYSTEM IQ

Figure 8.1. (*Continued*)

Sample Meeting Audit Questions

Ask meeting leaders and participants to answer the following questions about the meetings they've attended in the recent past, using the following rating scale:

Almost Always	-	5	Seldom	- 2
Frequently	-	4	Never	- 1
Sometimes	-	3		

- Was there a clear purpose for the meeting?
- Did the right people, and only the right people, attend?
- Was there a clear, effective agenda?
- Was the agenda distributed in advance?
- Were participant roles and expectations made clear before the meeting?
- Did the meeting start and end on time?
- Was the meeting time used efficiently?
- Did the leader make clear which procedures would be used?
- Was conflict managed productively?
- Did the leader encourage differences and disagreement?
- Was the leader neutral and objective?
- Did the leader discourage "groupthink"?
- Were verbal summaries of progress provided during the meeting?
- Was facilitation used, if needed?
- Did the discussion stick to the agenda?
- Did the leader strive for consensus, after sufficient discussion?
- Was everyone, including shy people, encouraged to participate?
- Did the leader or facilitator ensure that no one dominated the meeting?
- Were participants allowed to express emotions, not just opinions and ideas?
- Did participants seem to trust one another?
- Were interruptions controlled?
- Was the appropriate technology (e.g., electronic whiteboards, overhead projectors, groupware, videoconferencing) used?

Figure 8.2. (*Continued on next page.*)

- Were decisions and action plans made clear?
- By the end of the meeting, did participants know their work assignments?
- Were minutes distributed to participants no later than the day after the meeting?
- Were individuals confronted if they did not complete their follow-

Figure 8.2. *(Continued).*

ute. Meeting managers now take meetings more seriously, prepare more diligently, question the timing of meetings (they no longer call a meeting just because it's Monday, for example), and cancel meetings if the purpose is unclear or preparation is inadequate.

Meetings in this organization are no longer viewed as isolated events but as part of a system for continuous improvement. In fact, the company has folded the meeting improvement initiative into its Total Quality Management program.

Guidelines for Conducting a Meeting Audit

Any organization can conduct an audit of its meeting systems. Following is a suggested format, based on the work of Dick Byrd and John Johnson. You may choose to follow this format, use pieces of it, add components (focus groups, for example), or devise an audit of your own. There is no one right way to conduct a meeting audit. The key is to develop an audit process that will generate an accurate picture of your present meeting systems and identify needed improvements.

Step 1: Written surveys. A good first step is to administer a questionnaire to meeting managers and selected participants throughout the organization. Figure 8.2 shows the kinds of questions to ask to uncover current meeting practices and processes, and to identify potential problems. Focus on recent meetings, which survey respondents will be able to remember more clearly.

To identify strengths and weaknesses in meeting leadership, ask managers to compare their own meetings to those led by others, and ask participants to evaluate meetings led by various managers. Comparing these responses will give you a more accurate assessment of the current situation.

Step 2: Personal interviews. By analyzing questionnaire responses, you can begin to develop a profile of the meeting systems in your organization. To build on the profile, conduct interviews with senior management, meeting leaders, and selected participants. Focus on problem areas uncovered by the written surveys, and probe for additional information regarding broader issues such as how meetings are coordinated, which meetings are most important to the organization, what type of training is provided to meeting managers and participants, and what steps can be taken to make meetings more effective.

Step 3: Meeting observation. To gain a more objective understanding of the current state of meeting management, select a representative sample of meetings throughout the organization and choose someone to observe them.

Before the meeting, the observer should interview the meeting manager to determine what he or she intends to accomplish. During the meeting, the observer's job is to determine if those objectives are met. He or she should also observe how effective the meeting manager is at maintaining control, encouraging participating, discouraging groupthink, helping the group to stay focused on the agenda, managing conflict, and performing other leadership functions (see Chap. 4). Finally, the observer must watch for other signs of meeting effectiveness, such as whether or not the right people attended, and how skillfully technology was used. After the meeting, he or she interviews the meeting manager again to determine if the appropriate follow-up actions were taken.

Choosing Observers

Those chosen as observers should have a good understanding of group dynamics and organizational politics. Otherwise, they may draw the wrong conclusions.

For example: If a meeting is poorly attended, it may signal that the topic is unimportant to participants. It may be that the leader is unpopular or ineffective. Or, it may simply mean that too many meetings are being scheduled. Likewise, if the agenda is too long, it may be that the leader needs more training in developing agendas. It could be that unresolved issues from a previous meeting were added to this meeting's agenda. Or, perhaps the leader is trying to avoid an issue by deliberately placing it at the end of a too-long agenda, knowing the group will have no time to address it. The knowledgeable observer will be able to determine some truth in each situation.

A Tool for Continuous Improvement

Once you have analyzed the results of your surveys, interviews, and observations, you can begin to develop a plan to improve meetings throughout your organization (see "The Improvement Plan" earlier in this chapter).

The meeting audit is not a one-time process but a tool for continuous improvement. At least a partial audit should be conducted frequently to measure trends and variations over time, determine where improvements have been made, and identify areas that need additional work or even a whole new approach. (Some companies do partial auditing at every meeting of important work groups.) Ideally, the meeting audit process should be integrated into the organization's total quality effort.

Training: The Missing Link

Many meeting problems, from inadequate preparation to ineffective leadership, stem from a lack of training. Thus, any serious attempt to improve an organization's meeting systems must include a training component.

Lynn Oppenheim, of the Wharton Center for Applied Research, notes that "there is abundant evidence that improving the skills of individuals involved in meetings can make a difference."[3] Despite the evidence, meeting management training is routinely ignored by most organizations. Meeting expert Roger Mosvick finds this puzzling: "I remain perplexed as to why management, which is now in the throes of helpful analysis on meeting quality standards for all the other business and manufacturing processes, still neglects the quality and efficiency of meeting management." Mosvick adds that, "It costs corporations millions of dollars each year and remains the one major area of containable costs which we can affect virtually overnight."[4]

Among other things, training prevents meeting managers from misusing techniques they may have heard about only in passing. Management consultant Ann Depta reflects: "A little learning can be a dangerous thing. For example, corporate leaders have been exposed to just enough information about brainstorming to be dangerous." She continues: "Perhaps you have seen a meeting leader attempt to lead a brainstorming session only to see it quickly disintegrate because the leader allowed censure, either verbal or nonverbal, or the meeting leader winced or otherwise nonverbally indicated an opinion about an idea that was presented. There is nothing wrong with the brainstorming technique itself," says Depta. "It can be highly effective in certain situations, but it must be taught as a skill like any other."[5]

At a minimum, everyone who is responsible for leading or facilitating meetings should be trained in formal meeting management techniques. Ideally, all participants should be introduced to basic meeting management concepts.

Leader training should focus on skills that have to do with the boundary setting of meetings, such as the development of the agenda, minutes, evaluation, and follow-up.[6] Leaders and participants also should be trained in various meeting procedures, such as brainstorming, Hall's Consensus Rules, and Nominal Group Technique.[7] Special attention should be given to areas of weakness identified through the meeting systems audit.

Address Problems, Not Symptoms

It's vital that training be implemented only after a thorough assessment of the organization's meeting systems has been completed. This will ensure that the training addresses meeting problems, not just their symptoms.

For example, training designed to address a surface problem—lack of preparation—will have little impact if the underlying problem is that leaders and participants don't have enough time to prepare for meetings. A meeting audit would uncover this deeper problem, which managers could then explore further.

It may turn out that there is insufficient time to prepare because too many meetings are being held. Digging even further, management may discover the reason for so many meetings: leaders have not been trained in problem-solving or decision-making techniques, so what should be accomplished in one meeting requires three or four. Armed with this information, management can now devise a training program that *will* have an impact—one that focuses on problem-solving and decision-making procedures, not on the symptom of inadequate preparation.

Smart Meetings[8]

With the recognition that meetings are interconnected events, and the implementation of training and other processes to improve meeting systems, the organization begins moving toward the ideal of *smart meetings*—carefully coordinated, parallel, concurrent, cross-functional events, tied to organizational need, at which the right people, processes, and information are engaged.

The concept of smart meetings is analogous to the coordination of parallel computer processing units. The units are tightly coordinated so that gates stop and start work appropriately, allowing units with longer tasks to catch up with units that have shorter tasks.

The organization that implements smart meetings can expect to see some of the following phenomena:

- The company's top management team gives ongoing attention to meeting systems, specifically their results, costs, productivity, progress, and needs for improvement.

- Development group A meets on its task immediately upon obtaining results of the preliminary work of development group B, without having to wait until participants can find time on their calendars or until the next regularly scheduled meeting, which might be several days or weeks later.

- Separate functional groups have instant progress reports from one another's concurrent meetings, even while the meetings are in progress.

- Meetings are held across time and space with the help of electronic and telecommunications technology.

- Meetings are designed with an understanding of how people learn and how they change their behavior and thinking individually and as an organization. The organization and each individual changes a little bit at each meeting.

- Management control is built right into the meeting instead of having to rely on separate report and approval sessions outside the meeting.

- Meeting managers are coached extensively in using techniques for conflict management and encouraging the sharing of differences. If a meeting manager is unable to handle conflict, he or she is not asked to manage meetings.

- Participants view meetings as sessions in which they will be pushed to work as hard as they can.

- Participants know what was done before the meeting and what will be done afterward. All participants, not just the meeting leader, have a great deal of work to do outside the meeting.

- Participants have been trained in effective meeting behaviors, have access to up-to-the-minute information from their respective work units, and are empowered to make decisions.

- Leaders ensure adequate preparation and follow-up, design outcomes, select the most effective problem-solving or decision-making techniques, and choose appropriate technology and visual aids, such as overhead projectors with computer-generated graphics.

- All meetings justify substantial investment and utilize what is learned from Total Quality Management programs and other process improvement initiatives.

Winning Companies

Most importantly, competitive position can be enhanced by consciously and systemically improving the organization that implements smart meetings. "The capacity to meet effectively allows an organization to change in a timely and coordinated fashion through all its units," note Byrd and Johnson. "It allows the organization to capitalize on opportunities and neutralize vulnerabilities in the business environment as market windows open, competition refigures, regulations are passed, technology blossoms, and alliances form."[9]

In short, effective meeting management enables an organization to change "faster and better than others."[10] And as John Johnson points out: "The companies that can change faster are the companies that win."[11]

A High Priority

The need for better meeting management is becoming crucial to competitiveness—even to survival. As Tom Peters puts it: "We are finally learning that we can't live without getting serious about this stuff."[12]

Unfortunately, meeting management is not given the serious attention it deserves—not only in corporations but in the business schools that prepare future managers to assume their roles. Despite the fact that managers spend the bulk of their days in meetings, these schools put little or no emphasis on preparing them to be effective meeting leaders or participants. The 3M Meeting Management Institute surveyed 1900 U.S. colleges and universities and found that only 2.5 percent had courses that were specifically focused on meeting management training.

If we are to remain competitive, as individuals and organizations, we will have to begin to take meeting management more seriously. "The most important point, in some respects, is to worry about it," says Tom Peters. But, he adds, talk isn't enough; it must be backed by action: "Most of us talk about how awful meetings are. We spend 50% of our days on it but no time working on it. There are 1000 ideas [about how to improve meetings], just as in the area of quality improvement. But," says Peters, "the average company doesn't invest in trainers, technology, facilitators and so on. It's the same as dieting—you talk about it, then reach for the ice cream bowl. There's so little action."[13]

The first action step, says Peters, is to "put meeting technology (with a small 't') on your strategic agenda—literally, the notion we'll invest time, training, facilities, etc. on the topic of how we meet together, at home and away."[14]

The second step is to assign a high-level manager to oversee the organization's meeting systems. Lynn Oppenheim points out that while it would be "unlikely to find ... that no one was responsible for product quality control or for managing the MBO system" in an organization, it's rare that someone is given the job of managing meetings—one of the organization's most important control systems. Instead, responsibility for meetings is often "so diffuse as to be no one's responsibility."[15]

Dick Byrd and John Johnson recommend that someone such as an internal auditor or vice president of finance or quality improvement be put in charge of the organization's meetings. This person would be responsible for monitoring the results, costs, productivity, progress, and needs for improvement in the meeting systems across all units.[16]

A third step is for senior managers to begin modeling effective meeting management behavior, which will then "naturally diffuse throughout the organization."[17] John Johnson reflects: "Especially the leaders of the organization should take care in modeling what they want to see throughout the organization. If you are calling for a demonstration of empowerment throughout the organization, manage empowered meetings. If you want strategic thinking to catch on," says Johnson, "model it at your meetings. Integrity and congruence in doing what you say are powerful. Likewise a disconnect between word and deed is powerful."

Finally, top management must make people accountable for improving the quality of the organization's meetings. What gets measured gets done. To make employees and managers take meetings more seriously, make meeting participation, leadership, and results an integral part of their performance appraisals. There may be no faster or more effective way to get people's attention.

Individuals and organizations can no longer afford *not* to pay attention to meeting management if they hope to thrive in the coming decades. Stuart Smith, senior vice president of Mount Carmel Health, a multihospital health system based in Columbus, Ohio, puts the situation into perspective: "The staggering cost of wasted, ineffectual meetings is crippling organizations," he writes. "Professionals and businesspersons must manage their meetings as if their company's bottom line and their own careers depended on it—because they do."[18]

Notes

Chapter 1

1. Adapted and reprinted from *Claw Your Way to the Top* © 1986 by Dave Barry, p. 25. Permission granted by Rodale Press, Inc., Emmaus, PA 18098.

2. Frank, Milo O. *How to Run a Successful Meeting in Half the Time*, New York: Simon & Schuster, 1989, pp. 15-16. Copyright © 1989 by Milo O. Frank. Reprinted by permission of Simon & Schuster, Inc.

3. *Making Meetings Matter: A Report to the 3M Corporation*. Prepared by Lynn Oppenheim, Ph.D. Philadelphia, Pa.: Wharton Center for Applied Research, 1987, p. 26.

4. Ibid., p. 25.

5. Ibid.

6. Selection from page 44 from *The Effective Executive* by Peter F. Drucker. Copyright © 1966, 1967 by Peter F. Drucker. Reprinted by permission of Harper Collins Publishers, Inc.

7. Monge, Peter R., McSween, Charles, and Wyer, JoAnne. *A Profile of Meetings in Corporate America: Results of the 3M Meeting Effectiveness Study*. Los Angeles: Annenberg School of communications, University of Southern California, November 1989.

8. *Making Meetings Matter*, p. 11.

9. Ibid., p. 2.

10. Ibid, p. 15.

11. Byrd, Richard E., and Johnson, John. "Meeting Effectiveness: A Matter of Strategy," Minneapolis, October 1992.

12. Kieffer, George David. *The Strategy of Meetings*, New York: Simon & Schuster, 1988, p. 18.

13. Ibid., p. 20

14. Sheridan, John. "The $37 Billion Waste," *Industry Week*, September 4, 1989, p. 11.

15. Jay, Antony. "How to Run a Meeting," *Harvard Business Review*, March-April 1976, p. 43.

16. Johnson, Virginia. "Meeting as Ritual: What Makes a Good One?," *Successful Meetings*, January 1990, p. 100. Reprinted with permission from *Successful Meetings* Magazine. Copyright © 1990, Bill Communications, Inc.

17. Langham, Barbara A. "Standing on Ceremony," *Successful Meetings*, December 1993, p. 66. Reprinted with permission from *Successful Meetings* Magazine. Copyright © 1993, Bill Communications, Inc.

18. *Making Meetings Matter*, p. 19.

19. Langham, Barbara A. "Standing on Ceremony," *Successful Meetings*, December 1993, p. 66. Reprinted with permission from *Successful Meetings* Magazine. Copyright © 1993, Bill Communications, Inc.

20. Leimbach, Michael P. "The Soul of the Meeting: Embedding Organizational Culture in Meeting Procedures," *Innovative Meeting Management*, Richard A. Swanson and Bonnie Ogram Knapp, eds. Published by the University of Minnesota Training & Development Research Center and the 3M Meeting Management Institute, 1991, p. 111.

21. Ibid.

22. Ibid.

23. Ibid.

24. *Making Meetings Matter*, p. 20.

25. Kieffer, George. *The Strategy of Meetings*, p. 54.

26. *Making Meetings Matter*, p. 24.

27. Ibid., p. 26.

28. Ibid., p. 20.

29. Ibid., p. 25.

30. *A Profile of Meetings in Corporate America*, p. 81.

31. Johnson, Virginia. "The Meeting Meter," *Successful Meetings*, May 1993, p. 99. Reprinted with permission from *Successful Meetings* Magazine. Copyright © 1993, Bill Communications, Inc.

32. *Making Meetings Matter*, p. 14.

33. Johnson, Virginia. "Budget Cuts," *Successful Meetings*, March 1991, p. 124.

34. Ibid.

35. Ibid.

36. "The Year 2000: Expect Meetings to Change, Not Decline," *Meeting Management News*, Vol. 3 (1): April 1991.

37. McGoff, Christopher J. "Business Meetings of the 1990s: Characteristics & Compositions," *Innovative Meeting Management*, Richard A. Swanson and Bonnie Ogram Knapp, eds. Published by the University of Minnesota Training & Development Research Center and the 3M Meeting Management Institute, 1991, p. 205.

38. "A Spicier Stew in the Melting Pot," *Business Week*, December 21, 1992, p. 29.

39. Adapted and reprinted from *Claw Your Way to the Top* © 1986 by Dave Barry, p. 27. Permission granted by Rodale Press, Inc., Emmaus, PA 18098.

Chapter 2

1. Green, Walter A., and Lazarus, Harold, Ph.D. "Are Today's Executives Meeting with Success?," *The Journal of Management Development*, Vol. 10 (1): p. 14, 1991.

2. *Making Meetings Matter: A Report to the 3M Corporation.* Prepared by Lynn Oppenheim, Ph.D. Philadelphia, Pa.: Wharton Center for Applied Research, December 15, 1987, p. 32.

3. Ibid., p. 13.

4. Johnson, Virginia. "Creative Breaks," *Successful Meetings*, September 1991, p. 125. Reprinted with permission from *Successful Meetings* Magazine. Copyright © 1993, Bill Communications, Inc.

5. "Master Meeting Leader Bob Bostrom Says 'Identify Tangible Outcomes,'" *Meeting Management News*, Vol. 5 (2): June 1993.

6. *Making Meetings Matter*, p. 21.

7. Ibid., p. 22.

8. "From a Bird's-Eye View," *Meeting Management News*, Vol. 1 (3).

9. The bulk of this section was adapted from Virginia Johnson, "Minutes Count," *Successful Meetings*, August 1993, p. 93. Reprinted with permission from *Successful Meetings* Magazine. Copyright © 1993, Bill Communications, Inc.

10. Adapted from Virginia Johnson, "Evaluating Meetings," *Successful Meetings*, October 1991, p. 120. Reprinted with permission from *Successful Meetings* Magazine. Copyright © 1991, Bill Communications, Inc.

11. *Making Meetings Matter*, p. 32.

12. Monge, Peter R., McSween, Charles, and Wyer, JoAnne. *A Profile of Meetings in Corporate America: Results of the 3M Meeting Effectiveness Study.* Los Angeles: Annenberg School of Communications, University of Southern California, November 1989, p. 32.

13. Ibid., p. 26.

14. *Making Meetings Matter*, p. 24.

15. Ibid., p. 13.

Chapter 3

1. Poole, Marshall Scott. "Procedures for Managing Meetings: Social and Technological Innovation," *Innovative Meeting Management*, Richard A. Swanson and Bonnie Ogram Knapp, eds. Published by the University of Minnesota Training & Development Research Center and the 3M Meeting Management Institute, 1991, p. 53.

2. Ibid.

3. McDonald, Edward D. "Chaos or Communication: Technical Barriers to Effective Meetings," *Innovative Meeting Management*, Richard A. Swanson and Bonnie Ogram Knapp, eds. Published by the University of Minnesota

Training & Development Research Center and the 3M Meeting Management Institute, 1991, p. 177.

4. Ibid.

5. Poole, Marshall Scott. "Procedures for Managing Meetings: Social and Technological Innovation."

6. Johnson, Virginia. "Following the Rules," *Successful Meetings*, November 1991, p. 78. Reprinted with permission from *Successful Meetings* Magazine. Copyright © 1991, Bill Communications, Inc.

7. Pavitt, Charles. "What (Little) We Know About Formal Group Discussion Procedures: A Review of Relevant Research," *Small Group Research*, Vol. 24 (2): p. 217, May 1993.

8. Doyle, Michael, and Straus, David. *How to Make Meetings Work*, Chicago: Playboy Press, 1967.

9. Ibid., p. 24.

10. This section, "A Sampling of Meeting Procedures," "Differences Among Procedures," "Guidelines for Selecting Procedures," "Resistance to Using Procedures," and "Eight Ways to Promote Use of Procedures" are adapted from Marshall Scott Poole, "Procedures for Managing Meetings: Social and Technological Innovation," except where noted.

11. Nutt, Paul. *Planning Methods for Health and Related Organizations*, New York: John Wiley & Sons, 1984.

12. New York: Charles Scribner's, 1953.

13. Ibid., p. 178.

14. Pavitt, Charles. "What (Little) We Know About Formal Group Discussion Procedures: A Review of Relevant Research."

15. Nutt, Paul. *Planning Methods for Health and Related Organizations*.

16. This section was adapted from Michael P. Leimbach, "The Soul of the Meeting: Embedding Organizational Culture in Meeting Procedures," *Innovative Meeting Management*, Richard A. Swanson and Bonnie Ogram Knapp, eds. Published by the University of Minnesota Training & Development Research Center and the 3M Meeting Management Institute, 1991, p. 111.

17. Ibid.

18. Poole, Marshall Scott. "Procedures for Managing Meetings: Social and Technological Innovation."

19. *Making Meetings Matter*, p. 31.

Chapter 4

1. *Making Meetings Matter: A Report to the 3M Corporation*. Prepared by Lynn Oppenheim, Ph.D. Philadelphia, Pa.: Wharton Center for Applied Research, December 15, 1987, p. 30.

2. Jay, Antony. "How to Run a Meeting," *Harvard Business* Review, March-April 1976, p. 43.

3. Ibid.

4. Depta, Ann. "The Leader's Impact on Meeting Success," *Innovative Meeting Management*, Richard A. Swanson and Bonnie Ogram Knapp, eds. Published by the University of Minnesota Training & Development Research Center and the 3M Meeting Management Institute, 1991, p. 183.

5. *Making Meetings Matter*, p. 31.

6. "Ground Rules, Preparation Are Keys To Meetings, Three Experts Say," *Meeting Management News*, Vol. 1 (5).

7. Johnson, Virginia. "Icebreakers," *Successful Meetings*, July 1992, p. 64. Reprinted with permission from *Successful Meetings* Magazine. Copyright © 1992, Bill Communications, Inc.

8. Ibid.

9. Depta, Ann. "The Leader's Impact on Meeting Success," *Innovative Meeting Management*, Richard A. Swanson and Bonnie Ogram Knapp, eds. Published by the University of Minnesota Training & Development Research Center and the 3M Meeting Management Institute, 1991, p. 183.

10. Ibid.

11. Depta, Ann. "The Leader's Impact on Meeting Success."

12. Jay, Antony. "How to Run a Meeting."

13. Ibid.

14. Ibid.

15. Jay, Antony. "How to Run a Meeting."

16. Excerpt. p. 51 from *Thinking Together* by V. A. Howard, Ph.D. and J. H. Barton, M.A. Copyright © 1992 by V. A. Howard, and J. H. Barton.

17. Ibid., pp. 51-52.

18. Frank, Milo O. *How to Run a Successful Meeting in Half the Time*, New York: Simon & Schuster 1989, p. 131. Copyright © 1989 by Milo O. Frank. Reprinted by permission of Simon & Schuster, Inc.

19. Ibid.

20. The remainder of this section was adapted from Virginia Johnson, "Emotional Rescue," *Successful Meetings*, January 1992, p. 142. Reprinted with permission from *Successful Meetings* Magazine. Copyright © 1992, Bill Communications, Inc.

21. Jay, Antony. "How to Run a Meeting."

22. Ibid.

23. The remainder of this section was adapted from Virginia Johnson, "Dealing with Stragglers," *Successful Meetings*, July 1993, p. 50. Reprinted with permission from *Successful Meetings* Magazine. Copyright © 1993, Bill Communications, Inc.

24. Johnson, Virginia. "Seating Arrangements," *Successful Meetings*, July 1990, p. 132. Reprinted with permission from *Successful Meetings* Magazine. Copyright © 1990, Bill Communications, Inc.

25. Adapted from Virginia Johnson, "On the Lighter Side," *Successful Meetings*, February 1991, p. 110. Reprinted with permission from *Successful Meetings* Magazine. Copyright © 1991, Bill Communications, Inc.

26. *Vital Speeches*, July 1, 1986, p. 563. Cited in Malcolm Kushner, *The Light Touch*, New York: Simon & Schuster, 1990, pp. 38-39.

27. Depta, Ann. "The Leader's Impact on Meeting Success."

28. "Master Meeting Leader Deborah Nicklaus Says Focus on the Participants," *Meeting Management News*, Vol. 5 (3): September 1993.

29. "Master Meeting Leader Chris McGoff Puts People Skills Before Technology," *Meeting Management News*, Vol. 5 (4): December 1993.

30. Ibid.

31. *Improving Meetings Using Computers and Facilitators*. Prepared by Robert Anson, Ph.D. Boise, Idaho: Boise State University, College of Business, August 1990, p. 11.

32. Ibid., p. 6.

33. Clawson, Victoria K. Ph.D., and Bostrom, Robert P. Ph.D. "The Role of the Facilitator in Computer-Supported Meetings," Athens, Ga.: University of Georgia, Terry College of Business, 1993.

34. Adapted from Clawson and Bostrom, "The Role of the Facilitator in Computer-Supported Meetings."

35. Adapted from Virginia Johnson, "Artistic Meetings," *Successful Meetings*, March 1992, p. 99. Reprinted with permission from *Successful Meetings* Magazine. Copyright © 1992, Bill Communications, Inc.

36. Depta, Ann. "The Leader's Impact on Meeting Success,"

37. Adapted from Virginia Johnson, "Listening With Empathy," *Successful Meetings*, March 1993, p. 122. Reprinted with permission from *Successful Meetings* Magazine. Copyright © 1992, Bill Communications, Inc. Based on *The Seven Habits of Highly Effective People* by Stephen R. Covey, © 1989, Simon & Schuster. Covey Leadership Center, 1-800-331-7716. All Rights Reserved.

38. "Ground Rules, Preparation Are Keys to Meetings, Three Experts Say," *Meeting Management News*, Vol. 1 (5).

39. Adapted from "Risk Taking for Jellyfish: Board Member Offers Exercises to Build Psychic Muscle," *Meeting Management News*, Vol. 5 (1): April 1993; and Virginia Johnson, "Taking Risks," *Successful Meetings*, November 1992, p. 113. Copyright © 1992 Bill Communications, Inc.

Chapter 5

1. "New Book Explores Meeting Innovations," *Meeting Management News*, Vol. 3 (1): April 1991.

2. "Groupware May Facilitate Meetings of the 1990s," *Meeting Management News*, Vol. 2 (2): June 1990.

3. Johansen, Robert, Sibbet, David, Benson, Suzyn, Martin, Alexia, Mittman, Robert, and Saffo, Paul. *Leading Business Teams*, New York: Addison-Wesley, 1991, p. 5.

4. "Groupware May Facilitate Meetings of the 1990s," *Meeting Management News*, Vol. 2 (2): June 1990.

5. *Research on the Productivity of Mediated Meetings*, Janet Fulk and Lori Collins-Jarvis. Annenberg School for Communication, University of Southern California, Los Angeles, Calif., March 1993, p. 1.

6. Adapted from Virginia Johnson, "Meet Via Telephone," *Successful Meetings*, June 1993, p. 66, except where noted. Reprinted with permission from *Successful Meetings* Magazine. Copyright © 1993, Bill Communications, Inc.

7. Burleson, Clyde W. *Effective Meetings: The Complete Guide*, New York: John Wiley & Sons, 1990, p. 178. Copyright © 1990 by Clyde W. Burleson. Reprinted by permission of John Wiley & Sons, Inc.

8. Ibid., pp. 173-174.

9. Ibid., p. 174.

10. Adapted from "Videoconferences: Getting It From the Top," *Meeting Management News*, Vol. 3 (2): September 1991 and Virginia Johnson, "Videoconferencing," *Successful Meetings*, April 1991, p. 114. Reprinted with permission from *Successful Meetings* Magazine. Copyright © 1991, Bill Communications, Inc.

11. *Research on the Productivity of Mediated Meetings*, p. 3.

12. Johnson, Virginia. "Videoconferencing," *Successful Meetings* April 1991, p. 114. Reprinted with permission from *Successful Meetings* Magazine. Copyright © 1991, Bill Communications, Inc.

13. Mogle, Phillip R. "New Technologies Enhance Group Communications," *Convene*, December 1992, p. 77.

14. Holcombe, Marya W., and Stein, Judith K. *Presentations for Decision Makers*, New York: Van Nostrand Reinhold, 1990, p. 178.

15. *Research on the Productivity of Mediated Meetings*, p. 44.

16. Ibid., p. 45.

17. Holcombe, Marya W., and Stein, Judith K. *Presentations for Decision Makers*, p. 179.

18. Ibid.

19. *Groupware: Computer Support for Business Teams* by Robert Johansen. Copyright © 1988 by The Free Press, a Division of Macmillan, Inc. Reprinted with the permission of the publisher.

20. Ibid., p. 29.

21. *Research on the Productivity of Mediated Meetings*, p. 4.

22. Poole, Marshall Scott. "Procedures for Managing Meetings: Social and Technological Innovation," *Innovative Meeting Management*, Richard A. Swanson and

Bonnie Ogram Knapp, eds. Published by the University of Minnesota Training & Development Research Center and the 3M Meeting Management Institute, 1991, p. 97.

23. Ibid.

24. Ibid.

25. *Research on the Productivity of Mediated Meetings*, p. 16.

26. Adapted from *The Use and Adoption of OptionFinder: a Keypad Based Group Decision Support System: A Report to the 3M Meeting Management Institute*. Prepared by Richard T. Watson, Mary B. Alexander, Carol Pollard, and Robert P. Bostrom. University of Georgia Department of Management, February 15, 1991, and Virginia Johnson, "Support Systems." *Successful Meetings* Magazine, August 1990, p. 104. Reprinted with permission from *Successful Meetings* Magazine. Copyright © 1990, Bill Communications, Inc.

27. Kirkpatrick, David. "Here Comes the Payoff from PCs," *Fortune*, March 23, 1992, p. 93. © 1992 Time Inc. All rights reserved.

28. Excerpted with permission from "Collaborative Computing," *BYTE* Magazine, March 1993 © 1993 by McGraw-Hill, Inc., New York, N.Y. All rights reserved.

29. From interview with Jeannine Drew, December 17, 1993.

30. Ibid.

31. Ibid.

32. Ibid.

33. *Research on the Productivity of Mediated Meetings*, pp. 18, 39.

34. Kirkpatrick, David. "Here Comes the Payoff from PCs," *Fortune*, March 23, 1992, p. 93. © 1992 Time Inc. All rights reserved.

35. Ibid.

36. Ibid.

37. Reprinted from *Medical Meetings* magazine, September/October 1992, Vol. 19 (6): with permission of the Publisher, The Laux Company, Inc., 63 Great Road, Maynard, Mass. 01754.

38. Excerpted with permission from "Collaborative Computing," *BYTE* Magazine, March 1993 © 1993 by McGraw-Hill, Inc., New York, N.Y. All rights reserved.

39. Poole, Marshall Scott. "Procedures for Managing Meetings: Social and Technological Innovation," *Innovative Meeting Management*, Richard A. Swanson and Bonnie Ogram Knapp, eds. Published by the University of Minnesota Training & Development Research Center and the 3M Meeting Management Institute, 1991, p. 53.

40. Ibid.

41. Schrage, Michael. *Shared Minds: The New Technologies of Collaboration*, New York: Random House, 1990, p. 126. Copyright © 1990 by Michael Schrage.

42. Johnson, Virginia. "Future World," *Successful Meetings*, October 1990, p. 122. Reprinted with permission from *Successful Meetings* Magazine. Copyright © 1990, Bill Communications, Inc.

43 Ibid.

44. Adapted from Alice LaPlante, "Brainstorming '90s Style," *ASAP: Technology Supplement to Forbes Magazine*, October 25, 1993, p. 45. Reprinted by Permission of *FORBES ASAP* Magazine © Forbes Inc., 1993.

45. Ibid.

46. Ibid.

47. "Support Systems," *Successful Meetings*, August 1990, p. 104. Reprinted with permission from *Successful Meetings* Magazine. Copyright © 1990, Bill Communications, Inc.

48. Ibid.

49. *Improving Meetings Using Computers and Facilitators*. Prepared by Robert Anson, Ph.D. Boise, Idaho: Boise State University, College of Business, August 1990, p. 11.

50. Burleson, Clyde W. *Effective Meetings: The Complete Guide*, New York: John Wiley & Sons, 1990, p. 184. Copyright © 1990 by Clyde W. Burleson. Reprinted by permission of John Wiley & Sons, Inc.

51. *Groupware: Computer Support for Business Teams* by Robert Johansen. Copyright © 1988 by The Free Press, a Division of Macmillan, Inc. Reprinted with the permission of the publisher.

52. Schrage, Michael. *Shared Minds: The New Technologies of Collaboration*, New York: Random House, 1990, p. 133. Copyright © 1990 by Michael Schrage.

53. Excerpted with permission from "Collaborative Computing," *BYTE* Magazine, March 1993 © 1993 by McGraw-Hill, Inc., New York, N.Y. All rights reserved.

54. Kirkpatrick, David. "Here Comes the Payoff from PCs," *Fortune*, March 23, 1992, p. 93. © 1992 Time Inc. All rights reserved.

55. "Groupware May Facilitate Meetings of the 1990s," *Meeting Management News*, Vol. 2 (2): June 1990.

56. Kirkpatrick, David. "Here Comes the Payoff from PCs," *Fortune*, March 23, 1992, p. 93. © 1992 Time Inc. All rights reserved.

57. "Groupware May Facilitate Meetings of the 1990s," *Meeting Management News*, Vol. 2 (2): June 1990.

58. Robert Johansen et al. *Leading Business Teams*, Chapter 26.

59. *Groupware: Computer Support for Business Teams* by Robert Johansen. Copyright © 1988 by The Free Press, a Division of Macmillan, Inc. Reprinted with the permission of the publisher.

60. Jessup, Leonard M., and Valacich, Joseph S. "On the Study of Group Support System Research and Development, *Group Support Systems: New Perspectives*, eds. Leonard M. Jessup and Joseph S. Valacich. New York: Macmillan, 1993, p. 3.

61. DeKoven, Bernard. *Connected Executives*, Palo Alto, Calif.: Institute for Better Meetings, 1990, p. 1.

62. Johnson, Virginia. "The Whiz-bang Meeting," *Successful Meetings*, April 1990, p. 138. Reprinted with permission from *Successful Meetings* Magazine. Copyright © 1990, Bill Communications, Inc.

63. *Groupware: Computer Support for Business Teams* by Robert Johansen, p. 114. Copyright © 1988 by The Free Press, a Division of Macmillan, Inc. Reprinted with the permission of the publisher.

64. Johnson, Virginia. "The Whiz-bang Meeting," *Successful Meetings*, April 1990, p. 138. Reprinted with permission from *Successful Meetings* Magazine. Copyright © 1990, Bill Communications, Inc.

65. *Improving Meetings Using Computer and Facilitators*. Prepared by Robert Anson, Ph.D. Boise, Idaho: Boise State University, College of Business, August 1990, p. 20.

66. From telephone interview with Jeannine Drew, October 19, 1993.

67. Bernier, Nichole. "Don't Shoot the Messenger," Meeting News, Vol. 16, April 1992.

68. Ibid.

69. Ibid.

70. Johnson, Virginia. "The Whiz-bang Meeting," *Successful Meetings*, April 1990, p. 138. Reprinted with permission from *Successful Meetings* Magazine. Copyright © 1990, Bill Communications, Inc.

71. From telephone interview with Jeannine Drew, October 19, 1993.

Chapter 6

1. Peoples, David A. *Presentations Plus*, New York: John Wiley & Sons, 1992, p. 67. Copyright © 1992 by David A. Peoples. Reprinted by permission of John Wiley & Sons, Inc.

2. Johnson, Virginia. "Presenting to Executives," *Successful Meetings*, April 1993, p. 122. Reprinted with permission from *Successful Meetings* Magazine. Copyright © 1993, Bill Communications, Inc.

3. "Ten Formats for Organizing Your Presentation," *Meeting Management News*, Vol. 4 (4): December 1992.

4. Wilder, Claudyne. *The Presentations Kit*, New York: John Wiley & Sons, 1990.

5. "Presentation Planning: Draw a Logic Tree," *Meeting Management News*, Vol. 5 (1): April 1993.

6. Peoples, David A. *Presentations Plus*, New York: John Wiley & Sons, 1992, p. 67. Copyright © 1992 by David A. Peoples. Reprinted by permission of John Wiley & Sons, Inc.

7. Johnson, Virginia. "Visual Literacy," *Successful Meetings*, January 1991, p. 97. Reprinted with permission from *Successful Meetings* Magazine. Copyright © 1991, Bill Communications, Inc.

8. *A Study of the Effects of the Use of Overhead Transparencies on Business Meetings—Final Report*. Prepared by the Wharton Applied Research Center, The Wharton School, University of Pennsylvania, September 14, 1981.

9. *Persuasion and the Role of Visual Presentation Support: The UM/3M Study*, by Douglas R. Vogel, Gary W. Dickson, and John A. Lehman. School of Management, University of Minnesota, Minneapolis, June, 1986.

10. *Use of Electronic Media in Presentation and Training Applications*, by Douglas R. Vogel, Department of Management Information System, College of Business and Public Administration, University of Arizona—Tucson, October 1992.

11. Adapted from "Visuals Keep Meetings More Focused," *Meetings Management News*, Vol. 1 (2).

12. Ibid.

13. Ventana Press, 1990.

14. Rabb, Margaret. "Design Crimes and How to Prevent Them," *Practical Presentations*, April 1992, p. 4.

15. Ibid.

16. Meilach, Dona Z. *Dynamics of Presentation Graphics*, Homewood, Ill. Dow Jones-Irwin, Second Ed., 1990, p. 53.

17. Johnson, Virginia. "The Power of Color," *Successful Meetings*, June 1992, p. 87. Reprinted with permission from *Successful Meetings* Magazine. Copyright 1992, Bill Communications, Inc.

18. Ibid.

19. *Persuasion and the Role of Visual Presentation Support: The UM/3M Study*, by Douglas R. Vogel, Gary W. Dickson, and John A. Lehman. School of Management, University of Minnesota, Minneapolis, June, 1986.

20. Johnson, Virginia. "The Power of Color," *Successful Meetings*, June 1992, p. 87. Preprinted with permission from *Successful Meetings* Magazine. Copyright 1992, Bill Communications, Inc.

21. Meilach, Dona Z. "Using Colors Constructively," *Presentation Products Magazine*, July 1993, p. 24.

22. *Persuasion and the Role of Visual Presentation Support: The UM/3M Study*, by Douglas R. Vogel, Gary W. Dickson, and John A. Lehman. School of Management, University of Minnesota, Minneapolis, June, 1986, p. 11.

23. Adapted in part from Virginia Johnson, "The Power of Color," *Successful Meetings*, June 1992, p. 87. Reprinted with permission from *Successful Meetings* Magazine. Copyright 1992, Bill Communications, Inc.

24. *Summary Report: A Winning Executive Presentation*, Montgomery, Texas: Genesis Training Solutions, 1989.

25. Meilach, Dona Z. *Dynamics of Presentation Graphics*, p. 188.

26. Ibid., p. 55.

27. Johnson, Virginia. "Desktop Presentation Software," *Successful Meetings*, November 1990, p. 118. Reprinted with permission from *Successful Meetings* Magazine. Copyright © 1990, Bill Communications, Inc.

28. Meilach, Dona Z. *Dynamics of Presentation Graphics*, p. 188.

29. Ibid., p. 191.

30. Nelson, Robin. "Graphics: The Wretched Excess," *Personal Computing*, February 1990, p. 49.

31. Holcombe, Marya W., and Stein, Judith K. *Presentations for Decision Makers*, New York: Van Nostrand Reinhold, 1990, p. 121.

38. Peoples, David A. *Presentations Plus*, New York: John Wiley & Sons, 1992, p. 189. Copyright © 1992 by David A. Peoples. Reprinted by permission of John Wiley & Sons, Inc.

Chapter 7

1. Wann, Al. "A Speech to Remember," *IABC Communication World*, December 1993, p. 22.

2. Adapted from Virginia Johnson, "Workforce Diversity," *Successful Meetings*, April 1992, p. 122, except where noted. Reprinted with permission from *Successful Meetings* Magazine. Copyright © 1992, Bill Communications, Inc.

3. Johnson, Virginia. "Piercing the Glass Ceiling," *Successful Meetings*, October 1993, p. 134. Reprinted with permission from *Successful Meetings* Magazine. Copyright © 1993, Bill Communications, Inc.

4. Langham, Barbara A. "Genderspeak," *Successful Meetings*, February 1994, p. 121. Reprinted with permission from *Successful Meetings* Magazine. Copyright © 1994, Bill Communications, Inc.

5. Ibid.

6. Tannen, Deborah. *You Just Don't Understand: Women and Men in Conversation*, New York: William Morrow and Company, 1990, p. 228.

7. Ibid.

8. Ibid., p. 18.

9. Ibid., p. 44.

10. Ibid., p. 24-25.

11. Ibid., p. 16.

12. Ibid., p. 298.

13. Ibid., pp. 297-298.

14. Langham, Barbara A. "Genderspeak," *Successful Meetings*, February 1994, p. 121. Reprinted with permission from *Successful Meetings* Magazine. Copyright © 1994, Bill Communications, Inc.

15. From telephone interview with Jeannine Drew, October 19, 1993.

16. Ibid.

17. "More International Meetings Pose Challenges for Planners," *Meeting Management News*, Vol. 2 (2): June 1990.

18. *Do's and Taboos Around the World*, edited by Roger E. Axtell, New York: John Wiley & Sons, 1993, p. 166. Copyright © 1993 by The Parker Pen Company. Reprinted by permission of John Wiley & Sons, Inc.

19. "More International Meetings Pose Challenges for Planners," *Meeting Management News*, Vol. 2 (2): June 1990.

20. *Do's and Taboos Around the World*, edited by Roger E. Axtell, New York: John Wiley & Sons, 1993, p. 16. Copyright © 1993 by The Parker Pen Company. Reprinted by permission of John Wiley & Sons, Inc.

21. Harquet, Marc. "The Fine Art of Multicultural Meetings," *Off-Site Training Meetings*, July 1993, p. 29. Reprinted with permission from the July 1993 issue of *Training* Magazine. Copyright 1993. Lakewood Publications, Minneapolis, Minn. All rights reserved. Not for resale.

22. *Do's and Taboos Around the World*, edited by Roger E. Axtell, New York: John Wiley & Sons, 1993, p. 162. Copyright © 1993 by The Parker Pen Company. Reprinted by permission of John Wiley & Sons, Inc.

23. Ibid., p. 165.

24. Johansen, Robert, Sibbet, David, Benson, Suzyn, Martin, Alexia, Mittman, Robert, and Saffo, Paul. *Leading Business Teams: How Teams Can Use Technology and Group Process Tools to Enhance Performance*, Redding, Mass.: Addison-Wesley, 1991, p. 206.

25. Harquet, Marc. "The Fine Art of Multicultural Meetings," *Off-Site Training Meetings*, July 1993, p. 29. Reprinted with permission from the July 1993 issue of *Training* Magazine. Copyright 1993. Lakewood Publications, Minneapolis Minn. All rights reserved. Not for resale.

26. "Ten Golden Rules When Working with Interpreters," *Meeting Management News*, Vol. 5 (3): September 1993.

27. Axtell, Roger E. *Gestures: The DO's and TABOOs of Body Language Around the World*, New York: John Wiley & Sons, 1991, p. 13. Copyright © 1991 by Roger E. Axtell. Reprinted by permission of John Wiley & Sons, Inc.

28. Ibid., p. 43.

29. Ibid., p. 113.

30. *Do's and Taboos Around the World*, edited by Roger E. Axtell, New York: John Wiley & Sons, 3rd Edition, 1993, p. 3. Copyright © 1993 by The Parker Pen Company. Reprinted by permission of John Wiley & Sons, Inc.

31. Ibid., p. 6.

32. Harquet, Marc. "The Fine Art of Multicultural Meetings," *Off-Site Training Meetings*, July 1993, p. 29. Reprinted with permission from the July 1993 issue of *Training* Magazine. Copyright 1993. Lakewood Publications, Minneapolis, Minn. All rights reserved. Not for resale.

33. "More International Meetings Pose Challenges for Planners," *Meeting Management News*, Vol. 2 (2): June 1990.

34. Ibid.

35. Ibid.

36. "More International Meetings Pose Challenges for Planners," *Meeting Management News*, Vol. 2 (2): June 1990, except where noted.

37. Harquet, Marc. "The Fine Art of Multicultural Meetings," *Off-Site Training Meetings*, July 1993, p. 29. Reprinted with permission from the July 1993 issue of *Training* Magazine. Copyright 1993. Lakewood Publications, Minneapolis, Minn. All rights reserved. Not for resale.

38. Adapted from Virginia Johnson, "Teamwork," *Successful Meetings*, May 1991, p. 92. Reprinted with permission from *Successful Meetings* Magazine. Copyright © 1992, Bill Communications, Inc.

39. Johansen, Robert, Sibbet, David, Benson, Suzyn, Martin, Alexia, Mittman, Robert, and Saffo, Paul. *Leading Business Teams*, New York: Addison-Wesley, 1991, p. 27.

40. Adapted from "Meeting Quality: A Chicken-Egg Question?," *Meeting Management News*, Vol. 4 (2): June 1992 and Virginia Johnson, "Total Quality Management," *Successful Meetings*, May 1992, p. 100. Reprinted with permission from *Successful Meetings* Magazine. Copyright © 1992, Bill Communications, Inc.

41. Adapted from Raymond R. Panko, "Managerial Communication Patterns," *Journal of Organizational Computing*, 2(1): pp. 95-122 (1992); Raymond R. Panko and Susan T. Kinney, "Dyadic Organizational Communication: Is the Dyad Different?," published in the *Proceedings of the Twenty-Fifth Annual Hawaii International Conference on System Sciences*, Kauai, Hawaii, January 1991; and Virginia Johnson, "Two-Person Interactions: Trifle or Treasure?," *Successful Meetings*, December 1992, p. 128. Reprinted with permission from *Successful Meetings* Magazine. Copyright © 1992, Bill Communications, Inc.

42. From telephone interview with Jeannine Drew, November 22, 1993.

43. Poole, Marshall Scott, and Billingsley, Julie. "The Structure of Dyadic Decisions," in Brinberg, David and Jaccard, James, eds., *Dyadic Decision Making*, New York: Springer Verlag, 1989. Cited in Raymond R. Panko and Susan T. Kinney, "Dyadic Organizational Communication: Is the Dyad Different?"

Chapter 8

1. Johnson, Virginia. "Meeting Audits," *Successful Meetings*, August 1992, p. 90. Reprinted with permission from *Successful Meetings* Magazine. Copyright © 1992, Bill Communications, Inc.

2. Adapted from Richard E. Byrd and John C. Johnson, "Meetings as Systems: Rescripting the Organizational Drama" (Minneapolis, August 1993) and Virginia Johnson, "Meeting Audits," *Successful Meetings*, August 1992, p. 90. Re-

printed with permission from *Successful Meetings* Magazine. Copyright © 1992, Bill Communications, Inc.

3. *Making Meetings Matter: A Report to the 3M Corporation.* Prepared by Lynn Oppenheim, Ph.D. Philadelphia, Pa. Wharton Center for Applied Research, December 15, 1987, p. 37.

4. "Ground Rules, Preparation Are Keys to Meetings, Three Experts Say," *Meeting Management News*, Vol. 1 (5).

5. Depta, Ann. "The Leader's Impact on Meeting Success," *Innovative Meeting Management*, Richard A. Swanson and Bonnie Ogram Knapp, eds. Published by the University of Minnesota Training & Development Research Center and the 3M Meeting Management Institute, 1991, p. 183.

6. *Making Meetings Matter*, p. 38.

7. Depta, Ann. "The Leader's Impact on Meeting Success," *Innovative Meeting Management*, p. 183.

8. Adapted from Richard E. Byrd and John Johnson, "Meeting Effectiveness: A Matter of Strategy" (Minneapolis, October 1992) except where noted.

9. Byrd, Richard E., and Johnson, John C. "Meetings as Systems: Rescripting the Organizational Drama" (Minneapolis, August 1993).

10. Ibid.

11. Johnson, Virginia. "Meeting Audits," *Successful Meetings*, August 1992, p. 90. Reprinted with permission from *Successful Meetings* Magazine. Copyright © 1992, Bill Communications, Inc.

12. From telephone interview with Jeannine Drew, October 19, 1993.

13. Ibid.

14. Ibid.

15. *Making Meetings Matter*, p. 37.

16. Byrd, Richard E., and Johnson, John C. "Meetings as Systems: Rescripting the Organizational Drama" (Minneapolis, August 1993).

17. *Making Meetings Matter*, p. 38.

18. Smith, Stuart M. "Managing Your Meetings for a 'Bottom Line' Payoff," *Innovative Meeting Management*, Richard A. Swanson and Bonnie Ogram Knapp, eds. Published by the University of Minnesota Training & Development Research Center and the 3M Meeting Management Institute, 1991, p. 19.

Index

Access, meeting room, 33
Accountable communication, 100
Acoustics, meeting room, 33
Active participation, 97-102
   communicating accountably, 100
   empathic listening, 97-100
   risk taking, 101-102
Afternoon sessions, length of, 26
Agenda, 26-29
   detail, including, 27
   distribution of, 28-29
   general guidelines for, 26-27
   items
      framing in positive terms, 26, 81
      limiting number of, 26-27
      sample of, 28
   meeting focus and, 27
   time, allocating, 27
   what to include, 27-28
Amphitheater setup, 36-37
Anderson, Karen, 169-170
Annenberg School of Communications
      (USC), 4, 9, 12, 29
Anson, Rob, 91
Applied Imagination (Osborn), 59
Attendees, 29-31
Audience:
   analyzing, 135
   monitoring, 163-166
Audioconferencing, 105-109
   cost of, 106-107
   participants, advice for, 108-109
   planning for, 107-108
   potential drawbacks of, 107
   verbal cues, power of, 106
Audit:
   meeting systems, 195-196
      choosing observers for, 205
      guidelines for conducting, 204-206
      purpose of, 206
      sample questions for, 203
      typical findings, 197-198
Auditorium setup, 36, 37
Axtell, Roger, 173, 178

Bailey, Suzanne, 96
Bar charts, 148-150
Barry, Dave, 1-2
Barton, J. H., 83-84
Bethel, Sheila, 38
Billingsley, Julie, 191-192
Body language, 178-178
Bostrom, Bob, 26, 92
Brainstorming, 22-23, 59-60, 66, 69, 70, 74,
      88, 168
Breaks, scheduling, 25-26
Bridging equipment, 106-107
Bright colors, use of, 146
Brown, Larry, 183, 190-191
Burleson, Clyde, 108-109, 127
Byrd, Dick, 6, 17, 101-102, 209-210

CD-ROM, presentations and, 162
Celente, Gerald, 15
Ceremonial meetings, 7
Chairs, meeting room, 35
Change, meetings and, 17
Classroom setup, 36
"Coincidences" exercise, 80
Communication, accountable, 100
Competition, out-meeting, 5-6
Computer conferencing, 114-116
   as a flexible tool, 115
   groupware, 115-116
   interpersonal computer, 114-115
Computer graphics, 157
Conference room setups, 36
Conflict:
   managing, 86-87
   reconciling, 22
Connected Executives (DeKoven), 129
Content analysis, 50
Costs:
   of audioconferencing, 106-107
   calculating, 10-13
      formula for, 11
   levels of
      actual cost outlay per time unit, 12
      delayed decisions, 12

Costs (*Continued*)
    ineffectiveness, 12
    perpetuation of ineffectiveness, 13
    poor decisions, 13
  Meeting Meter, 14
  weighing, 14-16
Covey, Stephen, 97-100
Crego, Ed, 180
Cross-company alliances, meetings and, 17
Cross-company team meetings, 186-187
Cross-cultural groupware, 177
Cross-functional teams, meetings and, 17
Culturally influenced behavior, minority
    groups and, 168-169

Deagan, Tim, 121-122
Decision tree, 61, 62
DeKoven, Bernie, 14, 86, 127-128, 129
Delphi Technique, 58, 65-68
de Mestral, George, 65
Demographic shifts, meetings and, 17-18
Depta, Ann, 78-79, 81-82, 96-97, 206
DeSanctis, Geraldine, 128
Devil's advocate procedure, 64, 66, 68, 69
Diagrams, 151, 153
Di Pietro, Carl, 124
Distractions, meeting room, 33-34
Diversity, 168-172
  in communication styles, 171-172
  culturally influenced behavior, 168-169
  gender gap, 169-171
  self-assessment checklist for managers,
    172
  training in, 171
Doyle, Michael, 55
Drawings, 153
Drexler, Allan, 183
Drexler/Sibbet Team Performance Model,
    183-186
Drucker, Peter, 3-4
Dual overhead projectors, 34, 40
Dyads, 191-193

Effective Executive, The (Drucker), 3
Electrical outlets, meeting room, 34
Electronic blackboard, 193
Electronic meetings, 103-131
  audioconferencing, 105-109
  computer conferencing, 114-116
  groupware, 115-130
  meeting technology, growth of, 104-105

  technology, limits of, 129-131
  videoconferencing, 109-114
Ellis, Skip, 129
Empathic listening, 97-100
Ethnic jokes, 88-89
Evaluations, 47-51
  designing/conducting, 50-51
  formal, 49-50
  Meeting Assessment Form, 48
  presentations, 166-167
  simple, 47-49

Facilitators, 90-97
  benefits of, 91-92
  definition of, 90
  functions of, 92-95
  graphic facilitation, 95-96
  as neutral third party, 91
  skills, developing, 96-97
Fanning, Shiela, 177
Finkel, Coleman, 15
Flattening of hierarchy, meetings and, 17
Flow charts, 154
Formal evaluations, 49-50
Frank, Milo, 2
Fulk, Janet, 105, 113
*Funny Thing Happened on the Way to the
    Boardroom, A* (Iapoce), 88

Gantt charts, 154
Gantt, James, 123, 125
Gender differences, 169-171
Geneen, Harold, 6
Genesis Training Solutions, 134
Globalization, meetings and, 18
Graphic facilitation, 95-96
Green, Bob, 173
Griggs, Lewis, 168-169, 171
Group decision-making meetings, 22
Groupthink, 58
Groupware, 115-130, 186
  advantages of, 123-125
  cross-cultural, 177
  disadvantages of, 126
  future of, 128-129
  getting the most out of, 127-128
  meetings, 115-116
  products, 116-123
    GroupSystems V, 123
    Lotus Notes, 121-122
    OptionFinder, 116-121

Hall's Consensus Rules, 58, 63, 66, 67, 69
Handbook for Effective Meetings (Sylvester), 44
Hayles, Robert, 182
Holcombe, Marya, 113, 137, 163
Horseshoe setup, 38
Howard, V. A., 83-84
How to Make Meetings Work (Doyle/Straus), 55
How to Organize and Manage a Seminar: What to Do and When to Do It (Bethel), 38
How to Run a Successful Meeting in Half the Time (Frank), 2
Humor, 87-89
    international meetings and, 176

Iapoce, Michael, 88
Icebreakers, 79-80
Ideograph, 96
Informational meetings, 22, 31
Information overload, meetings and, 17
International meetings, 29, 173-182
    acronyms, 175
    body language, 178-178
    computer technology, 176-177
    cross-cultural groupware, 177
    customs, 178-180
    humor, use of, 176
    idioms, 175
    interpreters, 177-178
    jargon, 175
    language do's and don'ts, 174
    language gap, briding, 173-178
    language training, 178
    making yourself understandable, 175
    meeting styles, 180-181
    planning, 181-182
    pronunciation, 173
    slang, 175
    software translation, 177
    visual aids, 176
Interpreters, 177-178
Intimate conference room, 193

Jackson, Bill, 112, 113
Janis, Irving, 58
Jay, Antony, 7, 78, 82-83
Jessup, Leonard, 128-129
Johansen, Bob, 104, 114, 121, 127, 128, 129-130, 183-184
Johnson, John, 6, 12, 22, 23, 209-210
Julius, Connie, 109, 113, 114

Kearns, David, 88
Keystone eliminator, 34
Kieffer, George, 6
Kinney, Susan, 191, 193
Korbus, Bill, 139
Kushner, Malcolm, 87-89

Lakoff, Robin, 170-171
Language training, 178
Latecomers, 86
Laube, Sheldon, 122
LCD projection panels, 159
Leadership, rotating, 82
Leader training, 207
Leimbach, Michael, 8, 69-70
Length of meeting, 25-26
Lighting, meeting room, 32
Light Touch: How to Use Humor for Business Success (Kushner), 88
Line charts, 150
Line drawings, 153
Listening:
    empathetic, 97-100
    levels of, 97
Logic tree, constructing, 137-138
Logistics, international meetings, 181
Lotus Notes, 121-22
Lunch breaks, 26

McDonald, Edward, 54-55
McGoff, Chris, 91, 103
Making Meetings Matter (Oppenheim), 2, 29
Managers, self-assessment checklist for, 172
Maps, 155
Meeting Assessment Form, 48
Meeting leader, 77-90
    closing the meeting, 89
    conflict, managing, 86-87
    discussion, joining, 83-84
    encouragement of participation by, 80
    establishment of meeting control by, 79-80
    humor, use of, 87-89
    quality of, 77-78
    rotating leadership, 82
    seating arrangement, changing, 82
    as servant of group, 78-79
    silent types, handling, 82-83
    sins of meeting leadership, 90
    See also Facilitators

Meeting Management News, 2
Meeting Meter, 14
Meeting minutes, *See* Minutes
Meeting notification, 30
Meeting procedures, *See* Procedures
Meeting recorder, 27-28, 45
Meetings:
   active participation at, 97-102
   benefits, 14-16
      cost vs., 15
   as a control system, 5
   costs, 10-16, 24
   dread of, 1-3
      reasons for, 2-3
   electronic, 103-131
   evaluating, 47-51
   failure of, 8-13
      cost of failure, 10-16
      reasons for, 9-10
   functions of, 7
   future of, 17-18
   international, 173-182
   length of, 25-26
   objective of, 24
   off-site, 15-16
   organizational culture and, 8
   presentations vs., 23-24
   purposes of, 3-4
   reasons for, 21-24
   as ritual, 7-8
   roles at, 77-102
   room selection/setup, 31-42
   size of, 25, 31
   smart, 207-209
   team, 182-191
   two-person, 191-193
   as vehicle for advancement, 6
   when to hold, 23-25
   See also International meetings;
      Presentations; Team meetings
Meeting System IQ Test, 199-202
Meeting systems, 195-210
   audit, 195-196
      choosing observers for, 205
      guidelines for conducting, 204-205
      purpose of, 206
      sample questions for, 203
      typical findings, 197-198
   improvement plan, 196-197
   profile, 196
Meeting technology, growth of, 104-105

Meilach, Dona, 143, 146, 159-160
Microphones, 33
Minority groups, culturally influenced be-
      havior and, 168-169
Minutes, 42-45, 176
   guidelines for taking, 44-45
   Post-Meeting Action Plan, 45-46
Monge, Peter, 11-12
Mosvick, Roger, 79, 87, 206
Mower, Judith, 189-190
Multiattribute Decision Analysis (MDA), 61-
      63, 66, 69, 70
Multimedia presentations, 162, 193

Namawashi, 180
Nervousness, controlling, 163
Neshek, Milton, 178-178
Nicklaus, Deborah, 90-91
Nominal Group Technique (NGT), 56, 58,
      60-61, 66, 67, 68, 73, 81
Notification, meeting, 30
Nunamaker, Jay, 123, 124, 128, 130
Nutt, Paul, 69

Office setup, 35
Off-site meetings, 15-16
One-way videoconferencing, 110-111
Open-ended questions, stimulating discus-
      sion with, 81
Oppenheim, Lynn, 2-3, 5, 7, 10, 29, 31-32,
      206, 210
OptionFinder, 116-121
Organizational charts, 154
Organizational culture, meetings and, 8
Osborn, Alex, 59
Overhead transparencies, 154

Panko, Raymond, 191, 192-193
Pardi, Maria Elena Perez de, 177
Participation styles, recognizing differences
      in, 81-82
Pavitt, Charles, 55, 68, 75
Peoples, David, 133-134, 138, 165-166
Personal anecdotes, 88
Peters, Tom, 79, 130, 171, 209
Phair, Harold, 112
Photographs, 156
Pictograph, 96
Pie charts, 147
Polling devices, 107
Poole, Scott, 55-56, 70-75, 191-192

Post-Meeting Action Plan, 45-46
Preparation time, 25
Presentation Design Book, The (Rabb, ed.), 142
Presentation equipment, 34
Presentation Kit, The (Wilder), 135
Presentations, 31, 133-167
  audience
    analyzing, 135
    monitoring, 163
  beginning, developing, 138-139
  effectiveness of, 134
  ending, developing, 138-139
  formats, 135, 136
  logic tree, creating, 137-138
  meetings vs., 23-24
  structure, developing, 135
  visual aids, 139
Presentation software program, selecting, 157
Problem-solving meetings, 22, 88
Procedures, 53-76
  benefits of using, 55-59
  brainstorming, 22-23, 59-60, 66, 69, 70
  closure and, 58-59
  comprehensiveness of, 66
  conflict and, 57-58
  control, 55
    variations in level of, 66
  defensive behavior and, 57
  definition of, 84
  Delphi Technique, 58, 65-68
  devil's advocate procedure, 64, 66, 68, 69
  group-member behavior and, 56
  group resistance to, 70-72
  groupthink and, 58
  Hall's Consensus Rules, 58, 63, 66, 67, 69
  instructions given by, 56-57
  managing, 71
  Multiattribute Decision Analysis (MDA), 61-63, 66, 69, 70
  Nominal Group Technique (NGT), 56, 58, 60-61, 66, 67, 68
  participation, 57
    variations in level of, 66-67
  promoting use of, 72-75
  restrictiveness of, 66
  Roberts' Rules of Order, 56, 59, 66-69
  scope of, 66
  selecting, 67-70
  self-evaluation and, 58, 74
  synectics, 64-65

  as tools, 55
  variations in, 60-61
Product demonstrations, meetings as, 23
Profile, meeting systems, 196
Progress reports, meetings as, 23
Projection screens, 34
Project proposals, meetings for gaining support for, 22
Pryor, Fred, 26, 86

Rabb, Margaret, 143
Racist jokes, 88-89
Radde, Paul, 32-33, 37-38, 40-42
Recording capability, 107
Repetitive voting, 58
Reviews, 31
Risk taking, 101-102
Roberts' Rules of Order, 56, 59, 66-69, 182
Robinson, Dana Gaines, 49-50
Room selection/setup, 31-42
  access, 33
  acoustics, 33
  chairs, 35
  checklist for, 43
  distractions, 33-34
  electrical outlets, 34
  group size, 32
  insisting on, 40-42
  international meetings, 182
  lighting, 32
  presentation equipment, 34
  projection screens, 34
  seating arrangements, 35-40
  sound system, 33
  special needs, 35
  storage space, 34
  ventilation, 33
  windows, 32-33
  See also Seating arrangements
Rumors, meetings to deflect, 22

Saito, Kieko, 180-181
Scale drawings, 155
Scheduling meetings, 25-26
Schematic drawings, 156
Schrage, Michael, 125
Seating arrangements, 35-40, 87
  amphitheater setup, 36-37
  auditorium setup, 36, 37
  changing, 82
  classroom setup, 36

Seating arrangements (*Continued*)
concave setup, 38
conference room setups, 36
conflict and, 87
office setup, 35
optimizing, 37-40
semicircular setup, 38
theater setup, 36, 37
Self-evaluation, procedures and, 58, 74
Semicircular setup, 38
Seven Habits of Highly Effective People, The
(Covey), 97
Sexist jokes, 88-89
Shared Minds: The New Technology of Collabo-
ration (Schrage), 125
Sibbet, David, 96, 183
Silent types, handling, 82-83
Silverman, George, 105
Single-chair aisles, 40, 42
Size of meeting, 25, 31
Slesinski, Raymond, 134
Slides, *See* 35-millimeter slides
Smart meetings, 207-209
Smith, Stuart, 210
Software translation, 177
Sound system, meeting room, 33
Speaker phones, 107
Special needs, meeting room, 35
Stein, Judy, 113, 141, 142, 163
Storage space, meeting room, 34
Storyboard, 60
Stragglers, 86
Straus, David, 55
Straw votes, 58
Suleiman, Anver, 49-50, 86
Surprise meetings, avoiding, 25
Sylvester, Nancy, 44-45
Synectics, 64-65
System demonstrations, meetings as, 23

Tables, 152
Tannen, Deborah, 170
Tapley, Jerry, 114
Team meetings, 182-191
cross-company, 186-187
Drexler/Sibbet Team Performance
Model, 183-186
rewards, 189-191

team leaders/managers, profile of, 188
training, 187-191
Teams, meetings and, 17
Tebbe, Mark, 126
Technology, meetings and, 18-19, 74-75
Text charts, 153
Theater setup, 36, 37
Thinking Together (Howard/Barton), 83-84
35-millimeter slides, 156-157
3M Meeting Management Institute, 47
Title charts, 151
Training, 206-207
Training seminars, 31
Tribal rituals, functions of, 7
Tritle, Gary, 129, 130, 176-177
Two-person meetings, 191-193
small vs. large groups, 191-192
work tools for, 192-193
Two-way videoconferencing, 111

United Technologies Corproation (UTC),
videoconference, 112
U-shape seating arrangement, 38-39

Valacich, Joseph S., 128-129
VanDelinder, David, 110-112
Ventilation, meeting room, 33
Verbal cues, audioconferencing and, 106
Videoconferencing, 109-114
applications for, 109-110
future of, 113-114
guidelines for, 112-113
one-way, 110-111
producing a videoconference, 111-112
two-way, 111
Video and laser disk technology, 161
Visual aids, 139-162
Voting devices, 107

Wadino, Mike, 173, 181, 186-187
Wann, Al, 168
Watson, Rick, 127
Whinston, Andy, 126
Wilder, Claudyne, 135
Williams, Harold, 6
Windows, meeting room, 32-33
Work flow, meetings and, 5